SECRETS *of the* SUPERSTARS

Excellence In Selling New Homes

BONNIE ALFRIEND

Illustrations by Barbara J. Lerch, 1322 South Glebe Road, Arlington, VA 22204

Printed in the U.S.A. by Alfriend And Associates, Incorporated
6915 Heathstone Court, Fairfax Station, VA 22039
ISBN: 0-9639500-0-2
Library of Congress Catalog Card Number 93-073919

Acknowledgements

No work is an island unto itself. This book is the labor of many who have contributed their wisdom and generosity to building excellence in new home sales. Special credit goes to the following people who have given me special encouragement and nourishment, and for which I am deeply grateful. They unselfishly handed me their "light" filled with knowledge and experience, with instructions to pass the torch to others. In the order in which they began to influence my professional life they are: My parents, Claude and Sunshine Chattin, who taught me that God's love empowers us all to reach any star we choose; Gerald R. Talandis introduced me to building and developing; Dave Stone, my first and continuous teacher and leader, his excellence and integrity is a beacon to all; W. Howard Rooks challenged me to find my creative self and gave me the opportunity to use my talent; Charlie Clark, a trusted friend and professional mentor, who is always willing to advise and coach me; Tom Richey, whose intelligence and instruction continues to encourage me to reach for new heights; Bob Schultz, a great educator and insightful thinker, whose work I admire and respect; Rich Tiller, my editor, who believed in this book, and challenged me to write my story. He walked with me through every page.

My heartfelt appreciation also goes to Suzanne B. Albee, Kim J. Alfriend and Esther A. Blythe for their literary input. They spent many long hours reviewing and correcting the manuscript.

Thank you.

For Terry

My best friend, most ardent critic and loyal fan.
Our life together makes me feel blessed.
Your love makes me feel special.

Contents

"To every man there comes a time in his lifetime, that special moment when he is figuratively tapped on the shoulder and offered the chance to do a very special thing, unique to him and fitted to his talents. What a tragedy if that moment finds him unprepared or unqualified to do the work which could have been his finest hour."

Winston Churchill

Introduction

The homebuilding industry is blessed with a large number of outstanding salespeople. People with a vision and purpose to become the best that they can be. I have had the privilege of learning from many of them because I see salespeople in action every day. I am a "mystery shopper." For those of you who are unfamiliar with shopping evaluations, let me explain. Our company is hired by builders, developers, managers, Realtors and salespeople to visit new home communities as potential buyers. The interview and visit is monitored, evaluated and analyzed in order for sales counselors to *hear* themselves during a selling situation. Guess what? We have heard some pretty terrific things.

Although I have been in sales my entire career, I had no concept of the magnitude of talent, commitment and skill that exists in salespeople across the country. *Salespeople are very special people.* I am eager to share with you the great things I have seen. Witnessing superior ideas and concepts coming to life in a proactive manner, and ending in positive results is most exciting. This adventure and revelation prompted Secrets of the Superstars. My motivation to tell this story is also driven by the "heinous" injustice served on salespeople.

I have seen many salespeople excel in extraordinary ways. They excel in both their ideas and their techniques. This book will focus on both. I will discuss *ideas* that star performers use to win sales. I will also give *examples* of how they really do it.

* * *

My passion for sales and salespeople began over 25 years ago when I entered one of the most challenging and difficult career paths — that of an on-site salesperson. Quite honestly my venture was not by design, nor had I been prepared for this undertaking. I just fell into this exciting industry. Many of my colleagues admit to the same malady. *"Someone must think we are pretty special."*

My own story goes like this: My husband, Terry, accepted a faculty position at Cornell University and we moved from our roots in Southern Virginia to upstate New York. The builder of our apartment building was in need of someone to settle tempers and calm the souls of those who found construction delays running into months, and a porcelain strike that left small incidentals like sinks and toilets on back order. My builder concluded that a Southern accent might just be the answer. For sure, we couldn't understand each other, and that may have been the secret of our success.

In those days, sales education and training was rather limited, and I must admit I had a love-hate relationship with selling in the beginning. One moment I was enjoying my work, the next I was knee deep in stress. This paradox was partly because I did not know why I succeeded, when I did, nor why I failed. My accomplishments seemed to be overshadowed by the fear of another crisis, which, of course, I blamed on the market. The peaks and valleys of the business were frustrating, to say the least.

That is, until one day when my boss came into the model office and handed me a tape recorder. He left me alone with a cumbersome reel-to-reel recorder placed in the closet, with words I shall never forget: "Listen to your next appointments and correct yourself." That may have been followed by " or else," but I didn't ask him to repeat it. I would say, however, that I am witness to the fact that fear motivation does work. I did listen. ("I can't believe I said that!") And I did correct! What at first appeared to be a painful process and revelation has changed my professional life. I shall always be grateful for the many things Gerald Talandis, my first builder, taught me. Secret number one: It takes more than a Southern accent to become a top sales professional.

I have continued the practice of using a recorder to listen to myself; evaluate the results; and strive to correct, improve and perfect my performance. My own positive experience with monitoring and evaluating myself, and the valuable rewards it continues to bring me are why I choose to include "mystery shopping" as one of the services my company offers. I believe it can play an important role in helping salespeople fulfill their individual potential.

* * *

There is much written about educating salespeople, the suggested training methods and learning environments. One that is most important, but often overlooked, is the use of self-evaluation and repetitive practice of sound techniques and fundamentals. Whether you use outside shoppers or monitor yourself, periodically tape recording your sales presentation is a must. Shopping should serve as part of the company's support system for the sales team. The shopping report provides one more tool among the many which are available to help new home salespeople achieve their maximum potential. It is not intended as a substitute for in-house corporate sales training; sales seminars from industry experts; books, tapes or videos. It is one more piece of the total puzzle, like athletes watching the tapes of their performances.

Athletes achieve greatness through a variety of disciplines. One of these is watching the post game videos. By seeing themselves in action they can witness first-hand what they did that was outstanding, and what skills they need to sharpen in order to broaden their abilities. This experience directs them toward two different, but equally important, plans of action:

1) To commit to a program to develop those skills which will make them better.

2) To develop strategies that will increase the number of opportunities for them to exercise those special talents which make them win.

The job of the mystery shopper is to provide a "verbal video" of how you "look" when you sell. The shopping report is like a mirror that you can look into in order to see what you have already achieved, and what further potential lies ahead. By seeing yourself from an outsider's perspective, you can determine what other steps you should take in order to gain every competitive advantage available.

The road to success requires that we motivate ourselves to consistently seek change; to stretch, improve, and grow even though it is often hard to see ourselves objectively. All of us have different strengths and weaknesses. In order to become the best we can be, we must begin by knowing ourselves. Once we can admit without shame that we have potential for improvement, we open up unlimited horizons of opportunity. At the same time, knowing the ways in which we are uniquely gifted can propel us toward *greatness*. It is this *greatness*, which I have seen in abundance, that will be revealed in this book. I firmly believe, if we can maximize our strengths and strengthen our weaknesses, we can rise to the highest level of our commitment. But first we must *see* ourselves. Hearing or seeing ourselves in action is a major step to knowing the truth about our performance.

* * *

In the course of my shopping experiences I have had the opportunity to watch a brilliant array of personalities, techniques, and strategies that have helped people succeed. The purpose of this book is to share these experiences with you — to give you a glimpse into the world of other champion salespeople to see what puts them at the forefront of their profession — and to help you determine which of their competitive advantages might also become advantages for you.

Research for this book started over three years ago when I began my expedition to validate the degree of professionalism among new home salespeople. Information documented in *Secrets of the Superstars* was gathered from over 1,000 interviews and taped "mystery shopping" presentations with new home salespeople across the country. As part of the research, we analyzed the skill proficiency of each salesperson through a numerical skill assessment rating. The overall cumulative score was 55%, with initial greeting and enthusiasm ranking a high of 75%, while closing and follow through were at the low end at 25%.

Tom Richey, president of Richey Resources, Houston, Texas, has conducted extensive research of a similar order, over a seven year period with 3,000 salespeople. The result of his findings parallel ours almost identically. Both reports show a definite pattern of the skills most challenging for professional salespeople.

From our reports we separated out those who demonstrated the highest form of superiority, in order to analyze what sets them apart from the norm. This book is about what the superstars do differently on a daily basis. In addition, we also discovered the following interesting data.

1. Excellence in selling is not related to a particular price point in new residential homes or specific customer demographics. We found peak performers successfully selling everything from entry level condominiums to million dollar estates.

2. The pursuit of excellence is not gender specific. Our survey, based on a numerical evaluation of the critical sales path, revealed

that male and female top achievers ranked equally high, both in relationship building and focused, assertive closing skills. Superstars were successful in breaking through gender stereotyping.

3. Success in new home sales is not limited to geographic areas with escalated market driven traffic and volume. Nor was the lack of sophisticated marketing tools limiting the performance of top professionals working with our shoppers. In fact, great salespeople had the ability to minimize the need for a lot of additional collateral materials, merchandized models and other marketing promotions.

4. We discovered that winners win because they react to a burning desire to be the best they can be at all cost, not because they are the most talented.

5. By far, the strongest outside influence on excellent performance was directly related to the degree of consistent and continual education, coaching and training made available to sales professionals, who were motivated to excel. We met motivated, goal oriented salespeople who were limted because they did not have the tools of knowledge to help them reach their potential. We also met salespeople who have been exposed to the best coaching, training and education available, and continue to wallow in mediocrity. Our revelation is no secret. Knowledge lies dormant without a willing recipient, and races can never be won, even by the swiftest runners, without a map to the final destination.

From these resources I have drawn information that I believe can be of value to all new home sales professionals. I will deal with "actual" situations in selling, and with the dialogue which succeeded in building the sale. I have chosen scenarios from motivated star performers who have worked hard to develop and perfect their skills. Naturally I do not use any names of salespeople, neighborhoods, companies or even geographical locations. The purpose of this book is to illustrate knowledge of a magnitude that can have far reaching value and which, of course, is not confidential in nature.

* * *

Words Don't Come Easy

Theory is fine, and theory is certainly the foundation upon which we build, but what salespeople tell me is that they want examples of what to say. Frequently we assume that, in selling, the words just come naturally. This is not the case. While many salespeople have a "gift for gab," that is not the same as having good communication skills. You will find helpful words and phrases from industry giants throughout <u>Secrets of the Superstars</u>. Some of these experts are veterans, and some are rookies, but all continue to meet the challenges of selling new homes with an open mind, a commitment to grow, and a willingness to change.

A legitimate response from many salespeople is: "The idea sounds fine, but in real life it just won't work. It sounds mechanical and a little contrived." Often they say: "I understand the principle, but what are the words that really work? I want to sound natural." These kinds of questions cut to the core in sales training. All too often, managers and builders lack the time or the expertise to counsel and coach their team in this area.

* * *

"What Words Should I Use?"

The *real words* are where I believe I can help. The words, phrases and dialogue are what I hear each day from across the country. Admittedly, sometimes the words are not great. But often they *are* great — more often than salespeople are given credit. My goal is to include as many of these great words as possible, in order to share ideas and success stories to help you succeed as a professional communicator.

One interesting and encouraging thing that I have learned when I have heard *great words* or seen *great techniques* is that they are almost never unique or isolated. I have seen the same great ideas come to life, again and again. Just because they are not *unique* does not mean they are not *original*. Great ideas are often generated by more than one person simultaneously. This often proves that the ideas can work successfully for many people. Rarely in this book will I include an idea that I have seen only once. It's not that I believe isolated ideas have any less value. In my experience I have discovered that sound techniques which work tend to repeat themselves.

Selling techniques can be compared to golf swings. No two are identical (so my golfing friends tell me); but you see several primary principles interpreted in a variety of different ways to fit the particular style of the individual golfer, and the playing conditions of each particular shot. The same is true in new home sales. You see primary selling principles customized to fit the personality and talents of the salesperson, the specific conditions of the community, and the personality and needs of the customer. This is what we will be examining throughout this book.

I will spend more time focusing on the more difficult challenges; areas where I have seen the most anxiety in the selling process. My primary focus will be to highlight those ideas, strategies and techniques that I see most frequently separating outstanding salespeople from average ones. Here are several examples of areas where I see the greatest differences:

* Preparation for the entire selling effort

* Using the phone

* Establishing rapport

* Identifying and fulfilling needs

* Establishing a competitive advantage

* Demonstrating the home

* Showing the homesite with enough impact to create fear of loss

* Overcoming objections

* Executing a strong close without being offensive

* Following up

These areas of difference conform to the structure of this book. In the remaining chapters I will move through the selling process, one challenge at a time, to share the experiences of strength and brilliance from the superstars I have encountered.

Secrets of the Superstars is a tribute to all the great men and women in new home sales who, through their positive attitudes, hard work, and commitment to excellence, have helped families everywhere realize one of life's greatest desires — owning their dream home! It is they who have housed America.

Preparing For The Sale

M y Mother is a wonderful example of someone who understands that being prepared is the secret to minimizing stress
and enjoying life. In fact, it would be difficult to talk about
preparation without thinking of both my parents. I have
always marveled at how much they seem to accomplish
while maintaining their sense of humor and zest for life.

Their *secret*: "Never put off anything you can do ahead of
time." Even in retirement, my Dad starts planning and organizing his garden long before the spring. Each row is designed on
paper; seeds are dried for next year's crop; and rows are staked
as he gets ready for a garden that will feed the multitudes. As
the vegetables come in, my Mother and Father pick, clean, can
and freeze with diligence that is a marvel to witness. The result
is the best eating you can ever imagine. Not long ago I asked
them why they worked so hard when they could relax and enjoy
those golden years. They responded, "You just never know who
will show up, and we want to be ready, just in case they are
hungry."

And so it goes in new home sales. We never know who will show
up, and we must be ready, just in case they are buyers. For my parents and their generation, getting ready and staying on top of every

situation was part of survival. I fear that we have lost some of this important ideal. Fortunately, this is not true of everyone. During our visits on site, one of the most striking differences that we see between top salespeople and average ones is that top salespeople are better prepared. At every moment during the interaction, they know exactly where they are going and how they will get there. They prepare the major points they want to make and anticipate the array of possible responses, and are prepared to handle each of those responses. It is through their preparation that they are able to gain control of the selling situation and direct it along a path toward the close. This path may be filled with twists and turns, but it is always headed toward the ultimate destination of the close. Prior planning and preparation plays an important role in our ability to establish and sustain *momentum*, which is critical in new home sales.

One salesperson shared her *secret*. ***"There was a time in my career that I felt I had mastered the trade. That was my big mistake. Looking back, I realize that each time I fell into a slump it had very little to do with the market. It was because I had stopped practicing and learning. Today I try to learn a new technique and skill each week which keeps me focused on a fresh, crisp and exciting presentation. I practice with my children, thus bonding us together and teaching them some important lessons in life."***

Excellence Is A Habit

A very important question has baffled me for years. Why does one salesperson succeed when another fails? What is the difference? Certainly on the surface both are quite similar. In fact, as a recruiter, I have been amazed that many for whom we had high expectations stopped short of excellence, when others with fewer "credentials" went to the moon.

My observation reveals only one difference between winners and losers. It has little to do with talent or intellect. The difference is *habits*. The dictionary defines a habit as "an acquired behavior pattern regularly followed until it has become almost involuntary; a constant, often unconscious inclination to perform some act acquired through its frequent repetition."

The key to successful *habits* is to make a conscious effort to internalize and personalize the skill or technique until it becomes a natural response to a given situation. The technical aspects of sales concepts can be learned from books, tapes, educators and industry experts. You must do more than gain knowledge; you must establish action. The secret to transforming this knowledge into productivity is practice. Here are some tips on how to acquire *successful selling habits,* learned from top salespeople.

1) Set Aside Time

New habits take concentrated effort and a time commitment. Don't approach the development of a habit loosely. A specific timetable must be set. Choose a time when you are free from stress and are fresh to practice with zeal and enthusiasm. Try to set aside a specific time once or twice a week for diligent practice. You will have conquered a learned concept when the technique becomes automatic. Learning a new technique is the easy part. Developing the technique into *your* selling habit takes commitment to change and dedication to practice. This proactive state is what propels the top performers we have seen to excellence. Remember it will take time, and at first you will feel uncomfortable. This will change as your selling skills become habits, and you start doing them unconsciously in a selling situation.

The first few times I went snow skiing I felt awkward and clumsy. I constantly fell down, I tripped over my feet, and I really hated it; all this before I even got on the bunny slope! I still haven't mastered snow skiing because I haven't taken the time to practice. I must admit, however, each time I go it does become more comfortable, and I am a little less frightened. With any luck, I'll leave the chair lift, next time.

"Maybe I should have practiced that snowplow!"

2) Develop One Skill At A Time

Focus on one area at a time. It is virtually impossible to develop three or four skills at the same time. After you attend a sales seminar or training class do not make the mistake of trying to change everything about your approach to selling. The frustration will stop you dead in your tracks. The fastest, most productive, and most rewarding growth comes in small increments - one step at a time. Commit to working on one phase of development until the response is natural, and second nature to you.

My daughter, Kim, loves to ice skate. In fact she has been playing ice hockey since the age of eight. Fortunately her love for the sport outweighs the downside of repetitive training on one edge of the skate blade for an hour at a time. What do I mean by that? Skating is not a natural skill. It must be acquired. Physically, each of us is born with one dominant side and one weaker side of the body. Therefore, each step in skating must be broken down into small increments. Each section must be practiced over and over again. Each blade, the inside edge and the outside edge, must be mastered to perfection in order to gain equal strength and ability with both skates. Power skaters work on this skill every day because it affects everything they do. There were times when Kim skipped out on practice or took the lazy way out. She then tried to fake it during the game by covering up her weak points, using her stronger skate to compensate. " Fake it until you make it" doesn't work. Her weaker skate just got weaker, and sooner or later she paid for it with injuries. As Kim would say, "trying to take the easy way out will catch up with you, and when it does it's not fun anymore."

Think about this, if you will. Let's suppose you are playing goalie for the Stanley Cup. You are a "left side weak". You have not worked on the left side as you know you should. Your right skate, as good as it is, can't stop a shot on your left side. The game is lost, the Cup is gone. You not only lost the game for you, you lost it for the total team. Salespeople have an awesome responsibility which must be taken seriously. There is accountability if you expect to win in this great game of selling. Professionals know they must always work to build up their "weaker side".

3) Implement An Action Plan

Practice each technique until it literally takes on a life of its own. Relax, think of the elements of the skill, but also visualize yourself using the skill with a customer. This visualization will allow you to develop your new internalized skill in conjunction with your natural talents and personality. It takes discipline to work with a particular technique until it becomes a habit. Discipline is very binding and inhibiting. Kim said that she would never be able to get through the practice of *drilling* her edges if she could not *see* herself fighting for the puck and "scoring the winning goal." The important key to acquiring successful habits is to practice, repeat and rehearse them until they are a part of you.

I believe that we will never reach to our highest potential until we learn how to develop sound habits and are willing to consistently seek out new skills to develop into habits. "No gain without pain" is right. The secret I've learned from the great ones is that for them the pain of missed opportunities and lost sales is far greater than the effort of developing sound techniques and skills. Success is not a sprint. It is a marathon.

The habit of planning includes having a distinct pattern to follow in every sales contact. Preparation builds confidence, and buyers want to deal with professionals who are self confident. In today's world, buyers are insisting on the best, and rightfully so. Preparation for the entire selling process is a large task. It cannot be accomplished in one sitting, and parts of it will continually be revised. There are many things for which to prepare, such as product knowledge and community environment. The rest of this chapter will be devoted to addressing the areas of preparation which deal with preparing dialogue and scripts, and developing a comfortable and practiced presentation. Here is an overview of items for which you will need to prepare in order for your knowledge and selling skills to have maximum impact:

* Answering the phone
* The initial presentation
* What information you want to obtain from the customer
* Getting from one stage of the sale to the next
* The model demonstration — value perception
* Showing the homesite
* Objections
* Closing
* What to do when the close fails
* Follow-up

* * *

Answering The Phone

There are several places in the selling process where it is helpful to have a script. Scripts often have a negative connotation. They imply that we say the same thing exactly the same way over and over to every customer who walks in the door — a "spiel" which leaves no room for originality or insight. That idea is not my intent here. The value of a script is that it helps you to *organize* your presentation and keep it focused. It is the nature of conversation to be spontaneous, and that is good. But in selling it is still necessary for you to keep a gentle rein on the conversation in order to keep your interaction moving in a selling direction. There is plenty of room for detours and improvisations.

My uncle is a great fisherman. He taught me to fish as a young child. The most important thing about fishing is to try to stay in control. After hooking the fish, he would reel the line in, and then let it out again, so the fish was not always moving toward the boat at the same steady speed. There were times, in fact, when the fish on the line was actually moving away from the boat. I was always sure the fish was getting away, but Uncle Hansel assured me he was in control of the line, and he knew that the fish would ultimately move toward the boat. The script is your fishing line. You use the same fishing line again and again, and then you adapt your use of the line to fit the unique circumstances of each catch. Fish may not want to be caught, but customers do want to buy their dream home. They want to be led through the process to make that dream possible. Customers expect to be served in a professional manner. They want leadership, expertise, and assertiveness working in their best interest.

We will get into the specifics of the script in the next chapter — "Answering the Initial Phone Call." The point to be made here is that the telephone *does* offer real selling opportunities, and it is worth organizing a brief presentation that will help you maximize the phone's unique opportunities for creating interest and for setting an appointment.

* * *

The Initial Presentation And Questions

The initial greeting is another situation where a script can help you create greater impact, and gain more of the information you need in order to fulfill the customer's needs. It is especially important at this stage in the selling process that you be well organized. You will have the customer's full attention for only a few minutes initially, so every second counts. Research has shown that impressions formed in the first 30 seconds are so powerful that they affect the life of the relationship. Establishing rapport during this time is vital, but so is conveying your message. Your selling message should be reduced to a concise statement that can be conveyed easily in a short period of time. Then it can be expanded as opportunities present themselves.

However, these opportunities are often limited. Customers may be in a hurry, or impatient, or have children sitting in the car, or they just may not be communicative people. Often they only want to know your prices and see your homes, and they don't want to be bothered by a salesperson. In situations like this a script helps you to have the most impact in the shortest time. The script does not have to be written out in its entirety, as though it were a play. It can be simply an outline. Whether it is a complete script or an outline, it should include the following points, which will be discussed in depth in Chapter Four:

* An introduction and handshake
* An explanation of your location
* A statement about your builder

* A statement about your community
* A summary of your product line
* Questions about the customer's buying ability and urgency
* Questions about the customer's needs and priorities
* Particular comments and questions which help you to establish rapport and common ground with the customer
* Any other information which is especially unique to your particular situation (financing, incentives, availability, success stories, etc.)

This type of preparation in no way implies that your initial presentation should be a monologue. On the contrary, it is very important that your first interaction be a *conversation* in which information is *exchanged*. Ideally, your rapport will blossom into a relationship. Preparation will help this to happen. Rapport building will not always be established quickly. It takes time and continues to develop throughout the interview. In these cases preparation is equally important because you need to be conveying your high-impact information as quickly and concisely as possible, hoping that it will gain attention and have significance to your customers as they see more of your product.

* * *

Getting From One Stage Of The Sale To The Next

Taking customers from the first contact to the close requires a plan for getting them from each stage of the selling process to the next stage. Your plan is designed to meet the following objectives:

* During the initial phone call, you must have a way to get them to your sales office.

* When they are in the sales office, you must get them to the model tour.
* From the models you must get them to the homesite.
* From the homesite you must get them to sit down and redefine the selection of their favorite home and homesite.
* From selection of one of a kind they must refine the financing.
* Finally comes persuading them to make a buying decision.
* And you must know what you will do if the decision is, "Not today."

In each stage of the selling process, you must be prepared in advance with ways to create anticipation for the stage that follows. You need to know how to build these transitions from one stage to the next. Each stage of the selling process offers a convenient moment for the customer to bring the transaction to a stop. Your goal is to keep the transaction going. This requires preparation — a written plan — so that you will not be caught off guard if your selling momentum starts to wane.

* * *

The Model Demonstration

It is not as important to have a *script* for the model demonstration as it is for the phone call or the greeting, but it is just as important to have a *plan*. Your plan should include:

* The primary "theme" of your demonstration.
* Ways your demonstration will show your superiority over your competition.
* How to use the demonstration to compete against the customer's current home.
* How to use the demonstration to deepen your relationship with buyers and to better learn their most important needs.
* How you will elicit feedback about your product.

* The anecdotes or testimonials you will use.
* Construction features you will point out.
* Architectural features you will highlight.
* Benefits and advantages you will use in describing your features.
* Where in the home you will want to start, and where you will want to finish.
* How you will position yourself to enhance space which will add value in your homes.

During the interviews we have experienced, we have seen a significant difference in impact between a demonstration which is well-organized and one which is simply played by ear. The demonstration that is organized does not need to sound canned. This is show business. Your demonstration should be as natural and believable as the last great movie you saw. The actors spent long hours practicing and working on the final cut.

Demonstration of your homes should feel as though it has a sense of purpose. It needs to make your customers glad you came along with them, instead of turning them loose on their own. Salespeople who plan their presentations feel more comfortable demonstrating a model than those who don't. Salespeople who have no plan often feel that it is more appropriate to let the customer go alone. Sometimes this approach is necessary, but remember there will be selling opportunities lost when customers tour the models alone.

* * *

Going To The Homesite

As with the model tour, having a plan for "site seeing" will give you a stronger presentation, even though the plan is often subject to change. By this time you have gained more insight into the needs and preferences of the buyer. When you prepare to show homesites, answers to the following questions will help you develop your plan:

* What are the strengths of each site and how will you demonstrate those strengths?
* What are the weaknesses of each site, and how will you deal with them?
* Do you fully understand the dimensions, grading, and drainage?
* What are the advantages and disadvantages?
* In what order will you show your homesites? How many will you show?
* How will you involve your customer in the site?
* What is the position of the house location (orientation to sunrise, sunset, views, etc)?
* What tools will you need for greater impact?

Planning will help you to maintain your own sense of purpose and confidence. It will also help you to show superior expertise over your competitors. With a strategic plan and preparation you can concentrate all your attention on your customers. You are now free to be creative and flexible in order to serve their needs without concentrating on *your* concerns and fears, due to lack of knowledge and preparation. You will be ready, as my Mother would say, in case someone drops by.

* * *

Objections

We know that objections are inevitable at some point in the selling process. They are often the first buying signals you will recognize. Welcome them openly. Objections, at the very least, tell us that there is interest in what is being seen or said. You need to anticipate these objections so that you can decide:

1) Should you bring up the issue before customers do?
2) If they bring it up first, how will you respond?

Keep a record of past objections and potential objections, and how you plan to handle them when they arise. If it turns out that you decide to change your strategy and improvise on the spur of the moment, that is fine. The important point is that if you have a plan you will be able to respond more confidently, maintain better control, and keep the selling process focused on your ultimate objective — the close.

* * *

Closing

Closing is a *total selling process*. Closing is not simply one clever moment at the end of the sale when everything suddenly crystallizes. Closing is a **series of initiatives** which occurs from the time you first meet the customer until the moment when you finally do ask for the order.

Nevertheless, there is a *final closing moment* when you must bring all of your work together by asking the customer to buy your home. Closing is one more *initiative* which must be executed in a clearly defined way. Why this is true, and what to do about it, are the subjects of Chapter Eight. For now, I want to make the point that closing is one more part of the selling process which requires serious preparation.

Once you get to the close, you need to know how you will execute it. There are many effective ways, and winners do not close the same way every time. It varies with the kind of relationship they have developed with their customers. Their closes are still prepared, and this preparation shows itself in the confidence with which the top closers execute this final moment.

Identifying and recognizing when you used a close, why you used it, how you used it, and your results from using it are most important. At this juncture I recommend that you write down several closes that *you* feel comfortable with. Direct closes come in many descriptions and are as numerous as the stars. Be sure to give your favorite ones a name. In the chapter on closing, I will share a number of successful approaches that I have seen.

Timing is an important element in closing. Closing too soon can create an atmosphere of antagonism, which shuts down communication. Closing too late can result in lost opportunities and a feeling that "you didn't care enough to give your very best." After you have gone through all the stages of the selling process which lead to the close, be prepared to close in some way, even if you are not receiving strong buying signals. Some customers just don't give strong buying signals. These are the times when you must have the confidence to "go for it" simply because you have reached that point. If you wait for buying signals, you could lose the sale.

* * *

What To Do When The Close Fails

When you prepare your close, you must also prepare for the likelihood that the customer will say, "No." Many salespeople are reluctant to close because they don't know what they will do if the customer says, "No." It is especially important to be prepared with a variety of responses which will allow you to continue your interaction after the customer rejects your *initial* closing effort.

A negative response to a closing question does not have to mean the end of the sale. In fact, it may give you the insight you need to help you complete the close. Never shy away from the close because of the fear that you will get a "No." You need to be prepared with strategies for what to do next.

Here's some advice from my first builder: ***"Always remember that every time a customer says, 'No,' they really mean, 'Not right*** *now; I don't think I'm ready yet.' Sometimes you don't hear the last part, but it's always there."*

* * *

Follow-Up

Follow-up is another part of selling for which salespeople must prepare in order to succeed. As with the initial phone call and the greeting, a complete script can give you a critical advantage. It will not only increase the comfort level of the call, but it will make the call more productive by giving you a specific agenda to accomplish. Weak follow-up habits cause the termination of many sales today.

Once again, a prepared call is not the same as a canned call. The script simply makes the follow-up call more organized, more effective, and more comfortable. These scripts should include personalized benefits specific to the customer's needs or wants. A script is easier to use on the phone because you can look at it while you talk. In fact, I recommend that when salespeople begin using scripts, they start with the telephone script.

* * *

Once you complete your preparation for each stage of the sale, the next step is to *practice* your script or strategy. Practicing does not require rote memorization, but it does require a complete knowledge of your plan. It also helps make your presentation concise and powerful. The following are several of my favorite methods of practicing and rehearsing scripts:

* Practice with a tape recorder, using the appropriate voice modulations.
* Practice in front of a mirror, using the appropriate gestures,

motions and eye contact.
* Practice in the actual setting where you will be selling.
* Record your practice session on a video.
* Role play with another salesperson, your manager/coach or mentor.

Salespeople who do extensive preparation, and then practice their presentations, tell me that it has increased their impact, as well as their comfort and confidence. They practice their presentations, not so that they can memorize them word for word, but so they can deliver them more effectively. These salespeople are still excellent improvisors, but their ability to improvise improves as they practice.

The Initial Phone Call

There's Gold In Those Calls

everal years ago I was speaking to a very successful sales
lady. I asked her how she consistently stayed on top, regardless of market conditions. She gave me her *secret to success.*
*"I like what I'm doing. I believe in what I'm doing. I'm suc-
cessful because I have never forgotten the importance of
being responsive to every call and every visit to my community."*
She went on to say that many salespeople do not realize the vast
opportunities in the calls coming to their sales center. *"I cherish
phone inquiries as much as I cherish visitors."* Much of her success was realizing the importance of meeting every call with the
attitude that "this one may very well be my next sale." She understood the value of those calls and the travesty of missed opportunities.

The telephone plays a significant role in the life of Americans.
Our world, perhaps unfortunately, has become one of never having
enough time. Hours have been dissected into megaseconds. "Let
your fingers do the walking," for many of us, has become our most
arduous exercise. We live in an instantaneous society. The attitude,
"if I need it or want it, I must have it now," seems to abound. Cata-

log shopping is enjoying a tremendous boom. The value of the telephone has increased because it saves precious time. The number of incoming phone inquiries to sales centers is increasing, primarily because consumers can get action and answers more quickly.

An example of urgency of the moment, and the importance of the telephone, happened to me as I was writing <u>Secrets of the Superstars</u>. Horror of horrors, the computer shut down right in the middle of a deadline. By now I am a slave to this awesome machine. I wouldn't go as far as to say that we are compatible; but we were beginning to tolerate each other. On this day, however, *IT* decided not to "speak." Rapport-building did not help. I called Bill, my computer repairman, who is never lonely.

"You must be here in 15 minutes! I am on a deadline, and my computer just freaked out!"

Bill told me house calls were more expensive. I needed my computer working right then. Money was no object. There may be a lesson for selling in there someplace. Bill called his field rep, and *The Machine* and I were back in business in no time. Computers may have turned us all into "technocrats." But let's not forget the greatest technology to ever surface, especially for salespeople, is the telephone.

With the introduction of sales offices on site, and the luxury of merchandized models, the value of the customer's phone call to the sales office is often underestimated. While some salespeople use the phone as an important selling tool, others use it primarily to answer questions and give out basic information, such as directions and office hours. Many salespeople do not believe that the phone offers a real selling opportunity, because it is impossible to close over the phone. The idea that new home sales can only be accomplished face-to-face is very widespread.

In this chapter, I would like to look at the phone call in a different way. I have seen surprisingly good results from salespeople who use the phone for more than just giving information. We may not be able to conduct an entire sale over the phone in our business. However, we can *begin* the sale in a significant way. Salespeople who are average in their telephone techniques believe that the initial phone call for information is, at best, a *preface to the visit*. A top flight phone user believes the same call is the *beginning of the sale*.

Although the phone call lacks some of the opportunities of face-to-face interaction, it does offer a different set of opportunities. The phone call to the sales office is *less threatening* for many customers because it is not face-to-face. They can take the risk of being more open because they have complete control over the situation. After all, they can hang up at any time, and you don't even know who they are. Imagine yourself in their position. Is there anything for you to feel awkward about? They are completely comfortable in this situation, and you can use this comfort to your advantage. Top salespeople use the phone to *build friendship*. In establishing this *telephone friendship*, salespeople find that the phone call lasts longer and produces more benefits, because the customer feels "safe."

"Walk in my Shoes."

I would like to digress for a moment, regarding one principle that is important in every phase of the selling process. When I said, "Imagine yourself in their position," I was referring to the fact that it is very easy to get locked into one's own mindset over a period of time, thus causing us to lose our perspective on how our actions are affecting our customers. Whether talking on the phone, greeting, demonstrating, closing or following up, if you can step out of your own mind, and put yourself in the customer's position, you will gain tremendous insight into which techniques will work, and which won't work.

Companies spend millions of dollars in advertising to generate interest and inquiries. Knowing just how much money it has cost your company merely to cause the phone to ring, may help you to understand the importance of good telephone techniques, and to give you the motivation to strive to commit those callers to an appointment to visit. Inquiries indicate the hottest kind of prospective customer. Many times callers have more information about your homes than those who drop in. The "just curious" generally don't call first. You already know the caller is interested, and that interest must be nurtured while the iron is hot, before he cools off. Telephone inquiries do not automatically guarantee you customers. Time is of the essence. The longer the caller waits to meet you the lower his interest becomes. Ignoring this critical concept in human behavior may result in losing him forever.

Note: Since the English language does not have a singular pronoun to refer to both genders, I will follow the traditional method, using masculine pronouns, when ease of reading and grammatical correctness are an issue. In those cases, the gender reference relates to all people, male and female alike.

The telephone is vital to the success of a new home salesperson. I am firmly convinced that many follow-up programs are weak because we have developed call reluctance due to lack of practice in creating a positive telephone image. Later, I will talk about the importance of the telephone, and techniques to use in follow up and prospecting. In this chapter, I am dealing with the lost art of handling the incoming calls.

For many years I worked with a brilliant sales lady who practiced a technique that earned her tremendous results, as well as a referral base from loyal customers. Louise learned, early in the game of selling, that the way she handled the phone made a significant difference in the response of the caller. She also believes that if you have a smile in your voice, and a sincere interest in the person, they will most likely return the favor. "Smile and the world smiles back." Louise kept a mirror by the phone to catch her expressions, and a check list of questions to ask. A day in the life of a salesperson can be hectic. It's not always easy to sound pleased to receive a call. A pause, to gather your composure and concentrate on the impression you want to send through the air waves before you pick up the telephone, will help. Louise would tell you to prepare your phone station for the call, in order to switch gears.

Visual images are also important for the salesperson. Draw, in words, a portrait of the caller, based not only on what was said but how it was said. Visualize the person at the other end. Also, remember that he is probably getting a mental picture of you. "A picture is worth a thousand words" is as true today as ever. I love to hear salespeople use words and phrases that create images and help the caller paint mental pictures of what he will see when he comes for a visit. Imagine the caller's face. Who is he? What is he trying to accomplish? What is his personality profile? How can I effectively communicate with him? The information gathered should be filled out on the back of your guest card in anticipation of the visit.

One terrific salesperson, who did not get a firm appointment, but did record information on one of our shoppers, recognized the voice when she arrived and said, *"Brenda, you called earlier today. Thank you for coming out to see Grand Acres. I am Bob Sanders. You said you are interested in a four bedroom home. I believe we have just what you are looking for."*

Proper recorded information from initial inquiries will give you a head start in relationship building when the customer arrives. How insulting to call ahead, give out personal information on needs and desires, only to have the salesperson act as though you had never bothered to call.

* * *

The Caller That Never Came.

Closing for the appointment is the ultimate goal on the telephone. Sometimes there are objections to committing to an appointment. These objections are usually for one of the following reasons:

1. The caller doesn't see any possible benefit in talking with you further.
2. He is just too busy right now.
3. He is afraid of being pressured to do something he is not ready to do.
4. He hasn't received enough information to excite him to commit.

Anticipate these objections, and plan a strategy to resolve them. You will find many resolutions in this chapter.

Creating urgency is a major step toward exciting the caller to come for a visit. Inviting the caller to drop in anytime between 10 and 5 Monday through Sunday will not create the immediate action that you know is in his best interest, as well as yours. In order to make an incoming phone call productive, you need to have a sense of purpose. The most effective way to create a sense of purpose is to have a set of goals for the call. I will list a set of goals here, and a sample phone call illustrating an example of how to fulfill these goals. The sample call is a composite of many calls I have experienced. I will use this composite in order to illustrate as many of my points as possible.

* * *

Turn Callers Into Customers

The following seven goals for an initial phone inquiry are designed to move the call toward an appointment, and onward to the sale:

1) Identify Why The Person Is Calling

The reason for the call can range from, "Oops, I must have dialed the wrong number," to, "I'm being transferred next month and would like to see your homes." Understanding about the caller's motivation can help you set your direction for the remainder of the call.

Two questions that can help you to gain this information are:

a) "How did you learn about us?"
b) "How much do you know about us already?"

Remember that in selling, the most effective strategy you can have is one that *identifies and fulfills needs*. As long as you are fulfilling the customer's needs you can *gain more control, and establish more momentum.*

2) Learn About The Caller

This goal, of course, overlaps the last one. The more you can learn about the caller, the better you can tailor your presentation to his needs. This effort should not be delayed until the customer walks in your door. It begins with the telephone call.

There is nothing wrong with asking questions on the phone. Salespeople have sometimes expressed reluctance, on the grounds that the initial call is too early. In fact, the opposite is true. Asking questions and expanding on what the caller is saying shows you are interested in him and want to help him. Think of other professions — a doctor, a repair person, or a specialist of any kind. If they ask you questions, you perceive it as a form of professionalism. They are using their expertise to your best advantage, as well as their own. Our business should offer this same level of service. We are professionals working in an office. Our job is to solve people's problems and fulfill their needs. To do this with our best expertise, we need to make a preliminary diagnosis. If the caller does not want to answer your questions, he'll tell you. Otherwise, just think of questions as part of your service.

You do not want to bombard the caller with questions. Nor do you want to qualify him, as such, on the phone. This is a time for the two of you to get to know each other. I often hear salespeople ask a few "knockout questions" on the phone, as though they want to decide whether the caller is worth talking to. The phone is not the place for this kind of qualifying. If you are busy when he calls, ask to take his number and call him back, but do it as quickly as possible. Remember, if he called you, he is probably calling others.

You want to engage him in a conversation by asking questions which can *help you to help him.* At the same time, you give him important information that is targeted at his hot buttons. The following are a few examples of questions I have heard that can allow you to be helpful without being "pushy."

"How long have you been looking for a new home?"

"What else have you seen?"

"Where do you live now?"

"If you don't mind, let me ask you one or two questions that will help me assist you better. In fact, I'll even make a few notes while we talk, so I'll be prepared for you when you come out."

3) Make The Caller Feel Important

The tone of your call should be that you are "at their service."

What they want is important to you. You care what they think. I especially like it when a salesperson says to me, *"I'll be interested to see what you think of our homes* (or decorating, community, amenities, etc.) *when you see them."*

This one goal can often have more value than all of the personality in the world. The fictitious Sherlock Holmes was depicted as having an abrasive, obnoxious, arrogant personality. He would not have succeeded in new home sales. Yet he always captured the admiration of his clients because he showed intense interest in them. His perceptive observations about them proved his interest, and made them feel important. They were able to dismiss the shortcomings of his personality because underneath his facade they knew, from his questions and his focused attention to their answers, that he truly cared about them. He was sincere. They trusted him. They also respected that he was an expert.

4) Show The Caller That You Are An Expert

Customers want to buy from experts. You will have more significant opportunities to demonstrate your expertise after they arrive. Knowledge is power, and you must be current with community and product information. On the phone, however, you can show that you are an expert if:

a) You can make a concise statement of why your homes have value.

b) You can ask intelligent questions designed to provide superior service to the buyer.

5) Get The Caller To Like You

We all know the permanence of first impressions. Likewise, we have all had both good and bad experiences when calling a business or service. When the experience was good, what was said, and why were you happy you called? Charlie Clark, of Charles R. Clark Corporation, says it this way: "Salespeople are the critical link between the builder and the consumer." The most important way to communicate the builder's reputation is through salespeople. Those first few words will set the stage for the entire relationship. Working to continue the relationship beyond the phone is our goal.

The best way to get a person to like you is simply to be likable. Always sound pleased that *he* called. ***"I really appreciate your calling Heavenly Heights today."***

Answer the phone with a "smile in your voice."

Give him your name.

Ask his name and then use it as often as possible.

Act as though you like him. *The phone is an opportunity to begin your relationship with the customer.*

Sound happy. On first contact, we are much more attracted to a happy person than a sad, brooding or stressed person.

Make *him* feel glad he called. And be sure he knows *you* are glad he called. Thank him at the end of the call. Some salespeople thank the caller at both the beginning and at the end of the call.

6) Create A Sense Of Anticipation In The Caller's Mind

One of the most valuable opportunities in the initial phone call is the chance to create excitement in the caller's mind about what you are selling. Give him something to look forward to — a reason to want to visit your site. Customers often call simply to decide whether or not to elimi-

nate you from their shopping list. They have seen ten advertisements in
the paper which attracted their interest, and they want to decide which
ones to visit first. Your goal is to put yours at the top of their list. After
seeing your homes, they might want to see others before they decide.
But at least you will have placed yourself in a position to set the standard, by stating your case for why your homes are best.

Not only can you create a sense of excitement and anticipation
on the phone, you can set the mood for their visit by getting them
to think about your homes in a certain way. You are *precondition-
ing* them for the visit by beginning to tell them what to expect
when they see your homes, and why your benefits are worth special
consideration. One top salesperson said to me on the phone, *"Let
me give you an idea of what to expect when you get here."* If you
set a mood of excitement on the phone, you will establish an immediate advantage over salespeople who use the phone merely to convey information. If customers feel a sense of excitement during
their phone call, they are more likely to arrive at your community
in that same frame of mind.

In addition to creating anticipation and excitement in the initial phone
call, you can also begin to create urgency. Urgency begins with excitement. There are three basic ways to create excitement on the phone:

a) Act excited.
b) Give exciting information.
c) Tell about the excitement of others who have bought from you.
   Simple, enthusiastic statements can often be enough.

"You've must see our homes. People just love them."

*"I look forward to meeting you. I can't wait for you to see our
homes. I hope you like them as much as I do. Working here has
been a dream."*

"We are having a great day today. Our new Jefferson model just

opened and the merchandizers are still here. I hope you can get here before they leave."

Giving particular pieces of information that whet the customer's appetite is another effective strategy.

"When you come to visit us, one of the things I believe you'll like is the dramatic exteriors of our homes. Many builders concentrate on interiors and leave the outside to dated elevations. Our design team recognizes the outside of your home is what everyone sees first. Therefore, we have created drama and excitement in each home, starting with the exteriors and continuing throughout every room. We also give our buyers the opportunity to personalize and customize several design features. Do you have a particular design or floor plan in mind?"

"We have two homesites in particular that are really special. One has beautiful mature trees on a quiet lane, and the other has a terrific view of the golf course and lake. I'll be sure to point them out to you when you visit if they haven't sold."

You don't want to go as far as to say, "We only have a few good sites left." You may stand to lose more than you gain by trying to create urgency on the phone that way. In new home sales, limited supply is a better strategy to use after the person has become involved than it is in advertising or on the phone. Special promotions, of course, are a different matter. They exist to be promoted before the customer arrives, as well as after.

7) Set An Appointment

Opinions among salespeople on this goal run the gamut. At one extreme is, "I never make appointments on the phone. The only people who show up for those appointments are mystery shoppers." A more moderate feeling is, "I don't want them to feel any pressure on the phone. I want to give them the information they called for, and make them feel comfortable about coming out. When they do come out, I can switch into high gear."

However, the approach of most top salespeople is this: *"My goal is always to work toward generating an appointment for a specified time. These appointments are my primary source of sales."*

A salesman who was fairly new in the business suggested that we not limit the appointment to just the serious callers. He loves to excite everyone he talks to about coming to see his homes. He uses the opportunity to show off his community to people who may send him referrals, if they don't buy. He also creates a positive image about his builder and himself. Sam believes that everyone who calls, or comes to his community, is either a prospective buyer, a friend of a prospective buyer, or related to a prospective buyer. He particularly likes the chance to practice his presentation when traffic is slow. Sam believes that conveying an effective telephone presence is in the power of the *persuasive words* he uses.

The goal of always trying to close for the appointment is the best approach, and the one which I have found to be the most statistically productive. Asking for an appointment does not make the caller feel as uncomfortable as many salespeople think it does. Most customers view our asking for an appointment as a sign of professionalism. We will look at an effective technique for this in our sample call in a moment.

In many markets, Realtors account for 50% or more of the total sales. It is important that we do everything we can to encourage those Realtor visits. A slightly different presentation should be prepared for Realtor calls. Following up those calls, and keeping a record of them, are as important as with the non-Realtor calls. This is a great source for your Realtor Hit List. For many salespeople Realtors are their #1 referral base. It is most important to gather as much information as possible on Realtor calls. Record name, company, address and telephone number. Inquire about the needs and wants of their customers. Encourage them to come out for a personal demonstration. Close your Realtor calls for a specific appointment, at their convenience, to give them a complete presentation. The more Realtors know about your community, your builder, and your homes, the better they can close their customers for an appointment.

Why should you set an appointment instead of just asking the caller to come out at his convenience? One reason is that making appointments really is more professional. It adds an element of seriousness to the visit, and helps to set you apart from your competition in that way.

Another reason is that it shows that your time is valuable, just as the customer's is. You do not want to give the impression that you are *too* available. You have a business to run. You have many customers and responsibilities. In the midst of all this, you also want to do the most diligent job possible for anyone who is interested enough to call. You don't want the customer to go to the trouble of visiting your community, and not receive the attention or information he needs and deserves. The appointment gives you a chance to prepare for customers, and to arrange your time so you can give them your total attention. Depending on the circumstances and traffic flow, you can arrange for back-up support. Giving the caller some information on what they may expect when they visit is helpful. Naturally we want to deliver more than they expect.

Another important reason to make a specific date and time appointment is that most people take a commitment of this nature seriously. They will make a concerted effort to live up to their obligation and word, even when their enthusiasm is waning. You will get a second chance that might not occur with statements like, "Just stop by anytime, I'm always here." Your chances of their coming for a visit will significantly increase with a definite appointment.

Last spring I called several garden centers to ask about annual plants. I needed help as to the types of plants to buy, and advice about a soil problem. After talking to three people, who either admitted they were too busy to talk or didn't know much about my problem, I reached a wonderful man who made me feel as though my flower garden was the most important garden in the world. Needless to say, I went out to see him. When I met him, he remembered my name and remembered my needs. He really cared. In fact, I was back in the garden shop recently, and Mr. Shipley mentioned that my flowers were looking great. When I asked how he knew, he told me he had driven by to see them. This gentleman went above and beyond what I would expect in service and caring for me as a customer. It is important to note that the same attitude and commitment must follow, from call to visit to purchase to service to customer satisfaction.

Some salespeople like to call back the day before the appointment to confirm. Again, it reinforces the fact that we are in a professional business, and that the appointment is a real commitment. This commitment also means that you must prepare for the customer's visit. Assemble the information that you have gathered on the phone and use it to organize a presentation that will be uniquely valuable to him. A *personal* presentation goes a long way toward proving to customers that you are an expert at meeting their needs. Preparation for their visits shows your respect for them, giving them a feeling of importance, which will gain their attention and loyalty.

Finally, be sure that your directions are clear and accurate. Using tenths of a mile from one landmark to the next shows that you went to the trouble to measure it for your customers' convenience. Keep written directions from all major roads near the phone.

Staying focused on these seven goals will help you gain as many selling benefits as possible from the phone. Of course, it will not produce a sale or visit from every call. But it will help you maximize the opportunities which do exist in each call, however great or small they may be.

My sample call will tie together the principles which I have discussed. It is a composite of a number of real calls, and every line is one that has occurred during a shopping assignment. Scripts are important in preparing for the phone call, so I will put this sample phone call in the form of a script. To help make your calls smooth and effective, keep your script, or outline, near the phone so that you can grab it quickly when the phone rings. Highlight your goals, the main points you want to make, and the main questions you want to ask. If you have particular circumstances or promotions which can help you create urgency, include those as well. One of the reasons that these lists, outlines, and scripts are important is that they help you to inject enthusiasm into each call you receive. Retaining enthusiasm is one of the difficult aspects of selling. We say the same exciting things, again and again, until we no longer find them exciting. It becomes hard to imagine that customers could find them exciting. We must remember that even though we have said the same thing over and over, they are hearing it from us for the first time. A written script can help to remind us how exciting this information really is, *if we put ourselves in the customer's shoes.*

Once the script is completed, practicing it becomes just as important as writing it. It is the writing that makes it organized, and the practice that makes it sharp and crisp.

* * *

A Sample Phone Call

Salesperson: **Good afternoon. American Builders at Timber Wood Forest. This is Bonnie Alfriend. How may I help you?**

Customer: **I'd like to get some information on your homes.**

S: **I'd be glad to help you. And your name is?**

C: Bill Allen.

S: Hi, Bill. I really appreciate that you called. What information in particular are you looking for?

C: Well, I guess mainly just the prices and the sizes.

S: Okay, I can certainly give you that. Where do you live now?

C: I'm in Hometown.

S: Oh, I've been to Hometown a number of times. I have a good friend there. So you're thinking of selling your place in Home-town, and buying a new home?

C: Well, we're thinking about something a little bigger. How much are the colonials with four bedrooms?

S: It sounds like an exciting time for you, Bill. Let me tell you a little about our homes and Timber Wood Forest. Our homes run from $175,000 to $250,000. Is that within the price range you were looking for?

C: I think so.

S: Okay, that's super. Our square footage is about 2400 to 2800 — four to five bedrooms. How many square feet do you have now?

C: I think ours is about 2200, so we're looking for something a little larger than what we have now.

S: Well, this all sounds perfect. We might have exactly what you're looking for. People get excited about our homes because of the styling and the way the space is used. I think you're going to love them. And the neighborhood, too. It's a beautiful community with lots of green space. We have a lot of terrific people enjoying their life here. It's been a wonderful neighborhood for me to be a part of. Do you have any free time this afternoon that you can come out and visit Timber Wood Forest?

C: No, not today. I'm calling from work.

S: How about this weekend?

C: I might be able to come out this weekend. I haven't made all my plans yet.

S: What's your family situation? Is there a wife?

C: Yes. Four of us altogether.

S: How old are your kids, Bill?

C: Ten and twelve. That's one of the reasons we need more space.

S: Yes, I know what you mean. I have a teenager, and it seems like there's never enough space. We have a number of kids in the community the same age as yours, and the schools are very good. So, it looks like this weekend will be good for you?

C: I'll ask my wife. She wants to find a place, too. We probably can make it, at some point.

S: Bill, I'm looking at my calendar here. I have an opening at 12:00 on Saturday. Would the two of you be able to meet with me then?

C: Do I really need an appointment, or can I just come out?

S: We feel that appointments are the best way for you to gather the information you need. We have had a lot of traffic recently, and I want to set aside special time for you. There's so much I want to share with you, and we want you to have time to browse on your own. We have a couple of very special homesites that are important to see while you're here. We also offer several homes without models. One in particular has a lot of custom features, like a sunroom, that I'd like to tell you about. So if 12:00 is a possibility it would give me a chance to give you the whole picture.

C: Well, I really do have something in the morning that could run past noon. Do you have anything any later?

S: I have an opening at 2:30 if that would work better for you. I have an appointment at 1:00 that might run past 2:00, but 2:30 should be fine.

C: We can make 2:30.

S: That's great. Bill, what is your phone number there?

C: 555-1234.

S: Thanks, Bill. And your last name is A-l-l-e-n.

C: That's right.

S: And what is your wife's name, Bill?

C: Sarah.

S: Bill, I really appreciate your calling, and I look forward to meeting you and Sarah on Saturday at 2:30. If it's okay, I'll check back with you on Friday to confirm.

C: That would be fine.

S: Thanks again, Bill. I'll see you Saturday. Good-bye.

* * *

I chose a fairly simple scenario, with a customer who was not especially communicative or motivated, in order to present a plan for maximizing an average situation. There will be times when the customer will be much more motivated by the time he calls, either because he is more eager to buy, or more eager to communicate, or perhaps needs a home more urgently than this particular buyer. In those cases the interaction will be easier. The important thing, then, will be to focus on fulfilling the goals, and exchanging as much information as the conversation will allow. It is not unusual for an excellent phone user to have conversations that last five minutes or more.

Even in this more difficult situation, the seven goals listed above formed a basic foundation for the salesperson's questions and statements. Notice that the salesperson did not back off from the customer's reluctance to make an appointment, but also never caused discomfort by being overbearing. The strategy of the entire conversation was to provide the best possible service to the caller.

* * *

One way to enjoy the best results from those initial incoming phone calls is to track your results over a period of time. Keep a record of the following information, and monitor your results, as your skills sharpen:

* How many calls are you getting?
* In how many of your calls do you attempt to establish an appointment?
* How many of your attempts result in a close for a specific, firm appointment time.
* How many times does the customer honor the appointment?
* How does the quality of your appointment traffic compare with the rest of your traffic?

* How many of your appointments wind up buying?
* How many Realtor appointments were made?

Tracking this information will give you an honest assessment of the value of the telephone in your total selling process. It will also help you to hone your strategies in order to "work the telephone smarter."

* * *

Many of the principles for handling phone calls are equally important in other stages of the selling process, and will therefore be discussed again in following chapters. I will be repeating the relevant principles for two reasons:

1) A valid selling principle is worth at least one repetition, especially if it involves a different application.

2) I want readers of this book to have the opportunity to use each chapter independent of the others so they can focus on specific phases of the selling process, as the need arises.

In the next chapter we begin the actual face-to-face part of new home sales — getting to know your customers and getting them to know you.

Getting To Know The Customer

The dynamics of building a *winning relationship* with everyone you meet is, in my opinion, the number one reason why some people succeed and others fail in new home sales. Some would say, "Oh, but it's closing. Closing is #1." *Qualifying/Closing - Closing/Qualifying.* They are so intertwined it is difficult to separate the two, and to see where one begins and the other ends. One thing for sure, you can't have one without the other. In Chapter Eight of <u>Secrets of the Superstars</u> we will discuss closing the sale. This chapter is all about *opening the sale* and getting started.

The sale begins with selling yourself. I am convinced you must believe that what you are selling is not only *good* for your customers, but is the *BEST*. Conviction is your most powerful asset. The successful salespeople featured in this book showed us a strong conviction about what they are doing. You can't fake conviction. It comes from a strong sense of ethics, and a moral commitment to give your buyers the very best. Your fixed belief in what you are doing gives you the persistence, credibility and enthusiasm to carry through.

Getting to know your customers is about communicating effectively, using positive persistence and enthusiasm with everyone.

When I say communicating effectively with everyone, I am talking about developing the skills that help you build relationships with a wide range of people with varied backgrounds, personalities, profiles and behaviors. Ask yourself, are you just as effective with a doctor as you are with a meter maid? Are you as comfortable spending time with an assertive, speak-your-mind sort of person as you are with a mild mannered, pleasing disposition? Do you tend to sell homes to persons similar in character and life experiences to yourself? If you and I are honest with ourselves, the answer to that last question will most probably be yes. What about other types of people and personalities? Can you identify sales you may have lost to any of them? In many cases, I would concede that my lost opportunities were largely because I never really understood who the person was, or his motivations.

I came into the home building industry in 1967. At that time the average age of a Real Estate Broker was 55 years. I, along with my colleagues, had two choices. We could hang out for 30 years, waiting for life's experiences to mold us into a superstar, or we could set about learning how to make it happen sooner. The choice was up to us. Strong interpersonal skills begin with projecting an impressive image of self confidence and professionalism, not only because you believe you can make a difference in someone's life, but because you know how to lead people into action to achieve their dreams and goals.

"You Are A Born Salesman, You Are A Natural"

Many of us have heard these words at some point prior to, or during, our sales career as a sales counselor. I would caution you not to listen to, nor heed these statements, given by well meaning friends and colleagues. Statements of this nature have had a negative impact on the potential of many would-be-great salespeople. The assumption is, "I like people; therefore, getting to know them is not a problem with which I need to concern myself." Liking people and "being good with people" is not a guarantee of success in this business. In fact, on the contrary, it may actually mask weaknesses that need development.

Please hear me loud and clear. No one — and I mean no one — is a "born salesman" any more than they are a born doctor, lawyer or teacher. My husband, Terry, is an accomplished scientist and educator. I am a salesperson. Neither of us was born that way. For Terry, it took many years of dedication, focus, education and hard work to accomplish what he has, in order to enjoy the sweet flavor of success. Likewise, successful selling demands perfecting the many disciplines of our complex profession. Terry likes math and science; I like working with people. But where do we go from here? I challenge you to never short circuit any phase of development because you have "natural ability." Certainly we all have talents and potential that lead us toward an interest. But I must say, after many years of selling, as well as recruiting and coaching salespeople, I find very little difference in potential. The difference lies in the desire to do whatever it takes to be the best that one can be. Please don't fall into the trap of believing your own press. It can work to hinder growth and change. It is my hope that you will commit to read and reread this chapter on the importance of effective and productive ways to learn who your customers are, and to strive to build a positive relationship with everyone who visits your community.

* * *

How to talk so people will listen, and how to listen so people will talk, is about communication. Basics, you say, and you are right. But if your desire is to become more productive and to stay on the cutting edge, you must continue to perfect these skills. People may not change, in theory, but their decisions, motivations, and behaviors constantly change with trends, demographics, and economy. Consumers are a product of their environment. Veterans in our business who keep their winning edge have committed themselves to improving the skill of interpersonal relations, each and every day.

"Congratulations, you just gave birth to a 7lb. 6 oz. salesperson!"

Understanding and mastering the mechanics of building good human relations is not to be taken lightly. One of the top priorities of today's best new home salespeople is *fulfilling the needs of the customer*. In order to do that, they must first know what those needs are. To learn about the needs of your customers, you must develop a relationship with them that allows them to feel comfortable revealing those needs. Customers must perceive that you really care about them, and they must see you as non-threatening. We have all heard the expression, "I don't care how much you know, I want to know how much you care." Your customers need to believe that you are trying to *match your home to their needs*, and not trying to squeeze them into what you are selling.

Getting to know the customer is a challenging aspect of selling. The customer is not always motivated to reveal the information that you want. Often he seems distant and hard to reach. Customers want to slip past you with as little communication as possible. In the face of their aloofness you are trying to get to know them, and to help them get to know you, in your first few minutes together. In addition to that, you also want to position your homes favorably for them, in order to gain their interest. You want to position yourself for positive impact, and yet be non-threatening. You want the customer's experience at your community to be powerful and memorable, and also enjoyable. You want to sell practical value, as well as emotional excitement. And you want to accomplish all of this in only a few minutes. How do the top salespeople make this happen?

This chapter will discuss a number of ways that salespeople whom we have visited establish productive, enjoyable relationships with their customers, and then use these relationships as the springboard of their selling strategies.

* * *

In getting to know your customers, I believe there are four major challenges:

1) *Greeting* the customer in a way that gets the relationship off to a good start.

2) Giving an effective *initial overview* of what you are selling.

3) *Establishing rapport* with the customer.

4) *Qualifying* the customer.

* * *

Greeting The Customer

Creating First Impressions

We can't journey far into the subject of communication, both verbal and non-verbal, without reflecting on the importance of being aware of the impact of first impressions. Should you start off on the wrong foot, it is difficult to right the wrong. You see, the customer doesn't know you well enough to know whether you are having a bad day; are a proverbial discontent; your boss just gave you a paper deadline; you are solving problems for a buyer; or resolving a construction issue. He can only perceive that you do not want to be with him. It's the little things that tell the truth about where your priorities are at this moment. "We only have one chance to make that positive first impression." Our chances of getting to know customers are increased substantially when we hit a home run on this field.

Receiving First Impressions

Are the first impressions, or image we receive about someone, true? How many times have you looked back on friendships and realized that the person you know now is not at all who you thought he or she was when you first met? People are far too complex to measure in a moment, yet that is the natural thing for us to do. As salespeople, we must caution ourselves against taking our own first impressions of our customers too seriously. Tempting? You bet it is! First encounters give out strong signals. Looking back, I can recall more times than I care to remember when first impressions got me into trouble. How about those who look the part, dress the part, and act the part of a buyer, only to reveal, months into the relationship, that they have been justifying their decision to rent for eight years. Conversely, we have all overlooked the person who, on the surface, appears not to fit our buyer profile, only to find out in follow-up they bought the next weekend from our competitor. Ouch!

The first few seconds of your relationship with the customer can set the tone for the entire selling process. This is the moment when you begin *building the sale*. The concept of "building the sale" is an important theme throughout this book. A sale is built, one stage at a time, just as a home is built. Your first few minutes in the sale are the foundation upon which the rest of the sale is built. The greeting is the footer that provides security — a feeling of safety and assurance — for the foundation. Throughout the rest of the selling process, it is important that you remain focused on how each element of your interaction is adding another building block to the total sale.

What happens in the first few seconds, and how does it affect the rest of the sale? The message is quite clear from your customer. "Please pay attention to me. I may want you to leave me alone, or I may want your undivided attention. No matter, I expect you to care about me, and how I need to be treated."

We can all recall being offended in a business relationship. This is my latest: Last fall I took my car in for service. Back in the service department to pick it up I waited 10 minutes before my presence was even acknowledged. Another 30 minutes went by without so much as a word from the woman at the desk. She avoided me like the plague. She moved her typewriter to keep from watching me pace the floor. Each time I approached the desk she grabbed the telephone. After thirty minutes of being totally ignored I was not a happy camper. "Would someone, somewhere just give me the time of day?" Though I am not sure, I suspect the person behind the desk does not beat her kids and probably is not a serial killer, however, I am convinced she has the makings of both. During this hostile takeover of my day and my attitude, another co-worker came over to her, and I heard this conversation:

" How long has she been waiting?"

" Just a few minutes."

Folks, I don't know about you, but 40 minutes is not a few. Wouldn't you agree? At that moment I made a decision. This company is history! Oh, by the way, my car was satisfactory, the bill was in line, and the service manager was cordial. Recently, I went to another service center for a lube job. Now just what do you think my attitude and my expectations were? I was among the walking wounded, and it showed. The people at the new service center were not just average, nor were they just good; they were superb, and this was what it took to reset my faith in mankind. I have found a new friend.

The best builder in the universe, the most innovative marketing plan, and the most competitive value pricing can be wasted if the relationship with the salesperson starts off on the wrong foot.

The Welcome

What happens in the first few seconds of meeting, and how does it affect the rest of the sale? Selling begins and ends on your feet. Energize yourself for the opportunity ahead. If you are seated when the customer first walks in the door, it is important to get on your feet immediately. Remaining seated is not more casual, more friendly, and less threatening, as some might think. Standing up to greet the customer is important for four reasons:

1) *It is a symbol of respect and appreciation.*

Showing your respect to customers will help you gain their respect more quickly. It is much easier for us to respect a person who respects us, just as it is easier for us to like a person who likes us, or to be nice to a person who is nice to us. Additionally, it is a symbol of appreciation for their visit.

2) *It is a symbol of professionalism.*

Professionalism is a very important, and often underrated, selling tool. It conveys expertise, that in turn conveys value. We have seen various techniques designed to enhance professionalism on site. One such technique is to pick up a clipboard as you move toward your guest, clipboard in your left hand as you shake hands with your right. The clipboard includes a guest card, a legal pad for taking notes, and any handouts you believe may be helpful during the course of the initial interview. A brochure should not be included. The guest card, the handshake, and the brochure will all be discussed in more detail, shortly. Some folks have suggested including a purchase agreement and other pertinent documents to the sales transaction under the legal pad, to help you stay focused on the goal of selling. It is also convenient to have these documents when the close takes place in other environments, such as on the home-site, or in the model. When the decision to buy has been consummated, it can be less stressful to proceed where you are, rather than risk a cooling down on the way back to a sterile closing room. Wrap it up where it happens.

3) Since the customer is standing, *it puts you on an equal level with him.*

Greeting customers from a standing position allows you to deal with them "eye to eye." Equality is an important part of a comfortable relationship. Contrived methods of developing a dominant or subservient position are self-defeating. The expression "eye to eye" became a cliche because it conveys an important principle of human interaction.

4) *Your energy is increased in a standing posture.*

Energy creates momentum and enthusiasm. It moves the blood from your feet to your head, and this is projected in your actions and voice. This is show business, my friends, and if adrenaline does not propel you out of your seat in anticipation of each "performance" you may be slipping into a slump. Check yourself.

The first thing a customer should notice about you is your *smile*. As simple and obvious as smiling may seem, its importance cannot be overemphasized. If the customer's first observation about you is your warm, gentle smile, it can go a long way toward increasing his comfort level. Customers form opinions quickly. A smile can tip the scales in your favor right away. Throughout the sale, smiling and laughing makes customers feel better about you, and about everything that is going on. It helps contribute to an atmosphere of joy, and it shows that you are happy with what you are doing and happy to be doing it with them. If customers believe you are happy, they can assume several things:

1) You must be successful.
2) Your company must build good homes.
3) Your customers must be treating you well which also means you must be treating them well.
4) You have confidence that is evidence of a knowledgeable person with a positive self image.

Customers don't necessarily think through all of this on a conscious level, but their comfort level will certainly be affected. They will be happier to be there.

The Handshake

The handshake can help set your tone. Because business etiquette differs slightly from region to region and culture to culture, local customs for shaking hands may vary somewhat. Some male sales counselors ask if they should shake hands with a lady, and I have been told by salespeople in certain parts of the country that it is sometimes considered ungraceful for a female associate to shake hands. I mention this to bring up the point that it is not my intention to suggest a practice that might offend. In most cases handshakes are considered the professional and courteous introduction to a business relationship. Here are a few suggestions:

1) Your handshake sends a message about you. Make sure it is telling the sincere, positive, confident and warm message you intend.

2) As the salesperson, you should take the initiative in shaking hands. Extend your hand immediately as you approach the customer. Give your name and ask for theirs while continuing to shake hands.

Every now and then a customer will not respond and the situation will become a little awkward. Don't let that concern you, but rather use it as your first source of information about the personality of this person. In this situation, as in other selling situations, do not form your approach based upon fear of the exceptions. Any approach you take will fail some of the time. If you occasionally have a customer who doesn't want to shake your hand, or answer your questions, or sign your guest card, or allow you to go with them through the models, don't let these "exceptions" derail a strategy that is nearly always successful for you.

3) Make sure your handshake is firm. A firm handshake shows confidence, energy and respect. Your mannerisms and actions in this initial interaction set the stage for you being in charge. Leadership is about controlling the situation in order to give the customer what he needs to know.

4) Accompany the handshake with a verbal greeting, such as, *"It's nice to meet you,"* or, *"Thank you for coming to see our new homes,"* or *"Welcome to Heavenly Valley."* Silent handshakes are awkward. While a smile helps to set a tone of comfort, a handshake sets a tone of trust.

What's In A Name? Everything!

Building trust and confidence by personalizing the sale early in the welcome is also important. Begin with the exchange of names. Let's be honest. Chances are, the person entering your sales center probably is not anxious to meet you. They, too, may be among the walking wounded, having been worked over and spit out by not-so-professional salespeople. Turning this attitude around takes patience and finesse.

When you give your name, give your position as well. Customers often do not know if they're talking to the community sales manager, the sales assistant, or to someone else. Give your first and last name as well. The following conversation is an example.

"Good afternoon. I'm Bonnie Alfriend. I'm the sales manager here at Timber Wood Forest. [Shake, shake.] You are?"

"Hi, we're the Pattersons. This is my wife, Mary, and I'm John."

"It's nice to meet you, Mary. You, too, John. I'm glad you came to visit us today. What brings you?"

During your greeting, and after you introduce yourself, if customers do not give you their names, ask them. ("What are your names?" "Who are you folks?") This is, after all, your place of business. You get to set the rules. Just be sure that your rules are 1) not offensive, 2) designed to help them gain comfort and familiarity, and 3) focused on selling homes. Most customers expect this in a business practice as long as the atmosphere is professional.

Incorrect pronunciation can be a distraction and turn-off. Make sure you pronounce their names correctly. If uncertain, ask. People are always willing to help and asking shows that you are interested, and care enough to pronounce their name correctly. I can remember the frustration my father-in-law always had with our name. Alfriend — it looks easy, however, because it is an unusual surname, many people do mispronounce it. I can hear Dad now. "That is A-l-f-r-i-e-n-d but it is pronounced A-l-l f-r-i-e-n-d." Likewise, make sure they hear your name correctly, and spell it if your name is unusual.

Once you have their name, it is important to use it frequently, as long as it sounds natural and spontaneous. Customers can tell when you are using their names simply as a selling technique. If you use their names earnestly, it will help strengthen your bond with them. There is tremendous power in the use of names. We all like to hear our name spoken, as it makes us feel important and individual. The sound of it is comforting to us. The use of a name also helps to personalize a relationship. There is an element of sincerity about it.

Some salespeople like to create a casual remark about the customer's name before moving on. An example of this would be, *"Your name is John, my father's name is John. And that's just what he wanted to be called. No Jack or Johnny for Dad. He is John."*

What do I call them? It goes without saying that if your customers introduced themselves as Colonel Anderson, or Dr. Stewart, or Ms. Miller, you should address them the same. Once they feel comfortable "giving you permission" to call them Susan, or John, or Helen, you know you are on your way to building a relationship. What if they give their full name. "Hi, I'm Susan Powell, pleased to meet you." Some years ago when I entered the business it was the customary to refer to your customers as Mr, Ms, Dr, etc. until they became buyers, or asked you to call them by their first name. In those days, we also answered questions with a "yes sir" and "no ma'am." Today, we see a more informal approach to addressing customers. Of course this will vary in degree, depending upon the personality of your prospective buyers, and the custom in your region. It is always important to be sensitive to your customers, and to treat everyone with respect and appreciation.

Remember Me

If you find it difficult to remember names, you will need to develop a mechanism to help you. Some people repeat the name after the customer says it, as in the example above. Sometimes we don't hear the name because when the customer says it, we are thinking about what we are going to say next. If you have that problem the best solution, simply, is to be aware of the tendency, and force yourself to focus on what the customer is saying, and to rely more on spontaneity or prior preparation for your own next comment. When you miss the customer's name, be straightforward and honest. *"I'm sorry I didn't catch your name. Is that spelled with a y or ie?"* Ask them to repeat their names early in the relationship. The longer you wait, the more difficult it will become.

I have found this area of rapport-building to be one that is frequently difficult for salespeople. A veteran salesperson admitted to me this is an embarrassing area for him at times, especially when he learns the customer's name for the first time as he is writing the agreement. There are memory courses and learning techniques for recalling names. The simplest way is to ask for it, clarify it if necessary, write it down, and repeat it often.

How can you get customers to remember you and use your name in conversation, as well?

1) Wear a pin with your name, your position, and your company.

2) Repeat your name in conversation. For example, *"One of my homeowners just told me, 'Mary, I am so happy we selected the hardwood floors.' "*

3) Have awards, honors, personal recognition, and educational achievements displayed with your name on them.

4) Have a name plate on your desk.

5) Display your business cards.

6) Ask fellow employees and your construction team to address you by name when showing customers around. *"Hi Jim, we are going over to the Henderson model, was the carpet installed today?" " Yes, Mary, it was and it really looks nice."*

Create A Positive Mood

Be sure that your initial greeting contributes three ingredients to the atmosphere:

1) Happiness — to create a mood of optimism and good feelings.

2) Enthusiasm — to create an environment of energy and success.

3) Warmth — to create a sense of caring and comfort.

While the above thoughts may seem basic and obvious, I wanted to spend a little time discussing them because I have seen the greeting make an enormous difference during my shopping experiences. Salespeople who use the principles which I have just summarized build rapport and create momentum more quickly.

Gathering Information

I want to spend a few more moments talking about the guest card before I move on to the "initial overview." Many salespeople feel quite comfortable asking customers to fill out the guest card right away. However, more and more of the top producers are moving the guest card to a later point in the sale, after a relationship has been established. Personally, I agree with the latter approach. I

believe that the later you can incorporate the guest registration, the
better the information you receive.

One approach that is even more effective is to fill the card out
yourself as you go. I alluded to this technique earlier, when I mentioned the clipboard. It comes across as very professional, and entirely appropriate to the business at hand. On occasion, we have heard
salespeople apologize for the guest card, or disclaim it as something
for "our marketing department." The guest card is not for the marketing department. If other divisions in your company can benefit
from the information, that's great. But the guest card is primarily for
the benefit of the salesperson. Charlie Clark suggests we refer to our
information cards as asset cards because of the tremendous value the
information is to our future success. Any and all information you can
gather about your customers is the greatest asset you have in this
business. The more you know about your customers the better your
chances of helping them make a decision to buy your homes.

One salesperson who used the approach of filling out the guest
card herself "got permission" to ask for the information by saying,
*"Sue, may I ask you to do a couple of things for me that will help
me to help you with your decision?"* Another version of that question would be, *"Sue, do you mind if I ask you a couple of infor-
mation-type questions to help keep me on track?"*

If you do ask customers to fill out the card when they first walk in,
be sure to pick it up, look at it and make comments about what they
wrote. *"Mary, I see you live in Hometown. That's a lovely neighborhood. Have you enjoyed it?" "Jim and Sue, you have two children, boys or girls?"* When they spend a minute or more writing
down information then watch you toss the card aside without looking
at what they wrote, it makes them feel as though they are not important, and they just wasted their time. Looking at the card and com-
menting on what you learn shows interest in them, and is another
way to convey professionalism. Of course, I hope that, in most cases,
you are collecting the data as you move through your presentation.

Some guest cards ask for so much information that they become cumbersome or irritating. The guest card should not take the place of the qualifying process, and it should not be used to decide whether or not the customer is a bona fide buyer. Customers may not include their total combined income. The "own or rent" box may also cover up a more complex situation than you realize. The "price range desired" box can cause as many problems as it solves. This type of information should be obtained verbally at the appropriate time. Beware of forming those first impressions and assuming something, when, in fact, it may not be true.

The guest card can also be used as the basis for your follow-up strategy. When a customer leaves, immediately jot down as much information as you can recall on the back of the card. It is also appropriate to write information on the card as you talk to him. It is not rude. On the contrary, it is another way of making people feel important. We always feel a sense of importance when someone writes down something we say.

The critical issue to remember is that information *must* be recorded. The use of guest cards varies from region to region. If you use guest cards, make sure you are using them primarily to gather information to *help you* build the sale.

* * *

The Initial Overview

The best salespeople I see are well-organized, efficient, and professional in their presentations. After their initial greeting, they structure the interaction to include a balance of:

1) Friendly rapport-building — establishing a relationship with their customers.

2) A preliminary evaluation — finding out who they are, and their level of motivation.

Some salespeople like to begin their questioning with "open probes" — questions requiring thoughtful answers that open up other areas for questioning. Others, like to start with "closed probes" — questions requiring short simple answers, so that the customer can open up after they become more comfortable. Both approaches are valid. It is important to know the difference and decide which approach you prefer. You must also be willing to shift from one approach to the other, depending upon how easily your customer opens up. This is something you can determine pretty quickly. My personal preference is for more general questions, or open probes, at the beginning.

Here are a few examples of initial questions which we have heard used effectively. These questions usually follow the greeting immediately, and are designed to uncover the customer's motivation, level of urgency, and current situation. How ready, willing, and able are they?

"What brought you out to visit us today?"

"What brings you looking at new homes today?"

"What brings you out to Timber Wood Forest today?"

"Thank you for coming to Timber Wood Forest. What brings you?"

"Welcome to Timber Wood Forest. American Builders and I really appreciate your visiting us today. What brings you out?"

"Are you in the market for a new home?"

"Have you been looking long?"

"What is your present situation?"

When you ask these questions, you must bear in mind that, although probing questions are necessary to find out if your customers are even in the market, the answers do not tell the whole story. Sometimes the answers are obviously yes or no. Other times they are more ambiguous, in which case you will simply need to go on about the business of allowing the rapport time to grow. Don't give up too quickly, based on ambiguous or "just looking" answers to your first questions. If customers are cool, then your next goal is to warm them up. Don't let their coolness affect your warmth. Some customers simply need more time than others. Move cautiously here. Don't jump to conclusions too quickly. I can remember, all too painfully, times that I misjudged a statement or failed to interpret it correctly, assumed they were hot when they were not, and conversely assumed they were checking out wallpaper when they were "buyers in disguise."

Moving Forward: A New Age

The future wave that is moving by leaps and bounds is the growing trend by salespeople to move their customers directly into a private setting for a brief preliminary "interview" before going too far into the presentation. We witnessed an award-winning superstar use this professional business approach. She explained, *"I owe it to my customers and to myself to do the best job for them. I cannot possibly give them the service they deserve until we spend time together in private, diagnosing their situation and working together towards a mutual goal."* The advantages of this approach are:

1) It causes customers to sit down earlier in an atmosphere that is pressure free. Later, when the time for decision arrives, the climate is not unfamiliar.

2) It creates a more businesslike atmosphere.

3) Questions and exchange of information are expected and appropriate in this environment.

4) When customers sit down with you, they are saying, in effect, "I would like to talk."

You can then ask your primary qualifying questions in this private environment, rather than standing amidst the displays and other distractions. Salespeople who are unfamiliar with this approach often ask, "Why would a customer agree to go along with this procedure?" The fact is, customers usually will go along with whatever program you request as long as they do not find it demeaning, and as long as you position it as your way of providing better service. The decision to pursue this type of approach should be made prior to planning your sales office, so you can design a closing room that is larger and more comfortable. The feeling becomes more like a parlor, meeting room, or library than a "closing" room.

The Selling Sequence

In recent years there has been a lot of debate about the critical path of new home sales. The truth is that a sales presentation really does have a logical sequence. The sequence can be flexible, but it must be complete. We see many top salespeople vary their presentations to adapt to the personality as well as the needs of their customers, or to the traffic pattern on a particular day. Using the critical path as a basis for *preparing* your selling strategy will help you keep your sales on track and keep you moving forward. Vary it as the situation requires, keep track of where you are in the path, and make sure that all stages are covered before you are through. Think of the critical path as an *outline for selling*. The following components of the critical path should be kept in their logical sequence unless there is a legitimate reason to change.

At the beginning of this chapter I spoke about the importance of the salesperson in the selling game. The sales counselor must be a professional communicator. The sale can never move forward in a productive way if the salesperson puts up a roadblock. He is the critical link to building the sale.

1) *The Location*

The aerial location map makes a good place to start the formal part of your presentation because this display most easily promotes customer involvement. The goal is to start your customer talking as soon as possible. Maps inspire questions and conversation. To gain the maximum benefit from your aerial map, spend time learning about your area. Visit the schools, shopping centers, recreation facilities and other primary areas of interest so you can speak with first-hand experience, and can paint a more vivid picture for customers who are unfamiliar with the surroundings. Use the map to discover the customer's current knowledge of the area, and where they presently live, if they are local.

"Is your present home on this map?"

"How familiar are you with this area?"

"Did you take Jefferson Highway by the Regional Park and Zoo?"

"Have you been to the new Metro Mall located right here (pointing)?"

If people are familiar with your area, they will become intrigued with trying to locate places they know on the map. The map becomes a tool to start them talking about themselves, their current location, and their current home. If they are not familiar with your area, then the map becomes a tool for building excitement about your location.

Location, Location, Location

Location is a primary factor in the buying decision. We have been surprised during our shopping visits that some salespeople overlook the importance of selling location. With all the cliches about the importance of selling location, many salespeople still skip over this stage of the selling sequence, and move right to the neighborhood and product. First start with the overall area, focusing on the benefits of your location. Sell your builder next, before zooming in on your particular neighborhood. Bringing all the benefits and advantages of your location to the customer is a key to creating involvement.

2) *The Builder*

Introduce your builder early on, and build on the corporate image in order to develop rapport and create value in your homes. Who are we? What do we do? How well do we do it? Where else have we done it? What are the benefits to you if you buy a home built by us? These are important questions to answer in your builder presentation. We do see salespeople move from the aerial map directly to the site plan, believing that it makes sense to sell the larger location, and then the more immediate one. While this is certainly logical, there is a benefit to presenting the builder before you present the neighborhood, especially if the builder is also the developer. If they are separate, you should generally present the developer first, then the builder.

The builder can be introduced with wall displays, booklets, awards, testimonials, or any number of visual tools. Builder displays should include pictures of the building team, including the owner or president, other communities, special achievements, and a mission statement about the company.

Earlier we spoke about the importance of a name. This also applies to your company name. Give the name of your company and/or builder at every opportunity, rather than say "the builder." Use your name, your builder's name, and the name of your community as often as possible, to enhance memory. With consumers visiting numerous communities, and often spending considerable time in the selection process, it is critical that they remember you.

The "builder story" is another one of those frequently missed opportunities in the selling process. When a salesperson shows pride in his or her builder, it creates positive motivation. Here are several examples we have heard, that had significant impact because of their sincerity.

"Quality Homes is a company that I've really been able to put my faith in. They don't let their employees or their customers down."

"Working for Quality Homes makes me proud of what I do."

"I don't think I could ever work for another builder after being with Quality Homes. This company is the absolute tops."

"I love to work for a company whose product is so good, my customers become some of my best friends."

"Quality Homes and I make a good team. We both are committed to total quality, service and satisfaction to our customers."

"I am very proud to say I have been a part of the Quality Homes team for six years."

These types of comments have more credibility, and therefore more impact, than the traditional, "We build a real quality home here," or, "Our homes have the best value of any around."

We see great salespeople everywhere who are committed and loyal to their companies. They truly believe the relationship is a partnership. With those sales professionals it becomes a natural sequence to become the "builder in fact." Use of personal pronouns is exciting to hear and evidence that the "marriage has been consummated." For example:

"One of my homesites will work beautifully for you. Let's take a look at the spacious yard with trees for privacy."

"I can finish this lower level for you with a jumbo bath off the family room. How does that sound?"

"I have a new plan in my custom series that I know you will love."

"My builder will be happy to hear how you like our clubhouse."

Particular *anecdotes* involving your company can bring its spirit to life, if time permits. However, you may want to save these for later. The initial overview should be brief. In most cases, you only have the customer's attention for about five to seven minutes (sometimes less) before it begins to wane. Your preparation should include a scripted overview which includes your location, your builder, your neighborhood, and your homes. In that short period, your goal is to hit the special highlights of what you are offering, while you gain the basic information from them that you need to help you direct your selling strategy toward fulfilling the customer's *individual* needs.

3) *The Neighborhood*

There are two primary displays for selling your neighborhood:

1) The site plan should normally be a floor display that you can stand around, positioned away from the entry.

2) Lifestyle photos or conceptual drawings for your community and selling situation.

This is the point in the critical path of the selling sequence when you not only describe the community, but also bring it to life in a way that will make your customers want to live there.

"The reason this community has been so popular is..."

"The people who live here love it because..."

"I love selling in this neighborhood because..."

"We are located in the center of convenience with..."

The community presentation includes not only what is available, but information on the homesites, the amenities, the site planning philosophy, and the people who have already bought. Your goal at this stage of the sale is to make customers begin to feel as though they belong there — that their lives will be better at your community than where they are living now, and better than at any other place they might choose.

You may have noticed that I have not said anything about a brochure at this point in my discussion of the critical path. This is another part of the selling strategy that varies from one salesperson to the next. If you feel you must hand them a brochure immediately after you greet them, you should go through it briefly with them, then close it, and hand it to them. You don't want them wondering what's inside and leafing through it while you are talking. More and more salespeople are learning to feel comfortable holding the brochure back as long as possible. Their goal is to concentrate on getting to know the customer, getting the customer to know them, and getting the customer to focus on their primary selling message. At this stage in the relationship, the salesperson doesn't know enough about the prospective buyer to prepare a customized brochure that includes information tailored to the buyers interest.

What should you do when they ask for the brochure? One

salesman handled it this way: *"Thank you for your request for information about our homes. I will be preparing some materials on Rolling Acres for you before you leave. Is that what you are looking for? Fine, let me point out on our map where we are located."*

4) *The Homes*

Once again, new approaches are appearing throughout the country. More and more companies are moving away from wall displays that feature floor plans and elevations. The displays in the information center focus more on selling the location, builder, neighborhood, and lifestyle, and less on selling the individual homes. If you introduce floor plans and elevations early in the relationship it requires extensive qualifying to narrow down the selection. Don't overwhelm them with too many choices. Be aware that floor plans are confusing to most people. Even when customers do understand them, the impact is often minimal. If you confuse them, you will lose them, especially when you have more than three or four plans. My recommendation is to keep floor plans out of sight until you know enough about your customers to make the plans work effectively to their benefit.

We have seen salespeople give excellent demonstrations using floor plans after they determined this is where the customer would like to live. In these presentations, the salespeople will typically move through the home, one room at a time, on the plan, describing functions and benefits as well as dimensions. They try to demonstrate the feeling of actually *walking through* the home. They ask for feedback in order to gauge the impact of the presentation. They compare features and benefits of each plan in order to help their customers achieve a deeper understanding of the product and assist them in narrowing down to their favorite choice." In pre-opening campaigns, or other situations with few models or homes under construction to show, the salesperson describes the various homes while seated at the desk or table in the sales office. A round table is more friendly than a desk.

Another effective approach that we have seen for describing the homes is the use of blueprints. The blueprints are "cleaned up" for use as a selling tool. For the salesperson who can use them dramatically, blueprints can provide more of a "rolled-up-sleeves" feeling than polished brochure renderings. Many customers like this approach because it feels more professional and more real. This is a great involvement strategy. Building a home is an exciting dream come true. Marketing tools are helpful, but when they are too slick they can distract from the fun of selecting a site and building a home. People can better understand the plans when they are seated in an office than standing in a pavilion, because the environment is less distracting.

When models, or homes under construction, are available to show, the preferred approach in the critical sales path is to take the customers from the site plan to the homes themselves for a complete, three-dimensional presentation. This approach is the topic of Chapter Five. The final three stages of the critical path will be discussed in subsequent chapters as follows:

5) *The Homesites* — Chapter Six

6) *The Close* — Chapter Eight

7) *Follow Up* — Chapter Nine

Before moving on to "Establishing Rapport" and "Qualifying," I would like to conclude this section with a few observations on some of the most effective strategy used in the "Initial Overview."

Differential Selling

Top salespeople use the initial overview to show how they are *different* from the competition. Knowing that customers have a limited attention span in the early stages, these salespeople want to give their customers an immediate sense of why their product is better than the alternatives which are available. How do you know the ways in which your product is better? There are two primary sources for this information:

1) Studying competition.

You always want to know your competition better than they know you, and almost as well as you know your own product. You never want your customers handing you a surprise about your competition. Anticipate comments and be prepared to compete. We had the pleasure of visiting a salesperson who had a wonderful secret to successfully eliminating her competition. The "customer/shopper" told her they were seriously considering purchasing from XYZ builders.

S: "Which model are you most interested in?"

C: "We can't remember the name but can describe the layout."

S: "Maybe this will help. I have a copy of their floor plans, right here."

She brought out a brochure complete with floor plans and information on her competition. She began to lead us into eliminating the other home by letting us work through the plans, pointing out the difference in square footage in those special areas the shopper had indicated were important, as she enforced the added value in her homes. *THIS WAS EMPOWERMENT!* I just love this technique and hope you will find it useful as well.

Studying your competition includes gathering and updating information about them by periodic visits to their sales office and models. Top performers track their competition monthly.

2) Analyze why your homeowners chose you over others.

Be sure you understand why your customers made the decision to buy your home as opposed to someone else's. If you aren't sure, ask them. You may not want to ask as they are signing their agreement, but you can always ask them after they have moved in. When you determine your advantages, you can introduce them to your customers in a number of ways.

"The reason that so many people have been buying homes here is..."

"The thing that people like so much about our homes is..."

"People get really excited about our homes because..."

"The reason that I'd rather be selling here than anyplace else is..."

"My homeowners tell me they chose to live here because..."

With customers looking at many communities over a long period of time before they make a decision, they must have a clear understanding of why your homes are the *best* in the marketplace. If you can make this point in a concise way, it will give you an advantage, because most of your competitors won't be doing it. We have noticed in our shopping that many salespeople do *not* make a claim that their product is the best. They will claim to be good, but not the best. The salespeople who make their claim to superiority in the marketplace, and then back that claim up with strong evidence, deliver a much more powerful and memorable message in their initial overview.

Customers must realize that your homes are different, and also that your builder is different, and even that *you* are different. The more differences you can establish in their total experience at your community, the more memorable and credible you will be. Here are several examples of *differential selling* we have seen create a richer experience for customers:

1) Using the clipboard and guest card as discussed previously.

2) Showing superior knowledge of the marketplace, of construction, engineering and financing.

3) Bringing the customer into your office for an "initial interview."

4) Describing the vision of the community ("what we set out to do here") and why it has been successful.

5) Describing the builder as a *person*, and why you like working for him or her.

6) Talking a little about your company's history and philosophy.

7) Telling one or two anecdotes about particular customers who have bought from you, or about rewarding experiences which you have had selling your homes.

8) Special concern for customer comfort; offering refreshments, toys for children, etc.

9) Describing ways in which your homes and homesites are *unique*.

10) Explaining the *concept* of the larger community and your intimate neighborhood.

Salespeople we have visited who use differential selling as part of their initial overview build a greater position of strength, and create more interest in their homes, than those who don't. Differential selling can also help create a sense of anticipation about what is to come, and this is another significant objective of the initial overview.

Creating A Sense Of Anticipation

Anticipation increases impact. In the last chapter on use of the phone I talked about the importance of creating a sense of anticipation before customers arrive. When they know that something is coming, and they are prepared for it to be important or exciting, they will be more attentive, their senses will be sharpened, and the experience will have greater impact. As you present your initial overview, give your customers a glimpse of what is to come.

"I'll show you what I mean when we see the models."

"When we see the homes, you'll love..."

"I'm especially anxious for you to see the family room in the Jefferson model. People just love it."

"I can't wait to show you the pool and clubhouse. They're really first class."

"I have to admit, homesite 28 is a favorite because of the slopes. But some folks like more level yards, and we have those, too. Do you have a preference?"

"Later on we'll go into what this all means to you."

"Picture the green space and stream behind this area. It is such a unique setting. I will drive you down for a look."

Your goal in creating a sense of anticipation is also to create excitement and involvement. These feelings are important elements in emotional selling. Your own enthusiasm may prove to be the spark that lights the customer's emotional fire, so be sure to let them see it early. I will talk more about this concept in the next section.

* * *

Establishing Rapport

We have all heard the phrase "bonding with the customer." Another popular phrase is "relationship selling." They both stress the *human* element in new home sales. Selling a home is not a salesperson trying to conquer a customer in a fierce battle of wills, in a cold business environment, in a dog-eat-dog world. It is one person trying to help another fulfill their needs and improve their quality of life. The goal is to work toward a win-win conclusion. Establishing this kind of relationship means you must first get to know them.

And they must get to know you! Often we are so concerned with our evaluation process that we forget how important it is for customers to know who we are, and what we are about. Just as we are sizing them up, they are sizing us up, too. These are the types of questions they are wondering:

1) Is this salesperson honest?

2) Is he (she) nice?

3) Does he really care about me?

4) Is he competent?

5) Is he successful?

6) Do other customers like him?

7) Does he like his job?

8) Does he like his company?

9) Does he understand what people like me want?

10) Will he take advantage of me?

11) If I act interested, will he try to pressure me?

How will they answer these questions about you? Just as you are prepared to ask a few questions about them, you should also prepare a few things to say about yourself. Comments about yourself should be brief and modest, but not groveling. The customer's dignity is important to you, and your dignity is also important to him.

Salespeople we have visited, who have been especially appealing while talking about themselves, have usually revealed personal information in response to comments made by the customer. For example, if the customer says, *"We have two kids in high school,"* the salesperson might answer, *"Is that right? I'll be looking forward to that myself in a few years. I don't know what to expect. I feel like I've been so fortunate up to now, and so far, I've really loved being a parent. What's it like when they're in high school?"* In this example the salesperson used a seemingly trivial piece of information to open up about himself, and also to create a deeper level of communication between himself and his customer.

Customers must *know* you, and they must also *like* you. Customers may not buy your home solely because they like you, but they will certainly be more receptive to your message, your questions, and your attempts to sell to them. Some of the characteristics which customers find likable in salespeople are:

1) A warm smile.

2) Enthusiasm.

3) Happiness.

4) A good sense of humor.

5) A pleasant laugh.

6) A straightforward, sincere demeanor.

7) Politeness and respectfulness.

8) Honest answers to questions.

9) Intelligent, knowledgeable answers to questions.

10) A well-groomed appearance.

Establishing rapport begins at the greeting and continues to build throughout the selling process, always remaining a top priority. As the customer warms to your homes, he is, at the same time, beginning to:

1) Like and respect you.

2) Like and respect your company.

3) Feel good about the idea of living in your neighborhood.

* * *

In establishing rapport we focus on making customers feel *emotionally* comfortable in our presence. It is also important for customers to be *physically* comfortable. Giving your environment a daily checkup is important. I was working with a salesperson a few weeks ago who said, " *Follow me, and let's talk while I do my light bulb check.*" She gave me a Windex bottle, and together we spruced up the model before opening.

Make sure your sales office and models are at a comfortable temperature on all floors. We occasionally visit models where the upstairs is very hot or the basement is cold. This not only makes viewing the models uncomfortable, but the customer assumes that the heating and cooling systems are inadequate.

Music should never be intrusive. If it is loud enough to distract a conversation, then it is too loud. Classical music adds a touch of elegance even to affordable homes. Don't worry that it may sound too stuffy. For a model home, it is always appropriate. Other forms of music are okay as long as they are gentle and pleasing in tone. Avoid styles of music which are discordant, or that some people in your target market might find demeaning.

Your sales center should have plenty of comfortable seating so you do not have to send waiting customers into another home just to find a place to sit. Comfort is important. Lush cozy sofas will entice them to hang around. There should be a place to hang coats nearby. Taking their coat may cause them to stay longer. "Take off your coat and stay awhile."

On a hot day, offer something cold to drink. On a cold day, offer something hot. Light snacks also lend an atmosphere of hospitality to your business environment. As with differential selling, if you can create an atmosphere that is more comfortable and hospitable than other environments your customers have experienced, you will gain a competitive advantage and a positive image.

On one particular visit we were treated with special hospitality by a salesperson. When she learned we were from another county some 30 miles away, she initiated a common courtesy, not unlike what you would offer a guest in your home. *"Wow, you folks drove in from Tompkins County. That's great. I have fresh coffee ready for you, or would you prefer something cold? By the way, if you need to freshen up, our facilities are to the right. Please make yourself at home while I get our coffee."* Our shopping couple was not only very grateful, but indicated this care and concern set the tone for the total interview. Ask yourself, "What am I seeing here?" Are these folks hot, tired, happy, sad, or frustrated?

How can I help them feel physically and mentally better at this moment?

Talk And Listen:

One question that is frequently debated in selling is, "How much should you talk, and how much should you listen?" Today it has become fashionable to say that you should spend 80% of your time listening, and 20% of your time talking. This theory is not practiced, and it is not practical in selling new homes. Rarely will even a serious consumer talk 80% of the time. And the fact is, we simply don't see salespeople who only talk 20% of the time, and still sell successfully. New home sales is just not that passive. The important thing to stress here is not percentages, but rather the understanding that information is gathered by listening, and information creates opportunities. All of us need to strive to spend more time moving the conversation away from *our product* and toward *our customers* and their wants and needs. In other words, as salespeople we must leave our own position and move into their position.

Listening is very important — that is how you "get to know the customer." Conveying your message is equally important. Most of the top salespeople we have shopped strike an even balance between talking and listening. This is not meant to be a scientific formula. It's just that the top salespeople orchestrate a fairly equal *interaction,* in which information is *exchanged,* and a mutually rewarding relationship is formed. Think of the interaction as a game of catch. Two people must throw the ball the same number of times in order for the game to work.

Top salespeople use questions to *create a conversation*, not simply to gain information. Instead of saying, "Do you own or rent?" ask, **"Where do you live now?"** Then use the customer's answer as a springboard for a total conversation about his feelings concerning his present home, and what his priorities are for the next one. His answers to those questions give you the opportunity to sell your community in a conversational atmosphere rather than simply a monologue.

Remember, the customer's attention span when he first walks in is only a few minutes. The more opportunities he has to talk, the longer he will stay involved in the conversation. Sometimes you will need to do most of the talking in the beginning. There are those people with whom interaction is awkward, especially in the first few minutes of meeting someone. For customers like this you need to prepare a short presentation of several minutes that highlights the major points you want to convey. You should take the approach that this type of individual could bolt for the door at any moment, and your goal is to fill them with as much of your most critical information as possible before he does. We have seen salespeople do this very well without much verbal reaction from the customer. It works because the salespeople are well-organized. Their presentation has impact because it is well-prepared, efficient, enthusiastic, and brief. In this situation you must be especially alert for any reaction from the customer that you can turn into a conversation. Be sure this brief presentation (three to five minutes) is fresh, interesting, and different from what you believe your customer has heard at other places he has visited.

Earlier, I stated we seldom see great techniques as isolated situations. Great minds run on the same track. Word trends and phrases will repeat themselves as they become popular. You need to be fresh, appear spontaneous, and not give a word-for-word dialogue that is in overuse. I know salespeople who rewrite their total presentation every few months to keep it crisp and new. This motivates them and sets them apart from the competition.

Animation

Animation is an important tool for creating involvement. By animation, I don't mean jumping around or being a clown. If you are not an animated person by nature, don't worry. There are still a few skills you can learn that will make your presentation more animated, without having to change your personality. None of the following skills are natural gifts. They all can be used by anyone. For some people it simply takes a little more practice than for others.

1) Eye contact

People feel more comfortable if you look them in the eye when you talk. Eye contact is just as important when you are listening. When you talk, eye contact demonstrates confidence and trustworthiness. When you listen, your eyes show that you are interested and not distracted. Eye contact is equally important in rapport-building as using a customer's name. It says, with body language, "at this moment you are the most important person to me."

2) Smiling

I have already discussed the importance of smiling, but I want to emphasize it again here, as an act of will that is exercised throughout the entire selling process. The smile conveys warmth and happiness, and tells customers that you like them. The more you show you like them, the more they will like you. Try to smile and to be depressed at the same time! Doesn't work, does it? Smile and the world smiles with you, and hopefully some of your customers will too.

3) Voice modulation

As in a speech, using a variety of pitches, levels, and inflections in your sales presentation makes it easier to listen to you, and your information easier to remember.

4) Movement and gesturing

Like voice modulation, physical movement allows you to hold

the customer's attention for a longer period of time with the same message. Action creates energy and keeps the interview alive and not boring.

5) Enthusiasm and energy

We've heard it many times before, but it's another one of those sayings that became a cliche because it's so true — *enthusiasm is contagious.* If customers see that you are enthusiastic, they will assume you have something to inspire that enthusiasm. If they see that you have energy, they will assume you must be enjoying a positive position at your community. Occasionally on our visits, we see salespeople who seem beaten down. Customers find this unsettling. Just as enthusiasm is contagious, so is discouragement.

It's not easy to be "front and center" all the time. Quite frankly, it is an ongoing challenge. Educational and motivational tapes are a big help. Play them in your car on your way to the sales office. When you feel yourself heading for a slump, call on your "spiritual" mentor for that lift you need. We all lose momentum and have off days. Strive to treat every day as *opening day.* But also keep in mind, not every performance earns a standing ovation. The secret is to try to do your very best. When you feel yourself slipping, call in the reserves: A book, tapes, a day in the park, exercise, and above all keep yourself healthy, both physically and mentally.

Practicing these five habits is an important part of your preparation. Using animation such as the examples above can offer your presentation two important advantages:

1) It helps you *create customer involvement* in what you are selling.

2) It *increases the impact* of what you are saying.

* * *

Salespeople who are most effective in the early stages of the sale treat their involvement with the customer as both a business encounter and a social encounter. They are able to treat it as a business encounter by being well-prepared with their message and staying focused on moving the sale toward a conclusion. They treat it as a social encounter by staying relaxed and generating a two-way interaction.

Imagine that you are meeting a stranger at a social gathering, and you want to get to know him. How would you act? What would you say? The principle is really very similar in getting to know a customer in new home sales. Your approach at the party would include the following:

1) You would take the initiative in the encounter, introducing your-self and shaking hands.

2) You might ask him how he happens to be there, and how he is enjoying the party.

3) You would smile and make an extra effort to be pleasant, friend-ly, and engaging.

4) You would start out with light conversation, and hope a question or two might encourage him to open up.

5) You would also tell him a little about yourself.

6) You would listen attentively to anything he says, and try to find ways to express interest in his remarks by following up on them with comments of your own.

7) You would try not to talk too much or too little.

8) You would try to find any possible common ground (occupation,

hobbies, family, special interests, etc.) with the other person to make the conversation more fruitful, and to draw him closer emotionally.

9) You would not be shy about asking more personal questions as the conversation progressed.

10) You would seize the opportunity to say anything that you know would be of interest to the listener.

Approach your initial interaction with a customer the same way. The only difference is that you are combining these social strategies with a selling agenda. It is extremely important to show a *genuine interest* in the customer from the beginning. In the last chapter, I used the example of Sherlock Holmes, who, despite a less than endearing personality, won over his clients because of his sincere, intense interest in them. Honest caring is worth a lot in the initial encounter. I have already discussed the type of demeanor that conveys this caring, and I will give examples of the types of questions which convey it, in the next section on "Qualifying."

Be sure to acknowledge *all* of the customer's remarks, regardless of whether or not they relate directly to your selling agenda. Even your responding with interest to an insignificant remark can make shy customers feel glad they spoke, and more comfortable speaking again.

One comment that is sometimes ignored by salespeople is a favorable statement about a competitor. The more confident salespeople whom we have seen will allow and even encourage their customers to talk about why they like a competitor *("What did you like about them?")*. In drawing these opinions from the customer, salespeople receive valuable information about the customer's likes and dislikes. They are able to develop a more appropriate strategy for competing, because they have a better idea of what they are competing against. Customers respect salespeople for seeking the truth, rather than just trying to peddle their own product.

We have seen salespeople switch on their telephone answering machines when they become involved in conversations with customers. This shows your customers you want to give them your undivided attention, not just grab every opportunity that may pop up. Your goal is to give each customer you talk to a sense of importance and dignity. They will appreciate this treatment, and will be more inclined to treat you the same way.

Don't be afraid to be direct in your questioning. You do not want to hit customers with a series of rapid-fire questions. But when you do ask a question, it is better for the question to be straightforward. *"Do you mind if I ask you a few questions about your situation? It will help give me a better idea of whether or not I can provide what you're looking for."* A straightforward approach builds rapport more effectively than an approach that seems coy, subversive, or timid. The latter gives the impression that we are ashamed of what we do. A customer is more likely to trust us if we appear proud of what we do. He can begin to view us as a *counselor*, giving us a stronger position in the relationship. Straightforwardness is also more professional. Professionalism makes the customer feel "taken care of," which plays a positive role in the buyer's motivation.

Never be afraid to show empathy for a buyer's fears. You will not risk making the fear worse by appearing to agree with it. Empathy gains much more than it loses, as long as it is followed by a proposed solution. Customers want to know that you're doing more than just shrewdly overcoming their objections. They want to know that you understand how they feel. They want you to show them the light at the end of the tunnel.

"I can understand that this whole process is very intimidating. It's been the same way for practically everyone who's bought here, or anyplace else. It's even that way for me when I buy a home, and I'm

in the business. The good news is that the whole process doesn't take that long, and suddenly it's over. Once you've moved in, you realize that your life really is better than it was before, and you wish you'd done it sooner. My customers tell me that, again and again."

"I can understand how you feel. Standing where you are standing I would be feeling the same way. We will go through the process together so you will feel more comfortable."

Be sensitive to the personality of your customer. We have watched salespeople change their approach as different types of "shopper personalities" visit them. This is very refreshing to see. While no one expects a salesperson to develop a psychological profile on the basis of a minute or two of interaction with a stranger, it is still possible to be sensitive to obvious characteristics. When customers are serious, be serious. When they are jovial, you can be, too. When they are timid, be confident and reassuring. When they seem very formal, or conservative in their dress, an overly casual selling style may seem unprofessional. Likewise, when customers project a casual demeanor, stiffness on your part might be interpreted as coldness. Some salespeople refer to this adaptive approach as "being a chameleon."

* * *

One final thought on establishing rapport. *Rapport building is a part of selling, not a substitute for it.* Top salespeople establish a balance between relationship selling and staying focused on the sale. Salespeople who ignore the relationship aspect of selling get into trouble because they are not able to personalize their information, and relate it to their customers' needs. At the other extreme, salespeople who put too much emphasis on the relationship frequently wind up spinning their wheels, and wondering why their customers have no urgency to buy.

A successful salesperson recently said, *"When customers come into our sales offices, they're looking for a home, not a friend."*

There is a lot of wisdom in this remark. It is not intended to deny relationship selling, but only to put it in perspective. I have seen salespeople unable to generate selling momentum because they focus entirely on making a friend, and are unwilling to take the risks in the relationship necessary to make sales. They are so concerned with creating a comfortable atmosphere for the buyer that they are afraid to disrupt the comfort by qualifying, demonstrating, or closing. It is as though they are afraid they will lose them if they switch to the business of selling. Selling new homes is a very valuable service in which you play a major role in improving the lives of many people. I am proud to be a salesperson. Hope you are, too.

You do not need to have a gregarious personality to establish rapport, and you do not have to establish rapport in the first two minutes. With some customers, it simply takes longer. I know of a number of outstanding salespeople who establish rapport primarily by gaining the customer's respect. They are very straightforward, businesslike, and matter-of-fact. They are focused, and they have the ability to steer their buyers to become focused. These salespeople stay focused on illustrating the fine qualities of the builder and the builder's product. They demonstrate such a strong desire to serve their customers well that they establish their rapport through their credibility and confidence, more than through personal charisma. They use exciting words *("These homes are just terrific!"* — *"This master suite will take your breath away!")* without being exciting personalities. They are so involved in what they are doing that they are able to create customer involvement as well. This mutual involvement becomes the source of their bonding. And it is through this bonding that they become comfortable discussing the specific needs of their customers, and matching their homes to those needs.

For many salespeople, this approach may seem like putting the cart before the horse. The point that I want to make here is that if this more serious, focused personality reminds you of yourself, you can still be a successful new home salesperson, even though you don't fit the mold of the "relationship seller." It is always important to "connect with the customer," as one top salesperson put it, so you can personalize your selling style and your homes to fit your customer. Your goal always is to establish rapport, but there are a number of different ways to reach that goal.

* * *

Qualifying

Perhaps a better term for qualifying is *evaluating the customer.* "Qualifying" has an intimidating and judgmental ring to it. Your goal throughout this whole phase of the selling process is, once again, to "get to know the customer." There are four primary categories of knowledge which you need to evaluate:

1) Do your customers have the financial ability to buy?

2) Financing aside, are they otherwise ready, willing, and able to buy?

3) What is their source and level of motivation?

4) What are their needs and priorities?

Certainly these four questions can overlap. But a thorough evaluation must involve all of them, and we must begin to delve into these questions before the customers see our homes, in order to help them evaluate us in the most favorable light.

Qualifying does not occur at a specific moment in the selling process. It unfolds as our relationship with the customer develops. We can create a troublesome distance between ourselves and our customers by "over qualifying" too early. The answers to the four questions above will surface in the course of normal conversation.

"Rapid-fire" qualifying gives customers the feeling that you are trying to judge whether or not they are worthy of your time. At high-traffic communities this may be necessary. Just be aware that you risk damaging a potentially productive relationship if your qualifying strategy sounds impatient. Remember, your goal in your first few minutes with your customers is to make them feel comfortable, to like you, and to want to pay attention to you. "Qualifying" is not a separate process in itself. It is part of "getting to know the customer," and requires as much patience as time permits. Our "site seeing" visits have shown us many effective ways of working qualifying questions into the initial overview. Some salespeople believe you should always give before you take; that is, give a piece of information, and then ask for a piece in return.

S: *"Our homes include three to five bedrooms. How many are in your family?"*

C: *"We have two children."*

S: *"That's how many we have. How old are yours?"*

C: *"Our daughter is fifteen and our son is thirteen."*

S: *"Ah, two teenagers. I'll bet they keep you busy. What are their favorite activities?"*

In this example, the salesperson was using the information as a springboard for building rapport, as opposed to just "qualifying." By introducing the customer to the rhythm of a casual conversation with an interested person, the salesperson is setting up an atmosphere in which asking and answering questions becomes more comfortable. We have also watched salespeople move in, and then back off in their qualifying. They will ask a few qualifying questions, then move to a more casual climate, and then return to the business at hand. Others make their customers more comfortable by asking permission to ask question.

"Do you mind if I ask you a couple of things to help focus me on what you need?"

One salesperson used the following approach: *"My goodness, let me see. Allow me to ask you a few questions to see if I can help you. What is your price range?"* When the customer answered, the salesperson responded by saying, *"If you don't mind, let me find a piece of paper and a pen to write down what you are looking for, and your special needs."* This salesperson was getting down to business, but was also demonstrating that she was genuinely interested in her customers, and in providing good service. Discovering what customers *want* is an important part of qualifying.

Earlier I mentioned the greeting question, "What brings you out to see our homes today?" This is a good place to start the process of learning what they want. Asking your customers to list all of their desires can be very risky, because the chances are pretty good that they want more than you, or anyone else, can offer them. A safer strategy is to try to learn their top one or two priorities. You can begin to gather this information by asking about their current home. Keep in mind it is our emotional wants that outweigh our logical needs in most cases. When wants and needs are in conflict you're better off satisfying wants. "Show me how to get what I want, and I will take care of the rest."

S: *"Where do you live now?"*

C: *"We live in Hometown."*

S: *"Oh, I know a little about Hometown. I have a couple of friends who live there, and a few families in this community used to live in Hometown."* Then you can begin to move into your probing about their current home. *"How do you like it?...What kind of a home do you live in?...Will you be selling your home in order to move?...What is it that you would most like to have in your next home that you don't have now?"*

This last question is a critical one. It begins to delve into the customer's needs and motivations.

In markets where homes are appreciating rapidly in value ("Are there any out there? Lucky you, if so!"), there is a built-in urgency factor, because everyone agrees that waiting is costly. But what about slower markets, where the investment aspect is a smaller factor in the decision to buy a home? What inspires urgency in those situations? It comes primarily from *the customers' desire to improve their lives.* If they can be convinced that buying your home will give them a better quality of life, then you can take the next step in creating urgency by showing them the sooner they buy, the sooner their lives will improve.

In most housing markets this is a more important element in the selling process today than it has been in the past. Your main competition may likely be the customer's current home. You must encourage them to articulate their dissatisfaction with their home. With this information you can begin to show that you can offer them something better. You must also show why your homes are better than the alternatives which are available to them. Then you eliminate all but the one specific home and homesite that is better for them than any other. Finally, you have a basis for creating urgency in a market in which inflation is not a primary motivator.

Learning about the customer's current home can help you build a stronger selling position. We are surprised when salespeople do not ask about the current home, other than whether or not the customer needs to sell it. An old Indian proverb goes like this: "Walk in my moccasins for a mile, and you will be my brother." Helping them let go of their home is your job. There are several ways to ask questions about the current home. Here are some of the better ones we have heard:

"How do you like your present home?"

"What are you looking for that is different from what you have?"

"What is it that made you think about moving?"

"What is your number one priority for your next home?"

"What is the main thing you need in a home that you don't already have?"

"Which room in your present home would you most like to bring with you, and which one would you most like to leave behind?"

"Tell me a little bit about the home that you're leaving, what you like about it, and what you would like to see again in another home?"

"I am familiar with Hometown. You made a wise choice when you bought there twelve years ago. That community has increased in value nicely for you, hasn't it?"

*"When you bought your present house what was the #1 reason you did so? Has that changed? Let's look at **our homes** and see which one will satisfy your needs today.*

Sue, a wonderful veteran salesperson, shared one of her secrets with me: "When I refer to my customer's present residence I use the word house, when I speak of the new situation I use the word home. This is a subtle change in words but it helps my customer's to psychologically detach themselves from their current situation and become more open up for a new adventure."

It is not risky to encourage positive comments about the current home. But what if the customer talks himself into staying there? I wouldn't worry about this. People consider their decision from every possible angle, no matter what strategy you employ. There is a reason for their discontent. By your being understanding, this reason will surface. To ignore their "castle" is to ignore them. They will usually go through a period of trying to talk themselves into staying put ("We're happy enough where we are.") This is a normal part of the decision-making process. You, however, want to learn the truth. If you know what they like about their home, then you know what your competition is, and you know whether or not you can replace it with something better, and how to show them how it will be better. Knowing the good parts of their current home is part of "knowing the competition." When customers make comments about their current homes, whether they are positive or negative, be sure to follow up on these comments to show that you are seriously concerned with fulfilling their needs. Information about the current home can also become a helpful tool in your follow-up strategy.

You must convince your prospective buyers that change is good, and that living in your community will improve their lives. You can give them what they already have, and more. Yet, it is also important to be sensitive about their present home. Don't insult it. It is still part of their identity. Even when they really want to move, and improve their life their present home is still their castle, and their feelings about it are complex and ambivalent. They may not like everything about it, but they still love it. "Home is where the heart is." Questions about their home provide the springboard for other questions about the customer's needs. They give you insight into those needs.

If the discussion of their current home does not provide you with all the information about their needs, then you can follow up with additional questions. Here are two questions we have heard that require thoughtful answers from the customers. The first is the more obvious of the two: *"Tell me what you're looking for in a home."* The second is more intriguing: *"What is the total feeling you want in a home?"* You do not want to ask too many questions about needs and wants at the beginning. You want only the very basics in order to know:

1) Whether or not they are really prospective buyers.

2) Whether or not they can be motivated to buy.

3) What their priorities are, so that you can begin to personalize your strategy.

4) What highlights to focus on in your model demonstration (or your blueprints, if you don't have models).

Should you only ask questions that elicit an affirmative response? The more "yesses" you receive, the more momentum you achieve, so the theory goes. I believe this approach is transparent. Just because customers have the habit of nodding and saying, "yes", does not mean they will suddenly say "yes" to our final closing question. The idea that we will establish a position of selling strength by hearing a string of affirmative answers to contrived questions is a myth. We develop a much stronger position with honest feedback, and showing that we really care what customers think, whether or not they agree with us. Our ultimate objective still is to fulfill their needs, and as long as they believe this they will be more willing to work with us.

Negative responses do not kill sales. A new home sale is like a bumper car. A collision is not fatal. It simply tells us to turn our car in a different direction. Honest questions and answers are the most productive form of communication, so don't worry about an occasional negative.

There is still, however, a way to establish momentum through positive responses, and that is with *tie-downs*. A tie-down is any short phrase or question that asks the customer to agree with you. You are getting them to affirm your position, and in this way you can create an atmosphere of positive responses. This is not the same as contriving questions which insult the customer's intelligence, in order for them to agree with you. It is simply getting them to agree that you are providing benefits which will improve their lives. Help your customers to verbally "buy into" what you are telling them, and reaffirm the attributes of what you are selling. A few examples of tie-downs would be:

"This is a wonderful family room, __don't you think?__"

"__Don't you feel__ that these cabinets really add a touch of class to the kitchen?"

"Today's interest rates actually make the cost of buying, after taxes, less than renting. __Isn't that a pretty strong incentive?__"

"Everybody tells us that for the money, this is the best master suite they've seen. __Does that sound like a fair statement to you?__"

"This area is so spacious, __wouldn't your computer fit nicely in that corner?__"

If you use several tie-downs, put them at the beginning of some sentences and at the end or in the middle of others in order to prevent monotony. Naturally there is still the chance that the customer will disagree with your tie-down. That's okay. A tie-down is one form of a trial close. You are "testing the waters." A negative answer can still provide valuable feedback, and is nothing to fear. Normally, tie-downs serve a better purpose later on, especially during demonstrations and closing. Do not force a tie-down into an early conversation if it does not seem natural. A tie-down that sounds manipulative can do you more harm than good by making customers feel that you are using rhetorical questions to treat them like children. I wanted to raise the subject of tie-downs now, however, because they can be a momentum-building tool at any point in the sale, if used wisely.

* * *

I will conclude my section on "Qualifying" by giving examples of other effective qualifying questions we have heard on our shopping visits. I have divided these questions into five categories:

1) *Level of urgency.*

"How soon are you planning to move?"

"Are you planning to move in the next six months to a year?" This question may sound less threatening than the first. If customers are looking sooner than six months, they will answer accordingly.

"How long have you been looking?"

"Are you just beginning your search, or have you been looking for awhile?"

"How have you enjoyed your search, so far?"

"How has your search been going?"

"Have you seen anything, so far, that you've liked?"

"What is the reason you didn't purchase the one you liked?"

"Will you be selling your home? Is it on the market?

2) *Size of home.*

"Have you decided what size home you're looking for?" (Let them define size in whatever terms are important to them — square footage, number of bedrooms, etc.)

"What size home are you living in now?...How would you like your new home to compare in size with your present one?"

"How many are in your family?"

"How many bedrooms are you looking for?"

3) *Location*

"In what other locations have you been looking?"

"Where do you work?"

"What items about location are important to you?"

"Where are you presently living? Why are you considering making a move at this time?"

4) *Financial Questions*

This is the category of qualifying questions that often causes salespeople the most anxiety. We have seen salespeople begin the financial qualifying too soon, because they fear if they don't, they could be wasting their time. However, top performers are moving away from doing a lot of financial qualifying up front, and working more on the relationship. The theory of this approach is that the time wasted on unqualified customers is more than compensated by the better rapport established with the qualified ones. In addition, if financial qualifying is initiated too soon it may limit your opportunities for the best information. Financial qualifications go far beyond the dollars and cents of income. Don't misunderstand me — if prospects are unemployed, and are not independently wealthy, there could be a problem. But don't assume that a low income is always a dead end. Keep in mind that people are willing to spend more money and work harder in order to have what they really want. Persuade them that they really want it first. Don't limit the potential of your prospective buyers with stringent financial guidelines before you have "unveiled" their potential new lifestyle.

In markets where qualifying is a major problem, or where customers want financial details explained to them early in the presentation, financial qualifications should be explained early. In certain "starter home" markets, for example, part of the *counselor's* relationship is actually established through up-front qualifying and detailed financial explanations. But if this is not the situation, consider being more patient with the specific financial qualifying until after the customers have seen your homes and understand the value and benefits you are offering.

In markets where you want to take financing a little farther in the beginning, another approach is to give a thumbnail sketch of the financial information in one or two sentences, by telling approximate prices, down payments, and monthly payments of typical homes. You can determine if your customer is in the ball park in terms of income, by saying, *"Most folks who borrow 90% of the total price here, wind up needing to earn about $_____ to qualify for their loan. Are these the kinds of numbers you were hoping to hear?"*

While I believe that the trend away from aggressive qualifying at the very beginning is generally a good one, I also want to emphasize that it is important not to shy away from financing altogether. Determining financial qualifications should not solely be placed with the loan officer. Otherwise, your efforts may have tied up everyone's time. As a professional new home sales counselor, you are entitled to ask certain types of personal questions. Naturally, the better you know your customers, and the stronger the bond you have developed with them, the easier it will be to ask these questions. Just as doctors, attorneys, psychologists, marriage counselors, and ministers are entitled to ask questions that relate to the special services they provide, the same is true in our profession. If an occasional customer chooses to back off, we should nevertheless realize that most customers accept questions as part of our business, and they need this information to move forward. To ascertain the customer's level of sophistication about financing, there are several questions you can ask:

"Are you familiar with new home financing?"

"Have you talked to any lenders about the types of financing available and the terms that would suit you?"

Of first-time buyers you might ask, *"Has anyone explained to you the 'ins and outs' of obtaining a mortgage, and how the tax benefits work?"*

"Later, I will work up a cost analysis that will include your monthly investment, as well as your initial investment. Would that be helpful?" With these customers, you may even need to investigate whether or not they have bought into the concept of home ownership, versus renting. Of move-up buyers, you might ask, *"How long has it been since you bought your last home?"*

"Would it be helpful to go over some numbers reflecting the current low interest rates?"

5) *Who is the decision-maker?*

Salespeople have shared their discouragement of having to deal with one-half of a married couple. They feel they jump through hoops for nothing. The other party to the transaction probably didn't show up because he or she is not interested in buying. The one who did show up is the family's designated "fantasizer," while the stay-at-home partner will veto everything, sooner or later. While this may, in fact, be the case, it is important to ask. Don't forget to uncover other "higher authorities" such as parents, attorneys, tax accountants, etc. This is one area that merits very frank questioning. The best way to find out is to be direct.

"Are there any other folks who will be a part of your decision?"

"Are you the primary decision-maker in the purchase?"

"Will I be able to meet your wife/husband/parents soon?"

"Will you be consulting your attorney (accountant, banker) prior to making your decision?"

It is important that you not be discouraged by this situation. If your customer is seriously in the market to buy, but does not have sole decision-making power, you can still gain a competitive advantage by doing a better job with him than your less patient competitors do. They will be more likely to come back accompanied by the other party, and, when they do, you will have a head start because you took them seriously when they were alone.

The other possibility is that they may, in fact, be the decision-maker. Many couples decide in advance that one of the two will do the shopping and the decision-making, and the other will simply see it once to make sure he or she agrees. Customers will willingly reveal this kind of information if you ask them. Just be sure that it doesn't sound like you're asking them solely because you don't want to waste your time on them. Then be courteous and attentive regardless of their answer.

"I forgot to tell ya', I must talk to Uncle Harry before signing."

I can remember several occasions when I failed to ask about the "phantom" buyer, only to have it boomerang during the final moments of the transaction. One I remember so well. A young couple had been back several times. On the third visit it was evident we were moving toward the purchase. The decision was made, the paperwork was progressing, and in that split second when I handed them the pen, I found out about their uncle, the C.P.A. Was it a stall? Perhaps, but I had not prepared them or myself with how to handle Uncle Harry, who turned out to be the deal killer of all time. I wonder even today whether Lois and Jim ever bought a home. Certainly not if Uncle Harry has anything to do with it.

* * *

As I mentioned in Chapter Two, it is very important that your initial interaction with your customers be well-prepared. The impact of these few minutes can be crucial. As you prepare and practice, make sure your approach is always fresh. This may be difficult for a presentation in which you say the same thing again and again. I am always impressed at the wonderful job which is done by tour guides in national parks as they convey genuine enthusiasm for an hour or two at a time, even though they conduct several tours a day, five days a week. I get the same feeling in my shopping visits when I see a salesperson who is fresh and vibrant, even though I know he has made this same presentation hundreds of times before. We see many great presentations that successfully build a relationship and are a delight to witness.

* * *

No, we are not born salespeople. The selling process, and in particular "getting to know the customer," is a series of trained and learned, practiced and rehearsed, technical skills. This is as much of a scientific endeavor as my husband's ability to send a satellite into orbit.

Finally, remember that in your initial interaction it is as important to get to *know your customers* as it is to *sell your product.* Getting to know your customers, and knowing as much about them as possible in these early stages, will help you to create a presentation that will be more personal, and will provide greater impact and appeal.

What Is A Customer?

A Customer	Is the most important person in any business.
A Customer	Is not dependent on us. We are dependent on him.
A Customer	Is not an interruption of our work. He is the purpose of it.
A Customer	Does us a favor when he comes in. We aren't doing a favor by waiting on him.
A Customer	Is part of our business - not an outsider.
A Customer	Is not just money in the cash register. He is a human being with feelings and deserves to be treated with respect.
A Customer	Is a person who comes to us with his needs and his wants. It is our job to fill them.
A Customer	Deserves the most courteous attention we can give him. He is the lifeblood of this and every business. He pays your salary. Without him we would have to close our doors.

- Author Unknown -

Presenting Your Homes

Help Them See What You're Saying

When presenting new information to people it is important to be aware that although what you are saying is clear to you, it has not yet even been imagined by your listeners. For maximum impact it is critically important to help them visualize what you are saying, and how it will affect their lives. Research has found that we retain only about 15% of what we hear, but we remember a striking 80% of what we see. Visualization makes your message more memorable, but communication will never be effective until the listener is seeing the same "picture" that you are. Bringing the customer up "to speed" takes patience and understanding of their perception.

In Chapter Four, I talked about the importance of an equal balance between talking and listening. Now I am suggesting that your "talking" be split between words and pictures. The visual impact will always retain more permanence. "A picture is worth a thousand words," "Seeing is believing," "Show me, I'm a doubting Thomas," are not just old fashioned cliches. They are concepts necessary for people to take ownership of information and ideas.

Does this mean that we must have models to show before we can sell? Of course not. Does it mean people will not buy what they cannot see? No, they won't. Whether or not you have merchandized models, inventory homes under construction, or are selling from blueprints, your job is to perfect a visual demonstration that helps your prospective buyer "see" what they must "see" in order to make a decision.

Our society has become even more visual in recent years due to the strong influence of television. Admittedly, most of us have a problem paying attention to anything for very long. The chore of reading through detailed information to draw a conclusion is a thing of the past. Television leaves little to the imagination, and draws conclusions for us in "bite size" dialogues and graphic pictorials. We are no longer left to our own devices to gather, sort, evaluate and conclude. The challenge for salespeople is to get the message across in a way that will create interest and hold attention. *Words are out, pictures are in.* After 12 minutes we are conditioned to mentally leave the scene and "go to the refrigerator".

My daughter Kim, who majored in TV-Radio communication, worked behind the scenes for a national news team after college. She shared with me some of the secrets to successful newscasting. Kim told me that sound bites generally run for ten seconds unless you are a politician, then you get 30 seconds (who can figure?). A sound bite is a single statement that succinctly conveys the point the speaker is making. If the statement runs too long it will be edited out because the newscasters know if they don't, the audience will. More than a "talking head" (as an interviewee is called) is needed, or the audience's attention will be lost. Pictures along with words are critical not only to maintain the attention of the viewer, but to enhance the understanding of the story.

The Statue of Freedom that sits atop the Capitol building in Washington, D.C., was going through repair and renovation recently. The challenge for the team was how to make this newsworthy happening interesting to the public. Putting a man in the street reporting would be boring. They solved the problem by creating a delicate balance, cutting from the newscaster to shots of the helicopter on the roof and back again. The integral relationship between the media and the public is one of balance. The interaction is critical. A long debate exists, questioning whether the media gives the public what it demands or does it give us what it wants us to know? When it is the latter the public will surely edit the media out.

The relationship between words and pictures — showing and telling — and the role each plays in selling, is key throughout the sales process. The impact of visualization and imagination is paramount when discussing your product. I felt it important to review the significance of visualization before proceeding to showing and selling the product.

Selling homes without a model will be covered in Chapter Eleven. In this chapter I will discuss how to show and sell your homes when you do have models.

* * *

Four Arenas For Selling

In New Home sales there are four primary "arenas" for the selling process:

1) The sales office
2) The model home(s)
3) Homes under construction
4) The Homesite (Lot)

During the initial overview you don't have very much time to devote to the "product." You are more concerned with getting to know the customer and getting him to know you. You need to establish rapport, and to present a concise message that explains your location, builder and community. Also you want to learn enough about the customer's needs, motivations, qualifications and level of urgency to be able to *personalize* your selling approach. However, you can still make a few inroads into product presentation before you go to the model.

In the last chapter I discussed ways that your visual overview could include a brochure or wall displays for product selling. Your goal at that point is to help the customer understand your product line as a whole and why it is special, and to be able to "see" themselves living there. I mentioned that an increasing number of sales offices no longer include wall displays of floor plans. The salespeople use the sales pavilion for the purposes of "building a relationship with the customer, and then take the customer to the model in order to present product. Even with the trend away from product displays in the meeting area (I highly endorse this trend), you can still use the display area as a place to set up your model demonstration for greater visual impact.

The "initial overview" affords a good time to summarize the most important advantages of your homes. The customer will begin to imagine those advantages *before* he sees your models; and then you can use the models to confirm your point. To reiterate, the customer's attention span is often fairly short when he first arrives, so you must limit product details in the beginning. Remember, to cut those sound bites. Customers will remember only a small percentage of what they hear in your initial overview, and that percentage will drop the longer you talk. Hit only the highlights of your homes in the initial overview.

If your product line has one or two key features that will gain interest and hold the customer's attention, then the initial overview is a good place in which to reveal these features. For example, if all of your homes have a particular look or style that people find appealing, mention it. If the floor plans have a special theme, explain it. If there are certain quality features, such as insulation; windows; crown molding; cabinets; vaulted ceilings; plumbing; heating; or flooring systems which allow your homes to stand out in the marketplace, you could introduce one or two of those very briefly. Do not list features which are standard for your industry. Your purpose in the sales office is to present only those few elements of your homes which make them distinctive. In the last chapter, I talked about the importance of *differential selling*. That is the principle that I am talking about here. Use the sales office to explain how your homes are different from the competition, not how they are the same.

"Trust me, I know exactly what you're looking for."

If there is something special about which your builder is known include it in the builder portion of your overview, and then tie it in with your product. Statements such as, ***"Our builder is known for innovative design,"*** can help set up your model presentation. When you make such a statement, be sure to offer an example. This is a good time to introduce third-party articles to back up your statements. Other statements would be, *"Our builder is known for energy efficiency,"* or *"Our builder is known for delivering defect-free homes."*

An example we witnessed of a special unique builder feature is as follows: *"Sally and David, as first-time homeowners, I know you consider energy efficiency important in planning your budget. Is that correct? Let me show you how Hometown Builders has taken the worry out of that for you. This is a copy of a report by the county energy review board. It lists my company as the top builder for efficiency and savings. You can see here how they compute the percentage. The board estimates that because of the added materials we include in our homes, you can expect your bills to run 30% less than in homes built according to the standards required by county code. That will give you approximately $50.00 a month, or $600.00 each year, back in your pocket. We are proud to boast of the best energy package available to home buyers today."*

Use the initial overview to introduce one or two *symbolic* features that prove the superiority of your homes or your company. Leave the rest of the product details for the demonstration when you can interplay sight and sound, seeing and hearing. The overview sets the tone, the demonstration brings it to life. If you can establish a "mood" of quality that sounds different from your competition, your customers will view your models with greater interest. You don't want to make those broad statements that customers hear everywhere, such as, "We're known for our quality of construction," or, "If a good home is what you're looking for, you've come to the right place." Specific symbols of quality are much more powerful than familiar-sounding generalizations.

Your symbols must be memorable. Customers see many homes during their search. When they get back to their "nest," and try to sort through it all, you want to stand out in their minds. Anything that you can show, say or do that will make your homes memorable, is an advantage, as long as the memory is a positive one. *Differential sell-*

ing helps you to stand out in the customer's mind. To make your differential selling more effective, you need to have *memory points* throughout your selling process. Examples of memory points in the initial overview include statements of unique ways in which your homes are best. Interesting sales office displays (area maps, site plans, lifestyle photos, builder story, etc.) can also provide memory points, as can displays that show your "symbolic quality features."

During our shopping visits we have seen displays and samples of windows, insulation systems and party wall systems which salespeople have used effectively to create memory points. These samples not only helped us to understand the feature, but also gave us the feeling that we were dealing with a builder who used a superior approach. Maybe the approach was not really so unique, but because it was explained to us so precisely, we developed a feeling of special confidence in the builder and the salesperson. *Showing expertise* is as important as *relationship selling* in increasing the customer's comfort level.

The most effective presentations we have seen use the initial overview to *set the stage* for the model viewing. The salesperson *creates a context* for the model tour by:

1) Giving a strong builder presentation.

2) Making a concise and powerful statement of why his homes are best.

3) Giving a brief overview of the product line as a whole.

4) Describing several "symbolic" highlights of the homes in order to establish credibility, show expertise, and *create a sense of anticipation* for the model home experience.

5) Setting up a smooth transition from the sales office to the model.

I have discussed the first four points in the last chapter and the beginning of this one. Let me talk now about the fifth.

* * *

Going To The Model

One of the awkward moments of the sales sequence, for many salespeople, is the instant when you must conclude the initial overview, and begin the model demonstration. This moment requires a *transitional step.* If your sales office is inside the model the transition is easier. But if it is in a garage or trailer separate from the model, the transition can be more difficult. How do you make customers comfortable with the idea that you are going to accompany them through the model? In fact, should you accompany them at all? Wouldn't they feel more comfortable if you let them go alone? And, after all, isn't creating a feeling of comfort what selling is all about? I will deal with the transition in more detail shortly. First let me tackle two of the key questions which confront salespeople as they face the model demonstration:

1) What are the benefits of demonstrating a model, as opposed to letting the customer go alone?

2) How do you make the customer feel comfortable with the fact that you are going with him?

Benefits Of Demonstrating Models

1) *The more time you spend with customers, the better chance you have of selling them a home.* The time you have with customers during the demonstration is perhaps the most valuable benefit of all. You have more time to become acquainted with them — their personalities, their needs and their "hot buttons." You can "diagnose" their situation more effectively, thus improving your chances of providing a "cure." During model demonstration cus-

tomers reveal much more about themselves. This visual atmosphere gives you an opportunity to become the listener, while watching their reactions to what is being seen. "Stop, Look and Listen," as the saying goes.

The Power of Listening

You also give your customers more time to learn about you, become comfortable with you and trust you. Listening gives power to the other person, and is one of the greatest gifts we can give to another human being. This gift allows your customers to become more open and sharing with you, as you become more trustworthy in their eyes. They see that you are really concerned with their needs, and have the expertise to understand and fulfill those needs. You are, after all, selling yourself, as well as your homes, during the model demonstration.

2) *You move from a two-dimensional selling environment into a three-dimensional one.* Some of the top salespeople we visit believe the model really is where the most important selling occurs. Their initial overview in the sales office is brief. Then they move into the more comfortable environment of the model. It is no longer a business environment; it is friendlier and more casual. This warm, friendly environment actively invites both the salesperson and the prospective buyer to become closer, relax their guard and relate more directly and openly.

The three-dimensional environment is better suited for emotional selling. Opportunities now exist for the salesperson to *create involvement*. The home has "come to life," and many salespeople believe that this is when the sale comes to life as well. The visual aspects of selling create emotions; the words give information to be transformed visually. Remember, it takes more energy to listen than to see.

3) *The model demonstration gives you the opportunity to present the home in an organized way, allowing you the greatest*

impact. Referring to National Park tour guides as examples of people who are able to keep their presentations fresh time after time, I would like to use them as an example again. Although many tourists might believe that going through the park alone would be more comfortable and convenient, there is no doubt that a guide enriches the experience. Guides convey valuable information, and answer questions one would not even know to ask. Guides direct and structure your trip through the park in ways which will make it more meaningful because they are experts. They can show you special features that you would not see on your own because you would know where to look. They can enhance the experience because they know how the experience has affected others. In the same way, you enrich the customer's experience in touring your model home. Also, you can use the model demonstration to *develop your own special selling agenda.* Turn the model experience into a selling opportunity, that it would not be if the customer went on his own.

4) *The model demonstration gives you an opportunity to justify and enrich your value.* Selling value becomes more important and more complex every year. Each product defines value in a slightly different way. You must help customers understand how you have defined value with your product. This is another way in which *differential selling* allows you to gain a competitive advantage. Features are, of course, an important element in value. If customers don't appreciate your features, they won't appreciate your value and your price will seem out of line. Cautious consumers are more value conscious than ever.

The Art and Science of Selling

Space is another important element in value. You need to help your customer appreciate how your space has been designed, how it has been used by others who have bought your homes, and what potential it can have for them. Certainly the space will be there for the customer to see whether or not you go with them. But you are the one who can *bring the space to life* for them. Space equals value and value justifies price. This is where selling becomes an art as well as a *science.*

What does it mean when one says that selling is an "art" as well as a "science?" The science of selling is the principles. There are certain fundamentals of selling that must be perfected and applied in order for you to succeed over the long term. Selling is a process — a system. The Critical Path that we discussed in the last chapter is one part of the science of selling.

The art of selling is the part that you alone create by applying your own personality and genius to the process. It is the flair, or flavor that you add to the customer's experience to make that experience unique. It is another way in which *differential selling* comes to life. Throughout this book I will be sharing not only the principles — or science — of successful selling, but also the variety of ways in which different "artists" have given their work an individual style, making it a masterpiece bearing a personal signature. As a salesperson, you are like a chef trying to satisfy your customers' hunger. You can feed them by giving them a price list, and pointing them to your model. But it is the unique flavor of the food you serve them that will keep them coming back for more.

All of this deals with the first of the two questions I raised earlier — "What are the benefits of demonstrating a model as opposed to letting the customer wander through alone?" Now I will move on to the second question: "How do you make the customer feel more comfortable with the fact that you are going with him?" The key here is to set up a comfortable transition for you and your customer from the sales office to the model.

* * *

Creating A Comfortable Transition To The Model Demonstration

One of the first challenges you face with customers is the fact that they came to your community primarily to see your models and ascertain your prices, but not to meet you. In fact, until you persuade them otherwise, your customers may believe the less contact they have with you the better. You must change their mind very quickly in order to have any impact at all. Then you must go a step further to convince them it is in their best interest for you to accompany them through your model. Skeptical? You bet they are! When someone is saying, "Give me the opportunity and the power to sell you," it is natural to become concerned and defensive. We ask questions of ourselves: Who is this person? Is she on my side? Can I trust her? What will happen if I give her control? Do I like her? Does she even know who I am?

Our shopping visits have provided us with opportunities to see many salespeople make this transition very well. One thing we have learned is that all top salespeople really do believe in the value of model demonstration. In fact, they use this stage of the selling process more than any other to set themselves apart from their competition. This is the point in the sale where they gain their advantage. How do they use the demonstration to move ahead?

In the last chapter I spoke of using your first few minutes with the customer to begin creating a relationship, and get the selling process rolling. Early in this initial conversation some salespeople put their customers at ease by telling them what will be happening to them. Yes, they will become acquainted with the prices, and see the models. There are also a few other things they will need to know in order to understand exactly what you're offering for the price. And there are a few questions you must ask in order to be able to apply your expertise to their situation.

We heard this example of a way to prepare customers for the process: *"We have two beautiful models for you to see. Before you visit them let me tell you a couple of things about our builder and the community as a whole."* The salesperson then proceeded into her "initial overview," discussing the location, builder and site plan displays, and asking questions.

Once you have learned about their needs, motivations, and qualifications in your initial conversation, you must then decide whether to accompany customers to your model or let them go alone. The question is not, "Does the customer want me to go along with him?" He honestly doesn't know whether or not he wants you to join him because he doesn't know what will happen if you do. If you ask him, "Would you like me to go with you?" there is a strong likelihood he would say no, simply because he is intimidated. *He doesn't have to want you along, but he must be glad you were, when all is said and done.* Your ultimate objective is to sell him a home, and if the customer is qualified, a good model demonstration *will* increase your chances of making a sale. This is where prioritizing and ranking your visitors becomes important.

To Show or not to Show

The question you must therefore ask yourself is, "Will the four benefits of model demonstration (those listed above) increase my chances of selling a home to this customer?" Sometimes the correct answer is "no." Not all customers can be bona fide buyers for your homes. In these cases, model demonstrations can be used to enhance your image and gather referrals or you may simply decide that your time and priorities are best served allowing them to go through the models alone. Just don't call the game too quickly. Many sales are made in overtime. The value of demonstrating is so strong that I am always concerned when salespeople miss this opportunity. You are the decision-maker; make those decisions wisely. If the decision is to demonstrate, and in most cases it should be, then the next step is to make a comfortable transition from the sales office to the model.

I want to spend a little time on transition, even though it is not a problem for all salespeople. I talk with a large number of top pro-ducers who say that going from the sales office to the model is a completely natural event, requiring no further explanation. They simply say, "Let's go," and then do it. For many salespeople it really is just this simple. But for many others it is perhaps the most difficult moment in the entire selling process. For people who do struggle with this part of the sale, I want to give you a number of examples of techniques and statements that successful salespeople have used, in my shopping visits, to set up the model tour comfortably.

To begin with, it is important not to ask permission to go along. If you ask the question, "Do you mind if I go with you through the models?" you immediately set up a situation for them to decline your offer and run through quickly on their own. We do not have to apologize for the fact that we are trying to sell people a home. For one thing, they know it's our job. Some salespeople are concerned that customers will in some way be annoyed if we go with them. The only time they will be annoyed is when they specifically tell us they want to see the models alone, and we won't let them. But that situation is the exception, not the rule." The rule is that you are a salesperson trying to give the customer the best service you can in order to help him buy a home. He accepts, and often appreciates the fact that this is true.

When you initiate the idea of going with your customers to see the model, take an *assumptive* approach. Assume that it is your job to accompany them in order to help them appreciate what they see. Approach the model tour with *enthusiasm* so that your customers will be able to see that your desire to enhance their model tour is the result of your own love of your homes and your builder. In the examples that follow, I will use wording appropriate to a situation in which the sales office is in the garage of a single family home. The salesperson will be taking the customer back outside and into the model through the front door in order to give him the impact of entering the home the way a guest would.

"I'd love for you to see our model now, if you have time. Let me take you into the home through the front door and get you started."

"First, let's start outside so you can get the flavor of the community and the streetscape for which my community is known."

"In the model I will point out a few things about the home which will help you understand exactly what it is we're offering."

"Let me start by pointing out the special features included in the base price; which ones are custom items; and what are design ideas."

"If you'd like I'll go with you into the first home and point out the standard features and the custom items." (This wording implies that you do want their permission, but then you simply proceed with them unless they stop you).

"There are so many features in our homes that are not visible. I'll point out some things of which we're especially proud."

One salesperson likes this method: *"Let me open up the front door for you."*

Some salespeople prepare one or two special items they want to point out to the customer, and then say: *"Let's go into the model so that I can show you...[the specified items]"; or "I want you to see..."*

Another approach that helps set up a natural transition is for the salesperson to include in the initial overview a general remark about the homes and then say, *"I'll show you what I mean when we see the model."* This is one way to create anticipation for the model tour. Other comments might be: *"When we go into the model one of the things you'll notice is..."*; or *"The first home we're going to see is the Birch model. While we're there I'll point out..."*

In each of the examples I've mentioned so far, notice that the salesperson has taken control of the situation without coming across as pushy or hard sell. He's not saying he plans to hound the customer for the rest of the day. He's simply getting the customer started in order to help make the tour more meaningful.

As you begin the process of "walking and talking," so important in developing your relationship with customers, you can look for opportunities to continue. "While I'm here, let me show you..." If you then sense that your customers need time alone, you can return to the sales office and let them continue looking on their own. *"Take all the time you need to enjoy the homes. I'll be back at the sales office if you have questions."* One salesperson also reappeared for a "light bulb check," to see how the customers were doing.

If you offer several models but have merchandised only one, you can use that model as the reference point for your entire line. *"The home you're in now is the Birch model. It's the only model we show, but if we go through this one it will be easy to understand all the others. I can compare it room by room as we walk through and explain the ways in which the others are different."* I will talk about this situation in more detail later in this chapter. You also want to show how your homes are different from the competition, and you can use *differential selling* to help set up your model tour. *"I'd like to show you several things we do that are different from the usual done by other builders."* Another approach we have seen is for a salesperson to request feedback during the tour. *"Let's take a look at our homes, and tell me how they feel to you."*

You want to develop your own transitional phrases that work best for you. The point to remember is that the transition should be a simple, comfortable moment, letting the customer know that you want to give him the most benefit from your expertise as a new homes counselor.

* * *

Creating Involvement

"Creating involvement" is one of the most important objectives of the model demonstration. Unfortunately, it is one of those phrases that has been thrown around a lot without always being explained. Two other phrases which often get the same treatment are "Bringing the home to life" and "Moving the customer into the home." These phrases are so critical to your success in selling new homes that I want to look at them in depth. The phrases go directly to the heart of the art of selling. One of the great things about top salespeople we visit is the brilliance with which they create customer involvement in what they are saying and selling. They "create involvement" by combining selling skills, knowledge of the customer and a double dose of their own personal creativity.

Where does involvement begin?

Involvement begins during the initial overview when the salesperson stops talking *to* the customer and starts talking *with* him — when the conversation moves from being a sales pitch to being an *interaction*. The customer begins to respond and to ask questions of his own. I discussed ways to set this interaction in motion in the last chapter. I will now show how the interaction can be raised to another level during the demonstration.

Money-back guarantee

To demonstrate the need for personal involvement, one only has to look at the way other product sales are presented. We are offered books, tapes and videos with money-back guarantees. "Try me, and if you are not completely satisfied within 30 days send me back with no obligation." Everything from jewelry, art, copy machines, to automobiles extend a "test run" offer. Get involved, try me on for size and see how I feel, and if you don't like me, send me back.

Several years ago a young car salesman stopped by my office, introduced himself and told me about his cars and his company. I was not in the market for a new car and promptly told him so. David learned early in his career that a "no" was a stepping stone to a "yes." His first visit was an expedition. He learned enough to know he shouldn't stop at that point. He followed up with a thank you note, a few phone calls and another visit to "just keep in touch", and see how my business was going. Several months later he appeared in my office again. "Bonnie, I noticed your car out front and wanted to stop by to exchange keys with you. The car I drove over here just arrived in our show room and as soon as I saw it I thought of you. It has your name written on it. Take the keys, drive it home and see what you think. While I have your car I will have it detailed for you." On Monday David stopped by, and I told him I was still not convinced. He suggested that I keep it until the end of the week, because my car wasn't ready. You know the end of this story. By Friday the new car was mine and nothing could take it away from me. After all, it did have my name on it. When Terry asked about other colors I had to confess that I had never been to the show room. This one was mine. Incidently, I'm still driving and loving my car. It will take a major event for me to give this one up. Unless, of course, David drops by again.

Involvement takes on a dimension in new home sales too. True, we don't offer money-back guarantees or test drives, but during the model demonstration the customer begins to *personally interact with the product.* How do great salespeople get customers to interact with them and with their product on this deeper level?

From the Outside In

Begin creating involvement with the home on the outside. It is important to sell the outside first, and then move inside. Although many customers will talk more about the inside of a home than the exterior, the outside is really what most customers buy first. After all it is the outside that caused them to stop. *Pride of ownership* begins with the *look* of the community and the home. Also, the outside is the place to begin showing your own enthusiasm for the home.

Make a list of the exterior details you want to highlight. Talk about the architectural style and the architect. This is a good time to talk about the look of the community as a whole. Explain why you chose the materials you did. Take your time outside in order to sell the exterior with the same detail you would inside. This is also the place to begin analyzing customers' reactions to what they see. As you offer words describing a particular feature, give them time to digest the message and to draw their own conclusions. Watch and listen for a reaction. What they *see*, outside and in, will create a more lasting impression than what they *hear*.

"We put a lot of care into the exterior details. A lot of builders don't think the outside is important because people live inside. But the outside of a home is its identity. It's the first thing people see. It contributes to the total look of the community. We think it's extremely important. For example, look at the detailing we put around the door and the windows..."

Listen to your customers' verbal responses to the exterior. Just as important are their responses through body language and facial expressions. If they are responding favorably, then you know you are beginning to build momentum. If they are not, then you know you must begin to ask questions which will get them to verbalize their preferences, which can help you direct your presentation. If they don't like the look of the home, discover this before you spend a lot of time trying to sell them on the interior. Find out if you have another home that has an exterior they find more appealing. Try to determine if they have even decided what type of look they want in a home.

I was really excited when a rookie salesman took me across the street to capture the total look and feeling of a home. As we walked back toward the model he pointed out features of the elevation. The one thing I noticed was that he was in no hurry to rush inside. He slowed down his presentation, gave me time to ask questions and ended with a confirmation of how much I liked the style.

Once you have completed your exterior demonstration, then open the front door for your customer. It's okay for you to walk in first, and if you do, you should *back in* for two reasons:

1) To maintain eye contact. The better eye contact you maintain throughout your entire interaction, the stronger the bond you can create with your customers.

2) To observe their *immediate* reaction to the home as they enter it. Again, if it is favorable, you are off and running. If it is not, you need to persuade your customers to do some talking. If they were expecting a larger foyer, you can explain that you have other homes with larger foyers, and why this one was designed to be smaller. Some people say you should ignore negative responses, but this approach will solve nothing. It will only dig for you a deeper hole of customer apathy.

Appeal to All the Senses

Once you are in the home you want to provide every opportunity for your customers to use as many of their *senses* as possible to enjoy the experience of your home. Naturally they will use their sense of hearing as you are speaking. It is important that they use other senses as well.

Sight

Customers must not only appreciate the features of your home, but also your *space*. The length and width of each room must be appreciated for their emotional as well as their functional benefits. The height of the room is important, too, especially if the room has a higher-than-average ceiling. Sell the importance of *cubic footage* as well as square footage. Extra cubic footage gives a home a sense of excitement and comfort which you must talk about and they must savor. If a room has extra windows, the positive effects of extra light upon their lives must be expressed. Customers don't always think through the benefits of what they see. This is one of the advantages of demonstrating over letting customers wander through your homes alone. Help customers experience a greater sense of space by *walking into rooms*, as opposed to just looking into them. Once you are in the room, put as much space as possible between you and your customers as you talk with them. Don't stand too close to them, especially when you walk through small spaces. If you believe you are standing too close, back off from them. This is not an awkward gesture. On the contrary, it will make them feel more comfortable.

Builders often commit large budgets to appeal to the sense of sight through landscaping and merchandising. Make sure the customer appreciates these efforts. Use your own senses of hearing and sight as you continue to ask questions and observe his reactions while walking through the home.

Smell

This is one of the senses that is often overlooked in new home sales. However, we have noticed a difference in the atmosphere of homes with pleasant fragrances. Appealing to the sense of smell can create warmth and intimacy. In romance, perfume is an example of this principle. In model homes, kitchen smells such as bread, cookies, cinnamon or hot chocolate give your model the feeling of home. The scent of fresh flowers and potpourri add a touch of elegance. Cigarette smoke or lingering food odors do the opposite.

Touch

I cannot overemphasize the importance of touch as a selling tool. Many of the best model demonstrations we have seen were the ones that brought the sense of touch to the forefront. The more customers can touch, the more involved in your product they will become. Allow them to feel and open cabinets. Encourage them to touch carpet and tile samples. Use the sense of touch to experience refrigerators, icemakers, ranges, dishwashers, faucets, and lazy susans. Ask them to run their hands along counter tops or under the water of special spigots. If your windows are especially easy to operate, have customers experience this benefit for themselves.

Some salespeople have told me they find this technique difficult to do without sounding contrived. Here is how some salespeople make this experience comfortable for themselves as well as for their customers: If they want the customer to experience a kitchen cabinet, they will run a hand along the cabinet first and then say to the customer, "Feel the wood on this cabinet, and then go ahead and open it so you can see what's inside." This is a very normal and casual remark which sounded very natural when it was said to us. Customers do not feel awkward with a request expressed in this way. Showing enthusiasm makes the situation of involvement through touch more natural.

"I love this icemaker! On a hot day in the summer I probably use it myself twenty times giving people cold drinks. Give it a try. By the way, can I offer you something?"

"You need to check out this faucet with the long neck. It stretches out like a goose. Whoever invented this must have been a genius! We use ___[brand name] plumbing fixtures and they are always at the forefront of technology."

You can use experiences of touching to introduce questions about the customer's current home. *"Do you have a lazy susan at home?... That door has a lazy susan behind it. Have a look."* Another approach you can use to help customers to experience a feature through the sense of touch is to ask for their opinion, especially if it is a new item. Even people who don't want to buy usually won't mind being helpful.

"We've just started using dimmer switches for our dining room lights. They cost a little more, but we felt that most people really wanted them. Would you mind giving it a try and telling me if you think we made the right decision?"

"We use Corian for our kitchen counter tops now because of the look and feel. Run your hand along it. Do you think it enhances the look and durability, or should we just stick with Formica?"

These are sincere questions that show the customer you are seriously concerned with what he thinks, and are not just trying to shove your assortment of brand names down his throat. Secret Tip: Salespeople who use the name of the manufacturer gain memory points. When they are familiar brands the benefits may be obvious. We recommend that, whether the brand name is well known or not, it is good to follow up with information about the manufacturer with value-added benefits, and the reasons for your selection. The use of brand names in your demonstration is important. It shows your commitment to quality. But when you mention a brand name, don't assume that the customer will recognize the manufacturer or know the benefits of the product. They may think it's just one more way to run up the price of your home if you don't explain why you thought the extra cost was worthwhile. Explain how the extra price will be more cost effective in the long run as well as more aesthetically appealing for them personally. Again, the sense of touch can help you to enhance the value of some of your customized items.

Taste

While taste is not normally associated with new home sales, offering refreshments can help a customer gain more enjoyment from your model demonstration. Some salespeople find an "assumptive approach" more comfortable when they offer refreshments, because they are less likely to be rejected. Instead of saying, "May I offer you some lemonade?" they might say, *"I think I'd like some lemonade. Will you join me?" "The coffee is fresh, would you like yours black or with cream and sugar?"* The customer is a guest in your home. Anything that can increase his comfort, and also cause him to pause and linger, can help you establish a more open relationship in which customers are more appreciative of your efforts.

* * *

Won't You Please Have A Seat?

The more you can get a customer to sit down, the better. As I mentioned in the last chapter, getting a customer to relax can change the dynamics of the sale in your favor. Sitting makes an interaction more relaxing and intimate. Sitting in a model gives customers more of a sense of being "at home" there.

When salespeople have difficulty asking a customer to sit down in the middle of a model demonstration, they can overcome this by simply sitting down themselves and saying, *"Would you like to*

have a seat for a minute, and I'll tell you a little more about..."
Chances are the customer will join you. Even if they say, "No
thanks, we're in kind of a hurry," there is no harm done. You just
stand up and continue with the demonstration. Many salespeople
find this approach more comfortable and less forced than, "Why
don't you folks stop, have a seat, and experience the spaciousness
of this lovely room. Imagine yourself here at Christmas."

Throughout the model demonstration it is important to be *natural*
and *sincere*. If you are, then it is perfectly appropriate to be *curious
as well*. Throughout the demonstration you want to know the customer's *real* responses and needs, so it is natural to ask them for
feedback. If they give a negative response or raise an objection, that
is not only okay, but welcome. The sooner you hear their objections, the better. Don't try to cover up situations that force everyone
to ignore objections. Pretending they don't exist won't make them
go away. Only resolving them will accomplish that. Even if you
cannot resolve an objection right away, at least you know what it is,
and you can search for ways to try to balance it, or have the customer rethink it in a different light.

Humor

The extra dimension of humor and lightness can be very effective
in the more casual environment of demonstration. We don't use
humor as often as we might. This is due in part to the seriousness
of our business, and the concentration of accomplishing our goal.
But there is power in humor. It demonstrates you have confidence,
are at ease with what you are doing, and that you are in control of
the situation. Also, humor breaks through tension, putting people at
ease and relaxing them.

We saw humor used in demonstration when a salesperson was
able to laugh about an unfortunate circumstance while keeping her
focus, and without breaking stride. We arrived at her models on a

hot and dry afternoon. Sprinklers were operating between the two models. "Jill" spotted us entering the sales center while she was next door. Forgetting about the sprinklers she dashed across the lawn, landed ankle deep in mud, lost a shoe in the process, and greeted us without shoes, and dripping wet. "Had I known you were coming I would have dried off." In that moment we fell in love with Jill. Her entire presentation was completed with no evidence of being uncomfortable with her condition. We laughed and punned our way through each room. It was a memorable interview with a great sales lady who never lost sight of a major human attribute — flexibility. If we take ourselves too seriously, for sure, our customers will not. Maintaining flexibility and a sense of humor, as well as the ability to roll with the punches, expand awareness, and allow the freedom of total involvement on the part of both the sales professional and the customer.

"Hi, folks, Welcome to Happy Homes!"

Teach Me

Your customers are there to learn about you, your company, your neighborhood and your homes. Presenting your product must involve the human and personal side of life. People need to identify with something that reminds them of life as they know it. Involvement includes learning. The more you can learn about your customers' needs and their responses to what they are seeing, the easier it will be to keep your momentum going. Follow your statements with questions whenever you can. This helps the conversation become an interaction instead of a lecture.

Beware of the lecture. Remember the very nature of listening takes concentrated effort. It is work. Dull monologues will not "win friends and influence people." Information, by its very nature, is automatically boring, and often confusing. Most of the time people will prefer to stay confused or bored rather than lose face by saying they don't understand or they aren't interested in what you are saying.

Check your presentation. Customers don't need to know everything you know. They are only interested in knowing what *they* need to know. The following is a great example of how a superstar caught herself, changed directions, and won the sale. Our "customer" was a single male in his late thirties. During the model presentation the sales professional had been talking for several minutes in the kitchen, pointing out every nook and cranny (with benefits of each). Noting her very bored customer, shuffling from foot to foot, she quickly retrieved herself by saying:

"Paul, let me ask you something. Are you a gourmet cook or do you just nuke it and run?"

"I guess you would call me a 'nuker'," responded Paul.

"Well, in that case, let me tell you that all our homes feature a

microwave oven. Let's take a look at the den, shall we?"

The following are some other involvement questions we've heard:

"We offer hardwood or ceramic tile in the foyer. Do you like one better than the other?"

"This master bedroom is a favorite room for many folks. How do you like it?"

"The family kitchen is the focal point of the main level. How does this compare with your present kitchen?"

"You mentioned your two children. This fourth bedroom could be an extra one. How would you use it?"

"We use prefabricated fireplaces instead of masonry because we can locate them more conveniently in the home, and also offer a variety of styles for the hearth and surround. Are you familiar with this type of fireplace?"

The more you can appeal to your customers' sense of hearing, sight, touch, smell or taste, the more they will think, feel and imagine, and the more involved they will become. At the same time, you must remain sensitive to their levels of interest and attention spans. If their interest is increasing, keep your current strategy on track. If you are beginning to lose them, it is time to regroup and move on to something else that will capture their interest more successfully.

* * *

Memory Points

The most effective demonstrations are also the most memorable.

I have always been aware of this fact in a vague sort of way, but it really sank in when I began writing Secrets of the Superstars. I realized that the more effective demonstrations we had seen included techniques that made the model tour easier to remember.

As you prepare your strategies, make a list of techniques and statements you can include throughout your demonstration to help your customers remember you more clearly when they get home. This is another of the important advantages of demonstrating. List the ideas, features, benefits and experiences you want most for them to remember, and then plan how you will go about making these items memorable. Most customers do not make their buying decision in a sales office or model. They make it at home. This means when they decide the home to buy, they are relying heavily on their memory of what they saw and heard. This makes us realize what a powerful tool the *memory points* in our demonstration can be.

I discussed ways to stimulate the different senses in order to create involvement. Appealing to the senses can also make our homes more memorable. Our senses are very much a part of our memory. The more senses involved, the more ways there will be for your homes to be remembered. Memory points are another opportunity for *differential selling* to come into play. Highlight those features which separate your homes from those of your competition. Make *yourself* different, too. Show a higher level of expertise, a greater level of concern, a warmer personality, a greater love for your company, more enthusiasm for your homes. Provide a more meaningful initial overview and model demonstration. Stimulate a more lively interaction.

Some salespeople make themselves more memorable by doing something that is unusual. I remember one salesperson who picked up a stuffed Garfield and held it while we talked in a child's bedroom. I still remember that image as clearly as if I were there now. I can picture the salesperson, what she wore, her facial features and expressions as she held Garfield.

Offer an unusual form of refreshment. Explain a particular detail of construction or engineering. Hum a particular tune to yourself. Wear a memorable piece of clothing. Have an unusual display, fresh flowers, music in your model to employ as you walk through. Provide some unusual fact about your builder, your homes or your community. Make yourself, your builder, your homes and your community more memorable by making them different in a way that *symbolizes* your superiority over your competition. Dare to be different and creative.

* * *

The Sequence For Demonstrating

One question often asked is: "In what order should I demonstrate a model?" My answer would be, "Don't feel as though you need to demonstrate the model in exactly the same sequence each time." For one thing, you want to structure your demonstration around information you received from the customer during your initial overview. If you know that a particular part of the home is especially important to him, you might want to go to that area first, to show him that this home could be the last one he needs to see. After showing the rest of the home, you want to end your demonstration in that same area. One rule of thumb that has proven to be effective, is to conclude the demonstration of each particular model in the best part of the home. This makes a good place for do trial closes.

I mentioned earlier that the demonstration should begin outside. When you enter the model, the main level is a logical place to start, although the room sequence may vary. The initial impact should be exciting. If the foyer in your model is strong, linger there for a few moments to savor it. If it is weak, then pass through it to a stronger area. On the main level you are demonstrating livability, overall design and the particular rooms you want to highlight. If the family room is the most dramatic room, then conclude your demonstration of the first floor in that room.

Many salespeople then move to the basement, if there is one. Their reasoning is that the demonstration will have less impact if they show the basement at the beginning or at the end. In the middle of the tour they can use the basement primarily to explain construction features which prove quality, but rarely stimulate emotion.

The upstairs becomes the third level to be demonstrated, starting out with the smaller bedrooms, then finishing in the more dramatic master bedroom. If the master suite is the most dramatic part of the home, the demonstration can wind up there. If the family room is the most dramatic, you can go from the master bedroom back to the family room. There is nothing wrong with visiting the same room twice during a demonstration, especially if it is an area of importance or concern. Remember that the room you choose as the most important varies, depending upon the customer.

This scenario gives you a sequence to think about. But you must tailor your sequence to your own agenda, and then be willing to vary it for two reasons:

1) To blend naturally with the conversation that you have had with the customer up to that point.

2) To give yourself a sense of variety, thus keeping the presentation more exciting for you.

We have discovered when we visit the same salesperson numerous times that salespeople who vary their presentations seem to have fresher, more exciting presentations than those who present the same thing, the same way, every time. In Chapter Two I talked about the importance of scripts in planning each stage of the selling sequence. Scripts help you stay organized and focused. However, you need to *plan variety into your scripts* in order to keep yourself excited.

You also need to stay aware of the customer's rhythm as you move through your demonstration. Some customers need to move faster, some slower. Some are more analytical, others more emotional. Some like more detail, some less. They may think more precisely or more conceptually. Observations like these must be factored into your own rhythm and strategy. You also need to be sensitive to the customer's level of interest. Your interaction can unravel quickly if you spend time dwelling on a particular feature or area of the home after the customer has lost interest. The more you can *mirror the customer's actions,* the greater rapport he will feel.

* * *

How Much To Demonstrate

If you have more than one model, how many should you demonstrate? This is a judgment call that must be made after the demonstration of the first model has been completed. Most salespeople whom we visit do not demonstrate all of the models to us, and this is not necessarily a mistake. Part of selling is *helping customers make a series of decisions.* As you gather feedback from them throughout your demonstration, urge them to "open and close doors" in their decision-making process. Throughout their presentations, top salespeople accumulate decisions through the use of trial closes such as these:

"You mentioned needing more space. Will these room sizes give you what you need?"

"You said you were tired of 'cookie cutter' houses. How do you like the style of architecture on this home's exterior?"

"How does this kitchen compare with the one you have now?"

"Lots of people tell us that this is the best family room they've seen in this price range. What do you think?"

"Is this the kind of master bedroom you were looking for?"

If you hear positive feedback throughout your demonstration of the first model, you can conclude the demonstration with trial closes such as these:

"You seem to like this home quite a bit. Is this the type of home you were hoping to find?...What did you like best about it?...Was there anything you didn't like?"

"Is this a home you would like to own?"

Demonstrate to Eliminate

Depending upon the answers to these questions, you may be able to eliminate one or more of your other models from their consideration. Suppose they have said: "We were hoping for something a little larger, but this might work out. We definitely can't go any smaller." Naturally, this tells you that you can eliminate any smaller models, as long as you know they will qualify financially for the one you just showed them. You want to keep the selling process moving, and you want to keep the demonstration process as simple as possible. When you have more than one model and you have accumulated information in your initial overview that gives you an insight into your customers' priorities, don't necessarily begin your model tour with the home closest to the sales office. Begin it with the model that you believe will best suit their needs. Remember, you don't know how long you have before the customer's patience or attention span expires, so go ahead and take your best shot first and see where it leads. If he likes the first home you showed him, and you believe that it will suit his needs better than your other homes, you should consider taking him directly to the homesite best suited for the model he selected.

Sometimes customers will say they want to look at the other homes anyway, just out of curiosity. If you have other business that demands your attention, you can say to them, *"Would you like me to come with you, or would you like to have some time just to talk between yourselves?"* That might be exactly what they need to do, but didn't want to hurt your feelings. Or they might simply be curious about the other homes in the community. In any event, you can say, *"Why don't you just take your time and enjoy them. When you're finished I'll show you our best homesite for the Birch model. There's one site in particular that I think you'll love."*

When your customers don't like the first model, you may have another one you believe they will like better. Then you could say, *"From what you've mentioned, the Cedar model will fit your needs better. It has a larger family room. The dining room is smaller, but you said that wasn't as important to you. And it has a little bit more of a contemporary feeling to it. The Cedar model is two doors down. Let's run over to that one next."*

Remember, the model demonstration is not just a tour — it's a vital step to the close. Keep your demonstration focused on the path toward the close by persuading your customers to make one decision after another as you narrow down their choices to the one that is better for them than all the others.

Which model do they like best? Which elevation? Which options? Which site? Which type of financing? In the end there is one unique combination of features that they believe is best. Keep that vision in sight from the moment the customers first walks through your sales office door.

Once the customer starts showing interest in a particular home, top salespeople begin to focus on closing him that day. Don't worry about statistics that speak to how rarely customers buy on their first visit. We see many salespeople *in all price ranges* who have sold a home to a customer on a first visit. Much of their success in closing customers on their first visit comes simply from their belief that it is possible. It is important to stay focused on the fact that your demonstration is your first real opportunity to move the sale toward the close, and it may happen much more quickly than you expect.

The application of demonstration differs if you do not have models. The fundamentals do not. We are dealing in this chapter with merchandized product. However, I must point out that selling without models or product offers the same opportunities and demands the same objective of narrowing down, selecting and closing on each initial meeting. We cannot risk losing sales because statistics say 95% of people buying new homes do so on multiple visits. You never know when you might be talking to the other 5%.

Personally I believe that decisions are made and mental ownership takes place, at least 50% of the time, on a first visit. Taking action on that decision on the first visit depends upon the ability of the salesperson and the confidence of the buyer.

* * *

Selling From One Model

The availability and number of fully merchandized models has changed from the 1980's. In light of the economic climate and more prudent business decisions, most builders now merchandise only one model home. If you offer more than one house type, but have only one model to show, your demonstration becomes more important than ever. In this situation customers really need you, in order to understand the total picture. In the sales office you can set up the demonstration by saying, *"Of our three homes, we mer-chandise one as a model. The model shows our included features and gives you the feeling of how our homes are built. You will be able to see how furniture can be arranged. I can use that model to explain how the others lay out."* In this situation the model becomes your reference point for the builder's image and priori-ties, and also for the features and floor plans of your complete line.

As you begin to interpret your customer's responses to the home you are showing, you can decide how much you want to talk about the other models, and which ones to talk about. This environment gives you an opportunity to sit down with customers. For example if you are in the family room and the customer says, "This room is just too small," or, "I don't like the way this room lays out," then you can bring out the plan of the home that you think would be more appropriate.

"Let's have a seat over here on the sofa and I'll show you the differences between this family room and the larger one in the Oak model...The room is two feet wider, so you'd have two more feet from here to here." Remember that most of us have inexact and inaccurate pictures of distance and size. Therefore you will sometimes need to explain measurements by comparing your spaces with other spaces customers know.

Try pointing, or even standing up and walking around for more animation while they remain seated. *"Then it's also two and a half feet longer. The fireplace would be here instead of over there, and you'd have larger windows on either side. The win-dows and sliding door on the rear wall remain the same size so that you actually have more room for furniture. The room also steps down from the kitchen so that the ceiling is six inches high-er. Six inches may not sound like a lot, but it makes a big differ-ence when you add it to the increase in the length and width and the extra windows. The step down gives the family room a greater sense of identity while it retains the feature of being open to the kitchen. Does that sound more like what you're looking for?"*

The next step would be moving into the dining room in order to explain your other dining rooms. Do not try to explain your whole product line from a single room in your model. You may as well be using blueprints in your sales office.

There will be times, of course, when you believe that demonstrating a model you know they won't like will do more harm than good. In this situation you might prefer to complete as much of the sale as possible from brochures, blueprints and homes under construction. This is a judgment call, depending upon the feedback you've received during your initial overview.

* * *

Selling Value In The Model Demonstration

The sales office is the place where you *claim* to offer superior value. The model demonstration is where you *prove* it. One salesperson who did a wonderful job of conveying value in her demonstration, conveyed it by punctuating her benefits. Each time she prepared to explain a benefit, she would increase its impact with introductions like these:

"I mentioned that we build more value into our homes, and this is one way we do it..."

"We put more attention into smaller details than do most builders, and here's one example..."

"My builder has an exceptional reputation for quality, and here's one reason why..."

"You'll notice as we walk through the homes that Hometown Builders always stays a step above in terms of design breakthroughs. For instance, look at..."

Whenever you make a generalization that could sound like someone else's generalization, or make a claim that your competitor might also make, be sure to back it up with an example right away. This is an excellent technique for building credibility for yourself and your builder and showing superior value in your homes. Statements like these also position you as an expert as well as a salesperson. You know what features are important, and why. You know what makes a builder superior, and your builder has done it. This selling strategy builds confidence in customers' minds, as it stirs emotions in their hearts.

If you are concerned about spending too much time on details your customer may not be relating to, you can always speed it up. It might also help if you simply explain your purpose in a straightforward manner. One salesperson we visited explained her " gushing" over details by saying, *"The reason I am pointing out these features in great detail is that it is important for you to know everything you can about the home you decide to purchase. Not every builder includes what my builder does. After awhile all the homes that you see can start to blend together and cause confusion. I want you to remember us."* This comment gave us confidence in her enthusiasm about her homes and her company, her expertise, and her desire that her customers understand how special her homes really are.

You want to show the customers that you are an expert, and you want to make them experts, too, especially in areas where you have an advantage. Then they can begin to question your competitors more deeply, particularly in those areas where you are superior. We all know the axiom that whenever we show a feature, we should also explain the benefit. Benefit selling is one way to "bring your home to life for the customer."

As important as emotional selling is, you must also continue to reinforce the functional advantages of your homes. Naturally, you don't need to insult someone's intelligence by explaining the benefits of insulation, but you can still show how your feature may provide a greater benefit than the customer might have expected. Also, he might not have thought through all of the consequences of a benefit. He might realize that a larger refrigerator holds more food without stopping to ponder the fact that this also means fewer trips to the store.

* * *

Demonstrating Homes Under Construction

In the next chapter I will discuss the approaches top salespeople take in showing homesites after the customer has chosen a favorite model. Here I would like to spend a little time discussing how to show homes under construction when you don't have a completed model of that home. In this case I'm talking about product selling, not site selling. The principles are, therefore, similar to those for demonstrating models.

Your ultimate goal in demonstrating any homes, whether they are models, homes under construction, or blueprints is not merely to allow the customers to see your homes, or even to teach them the value and benefits of your homes. Your ultimate goal is to persuade them to *choose a favorite model.* Only when they make this decision can you keep your selling momentum moving toward the close. You must give them enough understanding of the homes not shown as models in order for them to appreciate everything you offer and make an educated, as well as an emotional decision. You want to avoid the problem of customers always choosing the furnished model as their favorite because it's the only one they can see. If you have only one model and nothing under construction to show, you must work from the plans and the model you do have, as I described above.

If you've got it, flaunt it

If you have homes under construction that you can show, even if they are not in "pretty" condition, you still can use them effectively to take advantage of all the same opportunities you have in demonstrating models. Do not be reluctant to take advantage of these precious opportunities just because the home under construction may look messy. You don't have to feel embarrassed about showing homes under construction, nor do you have to apologize to the customer. It is, after all, a construction site. Your construction team should be encouraged to keep the site as neat as possible. But if they don't, go ahead and show the homes anyway. Many customers like the "roll-up-your-sleeves" atmosphere of walking into homes before they are completed. Generally, they are not expecting an immaculate presentation. They just want to understand as clearly as possible the features and benefits of what you are selling and to see how the different design may fit their needs. Seeing a home under construction does help make it more real. Since we are in the business of painting pictures, the larger the canvas, the better the image.

As shoppers we have been encouraged to visit homes under construction with salespeople in several appealing ways.

"We have one home shown as a finished model, and then I will take you to see the others close by. They're still under construction, but they're far enough along so that you can have a much better picture by seeing them than by looking at plans."

"After we see the model, we can go into the community and see a few 'real homes,' as I call them."

"It's good to see the model because it gives you a feeling of how

we finish our homes and also you can see how your furniture can be arranged. But many customers prefer to see our homes as they're being built. It gives you a chance to see the construction details and the level of quality. Naturally it will be a different experience from seeing a furnished model, but I'll be there to explain the layout and the parts of the homes that aren't finished."

As with the model demonstration, this experience gives you more time to get to know your customers and build their confidence. A good field demonstration provides you with additional advantages over competitors who don't offer their customers this experience. You can develop more of a counselor relationship by explaining issues that would not arise in furnished models, and by involving your customers with the technical as well as aesthetic aspects of your homes. You can ask them if they are interested in these details. Even with minimal interest you can offer several pieces of information that will help them appreciate the care taken with each of your homes.

You will need to walk through the homes alone, and practice various presentations that sound different enough from your model demonstration to make them interesting. First, walk through with your field superintendant and tape the demonstration as you ask questions. Practice ways of *creating a vision* of a completed home as you walk through a structure that may be only studs. During some of the presentations we have received in homes under construction, the salesperson walked through *as though it were a finished home*, pointing out various features which had already been installed or would be in the future. These salespeople would explain what they were showing us, and would help us experience the feeling of living there by showing various options for furniture arrangement, and ways in which the space had been used by other buyers. You may need to explain that homes always look smaller as they are being built because they are darker and because, prior to drywall, the lack of clearly defined spaces makes areas seem less functional.

Homes under construction are also an ideal environment for explaining any advantages you may have in your plumbing, heating, flooring, roofing, carpentry, foundation or insulation systems.

To conduct an effective field demonstration, you must to be well-trained in the technical aspects of your homes. This training is well worth the effort, however, since it can provide you with some of your most significant selling advantages over your competition. Again, the more time you are able to spend with your customers, and the more "selling arenas" you are able to enter, the better your chances will be of making the sale.

Your own enthusiasm is as important in this arena as in any other. Enthusiasm in a field demonstration adds warmth to an experience that could otherwise seem sterile if it is handled without imagination. Once again we are talking about the art of selling. The same principles of interaction that have been explained previously apply here. Obtaining feedback, observing reactions, explaining benefits and guiding customers toward making decisions are as important in this selling arena as in any other.

Finally, be sure you know your insurance rules for allowing customers to enter your construction site. Use of hard hats may be required. Check with your construction team about the status of work to be done each day. Preview your construction homes prior to opening each day as you check on your models. Construction zones can be hazardous. Be careful and demonstrate with caution.

* * *

In each stage of the selling process you should begin to create a sense of anticipation for the next stage. This is one way you gain momentum and keep it going.

In Chapter Three I discussed how to use the customer's

phone call to your community as a way to create a sense of excitement about their visit. Also I have discussed ways to create anticipation for the model demonstration. During your model tour begin talking about your homesites, especially as you are reaching the point of deciding which model is the customer's favorite. You need customers to believe that one or two of your sites are more special than the others, so they will be prepared to make the transition to the next stage of your selling process. Also, some discussion of the homesites can be accomplished around the site table during the initial overview.

As each stage of the selling process draws to a close it provides a convenient moment for the customer to terminate the process. The only time you want a customer to do this is when he has made a definite decision not to buy one of your homes. Otherwise, you want him to keep looking forward to the next stage as long as his time, interest, and energy permit. Your hope is that you can move them all the way to the final close before they leave. With each stage of the critical path sequence completed, the period at the end should be an attempt to test for the final close. Trial closes are fine but we hear many success stories in which salespeople go for the main event after a positive reaction to demonstration.

"After seeing the Birch model, it appears the larger family room next to the morning room is exactly what you want. You will be able to move in before school starts and the cul-de-sac site is quiet and private just as you want. Shall we finalize your decision today?"

At the beginning of this chapter we listed four primary selling arenas. We discussed: 1) Sales Office; 2) Model Home; and 3) Construction Homes. The 4th arena — The Homesite — will be covered separately in our next chapter. I have deliberately separated the lot or homesite demonstration from the others because I believe it has become, for some, a lost art. It is my sincere hope that you will commit to include this most important function of the selling process in each presentation and demonstration.

Selling The Homesite

"Under all is the land"

From the past comes one of the greatest success secrets of all times: "Under all is the land." During the 1980's many markets in this country experienced a shift of priorities in the selling process. Prior to that time, most building companies put major emphasis on training in construction and engineering for their salespeople. Those of us who joined the ranks of selling prior to 1980 learned more about how to build than how to sell. In fact, it was not uncommon for larger building firms to require people to spend time in the field, prior to going into sales. After all, who would buy from a salesperson who could not explain the flooring, roofing, or mechanical systems of their own product? The same was true of selling the homesite. An understanding of grading, drainage, easements, and setbacks was considered basic knowledge. In order to appear professional, salespeople would carry blueprints and site plans to the homesites. Customers had the satisfaction of knowing that they were buying from a "builder," not just a "salesperson."

Builders were attempting to create the feeling that they were building each buyer a home of his own — unique and individually personal. They were not just mass-producing housing. Oddly enough, as the demand for new homes increased, and housing prices began to skyrocket, the emphasis on salespeople knowing and understanding construction and engineering declined. There were several reasons for this:

1) As the building industry developed a better reputation for quality and integrity, the need for salespeople to "prove themselves" with construction details declined.

2) Skyrocketing housing prices gave builders a greater position of strength with buyers. Builders were in the driver's seat.

3) This same price escalation also created buyer urgency. Urgency was handed to us by a self-motivated society. If they didn't buy today, they would pay more tomorrow. And even if they wound up regretting their purchase, so what? They could just turn around and resell for a profit.

In sales strategy, the priorities shifted from selling the details of the product and the homesite to more sophisticated marketing and merchandising. Instead of being articulate about construction and engineering, it became more important to be articulate about financing, marketing and merchandizing. Many builders today do not want their salespeople to use a site plan for fear "they will get into trouble." Instead of training salespeople so that they won't have problems, some companies have decided to take away those tools altogether.

A decade ago a striking division developed between the sales team and the building team, each specializing in its areas of expertise, in more depth. I am not suggesting this was all bad. Quite the contrary. There was a wonderful revolution in marketing concepts and strategies that helped builders move with the times. I am, however, suggesting that some skills were placed on a back burner while we moved through the "boom."

Pick yourself up and dust yourself off

Today, in most markets we are seeing the pendulum swing back. Consumer attitudes and market trends are dictating that we bring out some of those skills and techniques, and polish up on them. My all-time favorite is the opportunity to get back outside. To learn the "lay of the land," and to walk the sites, dreaming with buyers, is the most exciting part of our business. I am just old-fashioned enough to believe that ownership never transfers inside a sales office, or, for that matter, inside a model home with "someone else's furniture." On the land, that's where it really happens.

Superior marketing and merchandising can still create a competitive advantage. But without the built-in motivation of rapid price increases, the nature of "urgency" in new home sales has changed. We now create urgency by persuading customers that our neighborhood and our homes will improve their quality of life. The sooner they buy, the sooner they can begin to enjoy the better life that we are offering them. We create this urgency by causing our customers to become emotionally involved, and rationally convinced. To accomplish this, we must show expertise and integrity in order to achieve credibility and build the customers' confidence. We encourage them to believe in us, convince them they want to live in our community, and finally to believe that there is one home and homesite that is better for them than the rest. These are the dynamics of urgency in today's market. They require greater skill and preparation in product and homesite selling.

Top salespeople emphasize the importance of owning a particular piece of property. In the case of single family homes and town homes, it is the parcel of land. In the case of condominiums, it is the unique location and identity of each home. In all three types of homes, it is still the basic notion of *pride of ownership.* For purposes of this chapter on homesites, I will be dealing primarily with examples of single family homes. The principles I will discuss will also apply to other types of home ownership.

* * *

"For The Beauty Of The Earth"
Pride of Ownership

Sticks and bricks will come and go. Land is forever. Certainly much work and detail goes into design and building. It's funny how, when the dust settles and buyers move in, it is the land that ultimately wins their hearts. Our home may be our castle, but our land is our territory and identity. Even Uncle Sam depreciates the home, but never the land.

The reality of this was made more evident to me recently when Terry and I were doing some yard work. Our neighbor came over and started chatting. During the conversation it was quite obvious that each proud and possessive owner was "selling" the other on the fact that he had the most trees and the largest property. The conversation led to checking out property lines and boundaries and comparing them. The afternoon ended with our neighbor bringing over a survey on *his* property. We conceded that he does have more frontage.

In the last chapter I talked about the importance of the home's exterior in "pride of ownership." Another element in this pride is the *excitement of owning land*. By "land" I don't mean an estate. I mean property, regardless of the square footage. Pride of ownership even applies to patio sites or townhome sites. There is one special piece of land that belongs to you and no one else. Creating customer involvement with the *individuality of property* is one key to creating urgency. For this reason the trip to the homesite becomes one of the most critical stages of the sale for setting up the close. The selection of a homesite is the point at which you receive your first clear glimpse of the "final closing moment." In fact, if financing is not the pivotal issue in the sale (and in most cases it is not), the next best moment to go for the close will be at the homesite. Although you use trial closes throughout the model demonstration, and sometimes even in the initial overview, now at the homesite is the time for the real thing.

Here is one example of the type of close that is appropriate at the property location when you want to create urgency through *fear of loss:*

"Bill, I need to ask you one thing. Think about this. Now that you have decided Timber Wood Forest is the place for you, and this is the best homesite, suppose you call me in a few days and home-site 12 is no longer available. Is that going to be a problem for you? Will you be just as happy with your second choice? Why not start the ball rolling today and not risk having to settle for second best?"

Closing is not the subject of this chapter, but I needed to touch on it briefly to stress the importance of the trip to the site in the total dynamics of selling. In most cases, when the prospective buyer is seriously interested in your homes, the sale will succeed or fail based on the results of your success in creating an attachment, in their hearts, to a particular homesite that you have today, but may not have tomorrow. The closing question mentioned above may not give you the answer you *want*, but it will at least give you the answer you *need*. I have said that selling involves persuading the customer to make a series of decisions. Showing the location brings the sale to the point where decisions become big ones — the ones, when addressed, that bring your selling effort to a conclusion. By the time you reach this stage in the sale, you have finally "earned the right to close." While Chapter Eight will be devoted to closing, I will use this chapter to talk about "earning the right."

Initially, people buy with emotion; therefore, we want to try to create positive emotional images in their minds. The thought of being "sold" stirs negative feelings in the minds of most consumers. You must overcome these negative feelings by creating positive emotions. I have talked a great deal about words throughout *Secrets of the Superstars*, and how words influence our customers. Here, I want to discuss eliminating those words which do not create positive and exciting imagery. One such word is "lot."

Whether or not it depicts a negative, or only a neutral picture, the word "lot" definitely does not give the warm fuzzy feeling that motivates one to run out and take a look. I suggest describing the site, location, property, or homesite in glowing terms to cause your customer to act with urgency to become involved with the land. In recent years, property has taken a back seat to product in the selling arena. Now is the time to "go *back* to the future."

Your lot in life

As with model demonstration, showing the land provides you with a number of selling opportunities which no other stage of the selling process can provide. The trip to the site is very invigorating. On the way to the homesite talk about the community. This is the time to talk about life in the neighborhood, to create a feeling of happiness — a feeling that life here is good. Greeting homeowners who are outside is a strong involvement strategy, but it requires sustaining your relationships with buyers after they have moved in. This walking and talking provides a more casual atmosphere for conversation than standing still. Also, it is more energizing. These advantages are partly because you have moved from the sales office to a more casual and energizing environment. You are now "where the action is." The dynamics of motion are a factor as well, and those dynamics create energy. Both the model demonstration and the homesite demonstration take you out of the business environment, and allow energy to enter your selling process.

Hang in there: Don't jump ship

What about the fact that you're leaving the sales office without staff? Don't worry about it. You can't afford to worry. If you have a customer who is moving with you through the selling sequence with interest, enthusiasm and ability, don't break your pace. He deserves your undivided concentration and attention. Naturally, you do not want to be away from the sales office for an hour on a Saturday afternoon with an unqualified or unmotivated person if you don't have an assistant. But here I'm talking about an "A" or "B" buyer.

What if you miss someone better? It could happen, but the odds are in your favor that you won't. If your neighborhood is busy, then, of course, you need to be adequately staffed. Management must be willing to endorse the value of your taking time to show property to a serious buyer. They must provide enough staff, and enough training to give you the freedom and the expertise to make this critical part of the selling process pay off. The same applies to demonstrating models. It is a shame for salespeople not to feel free to demonstrate models or show homesites because of a staffing shortage.

Let's suppose, however, you are alone on a Saturday afternoon and you expect to see ten visitors during the course of a seven-hour day. A couple has seen your models and selected one. You now have to leave your sales office unattended for perhaps an hour to take your customers to the homesites. Mathematically, you are likely to miss one or two visitors during the time you are away. Those are the worst odds. What are the chances that one of those two people whom you miss will be better than the one you now have? Then suppose one of them is better. What are the chances that they will come in immediately after you left, look through your models, like them a lot, be qualified to buy, and not wait around, or ever come back? It's a pretty safe bet that your best shot is with the customer you already know is interested and qualified. Sounds fair, doesn't it?

Sure, there will be times when you will walk out the door and five of your ten for that day will come in while you're gone. It often seems as though there is a holding bin just outside your community where customers gather until there is a crowd of them, and they all descend on you together. But realistically these occurrences are still more the exception than the rule, and should not dictate your basic selling strategy. If you lose a sale here and there (and I repeat, it is unlikely that you would really lose a sale because you're on site with a prospective buyer), you will still gain many more additional sales than you will lose by giving every *good* prospective purchaser your best effort. I mention this because at times salespeople seem reluctant to go too far from the office, phone and desk. They fear missing a greeting, have concern the boss might call, or truly misunderstand the importance of spending quality time with qualified customers in the community and walking the land. A nice-looking note should always be put on the door, welcoming the customer to look around and explaining that you are on site with another customer. People understand this.

You must also to be willing to shed a prospect who is clearly wasting your time. Some salespeople explain the situation in a straightforward way: *"I wish I could spend more time with you, but I'm here alone today and I need to be available to talk to everyone. I'd love to answer anything that's important, but otherwise I need to be getting back."* Other salespeople use approaches such as: *"Oops (looking at their watch), I almost forgot. I have some people who said they would be here to meet with me in 15 minutes. I need to do a couple of things to get ready for them. Is there anything else I can do for you?"* It's important not to be ashamed about politely excusing yourself from people who are not serious candidates, but demand a lot of attention anyway.

What about the concern that the boss might call and you will miss the call? If you have a potentially hot buyer, the manager should always be secondary. Let your manager express any exceptions to that rule. Managers need to endorse the property-showing process. It will gain significant income for the company, despite the occasional inconvenience it may cause.

One thoughtful approach that we have seen is to have two different messages for your answering machine: one for when you are closed and another for when you're open but on site.

* * *

The Selling Opportunities Of Showing Homesites

Showing homesites offers special opportunities. Here is a brief overview of the highlights of this stage of the selling process:

1) You have more time to *get to know the customer.* The homesite arena is usually the most casual one, and by now you have already had time to develop your relationship with the customer. You can now have a more open, honest interaction as the process moves toward the close.

2) You have additional opportunities to *create value* in your homes. I discussed creating value in homes under construction in the last chapter. With homesites, the emphasis expands to include demonstrating the benefits of your company's approach to site planning and engineering, as well as the unique benefits of each individual homesite. Once again, you also increase perceived value if your expertise exceeds that of your competition. Customers will assume that if the salesperson has a higher level of expertise, so must the company as a whole. This makes the quality of your training all the more important.

3) You can *sell the neighborhood.* One of your most important objectives is persuading the customer to want to live in your community. Customers sometimes don't ask as many ques-

tions about your community as they do about your homes or
even your terms. This does not mean the community is less
important. Some customers are just focusing in on product,
while others, simply, don't know what questions to ask. You
need to help them feel that they *belong* there. The sense of
"belonging" is a very important motivation, even if it is not
expressed. Sooner or later the community becomes an important factor in the home-buying decision. Be sure to take the
initiative to tell about your neighborhood, even if the customer
is not asking questions about it.

Welcome to the neighborhood

After your buyers have taken ownership, it is important for you to
keep in touch with them. Not only are they a good source of referrals, they are one of the most powerful selling advantages you can
have when you are walking through the neighborhood. We visit
salespeople who clearly have had a continuing relationship with
their buyers after they become neighbors. When we are conducting
a shopping interview with a salesperson and their homeowners
encourage us to buy, the effect is overwhelming. As you are walking
and talking with your customers, take advantage of opportunities to
wave to homeowners and exchange pleasantries. One scenario I
remember happened while we were visiting a sales professional in a
townhome community with several inventory homes. She encouraged us to visit the property with her, which we did. As we walked
through the neighborhood Barbara was greeted warmly by everyone
we saw. She knew their names and they knew hers. We met and pet-
ted a new member of the community, "Starky," a Dalmatian puppy,
who was with his proud owners. One neighbor ran out and asked
what model we were buying, and offered to show us around his
home. As we finished, Barbara said, ***"As you can see we are a family around here. Everyone is so friendly. Yet, you also have your
privacy. I believe it is because they are so happy to be living here."***
We agreed and "bought" on our first visit. EMPOWERMENT!

People seem more concerned about privacy today than ever before, so we need to be especially careful about the information we convey concerning our homeowners. Assume that they are sensitive about their privacy, and that your customer is also sensitive. Within those boundaries, proceed with discrete information that may help your prospective buyer feel a "common bond" with the neighborhood. Personal incomes are obviously off limits. Giving out names is sometimes questionable. If you have a question about possible invasion of privacy, either avoid the issue, or get the homeowner's permission to reveal the information to prospective purchasers. "Giving out children's ages," I am told, is now off limits; however, you can give out the school grades of the children. "Occupations" can also be helpful. "Incomes" should be discussed only in terms of the community as a whole when you are trying to reassure your customers. Some buyers would rather know that their incomes are in line with others in the neighborhood, than simply that they qualify for a loan. Generally, in the early stages, buyers qualify for more monthly investment than they feel comfortable giving up. Also, at this stage they may not feel completely trusting of lenders. Your assistance may be needed to get them through this period, but do not sacrifice the privacy and protection of your homeowners.

4) Be sure to *sell the amenities, in addition to selling the neighborhood.* It is important for your customers to see your amenities, or where the amenities will be located. Community amenities are a great selling benefit, and need to be brought to life in order to be appreciated. Amenities that are completed prior to construction are costly for builders. If they are not demonstrated, the salesperson is missing the opportunity of using this valuable tool to build lifestyle and convenience in the community.

5) Showing homesites offers another wonderful opportunity to *create customer involvement.* This objective is a complex one, so I will devote a separate section to it later in this chapter.

6) Persuade customers to continue with their **series of decisions** by *narrowing their focus to one favorite homesite.* Once they have decided that what you are offering is best for them, and that there is one homesite in your selection which is "the best of the best," you have reached the point where *fear of loss* can become a factor in their level of urgency. *Fear of loss* strengthens your position, so it must be an important goal in showing homesites.

Once again, *differential selling* gives extra power to your selling strategy. If your property is superior to that of your competition, your location and sites become a focal point. Great homesites are a salesperson's dream. They allow you to make "love of the land" a major force in your selling. Use differential selling to set your property apart from the competition. Then use it again to distinguish your sites one from another so your customers will decide which one is best for them.

However, if your land is average or below, you are selling value in a different way by showing that your homesites are the best way to give the most home in the best location for the money. When your homesites are mediocre, the sale becomes more of a "total package sell" and less of a "homesite sell." You must create a greater sense of involvement in the product and the community before you go to the homesites. But even in this situation, your goal still is to show you have one homesite that is best for your customer. You still create *fear of loss,* even if it is on a different level.

7) Showing property is the point at which you *set up the close.* When you reach this stage of the sale, you should be intensely focused on closing. Don't worry that it's their first visit to the community. Different people make buying decisions at different speeds, and your customers may already be 99% there before they even meet you. You just don't know. All you can do is push the button and see if the light comes on. While

you are "site seeing," let your customers know your procedure for selling a home (including the amount of earnest money deposit required — "initial investment"), so that when you reach the closing moment you aren't conveying this information for the first time. Create anticipation for the close during the homesite-showing stage, just as you always use anticipation for the next stage to keep your momentum going.

8) *Gather information for your follow-up effort.* Although your trip to the homesites sets up the close, you also know that, more times than not, the customer will not buy that day. This is the point at which you temper your determination with realism. You use this stage of the sale to set the stage for follow-up, in case it becomes necessary. Of course, you should be considering this objective in every phase of the selling process, but now it is more important than ever. If you don't close the sale today, how will you create a situation where the transaction can continue?

* * *

In the last chapter I discussed the transition from the sales office to the model demonstration. I gave examples of techniques which salespeople use to make this transition comfortable because so many salespeople have expressed concern about it. The transition from the models to the site is different. It is much more natural because you are already into the demonstrating process, your customers know you better, and they are now expressing interest in what they have seen. Even if they have toured the models alone, getting them to see the property is easier, assuming that they liked what they saw. However, if you do have concerns about the best way to start the trip to the site, here are several approaches you can take:

1) You can explain your whole process to your customers during your initial overview.

"I have two models I can show you. (If you're at a high-traffic community and you're talking to a marginal customer, it would be "two models you can see.") I also have homes under construction which can give you an idea of two others. Then I can show you the homesites we have available. There are several beautiful ones. We can talk more about those after you see how you like our homes." This approach makes the process familiar to the customer before he has to face it. They are more likely to go along with your program if they know where it's leading.

    2) Once customers understand your homes and have reached the point of selecting a favorite, you can take a very straightforward approach. This part of the selling process does not have to be fancy.

"Let's go and have a look at a couple of our best homesites."

"I have a few sites I'd love for you to see."

"Let's go down and have a look at homesite 24. You said you liked a corner site because of your gardening. Homesite 24 is great in the front and on both of the sides."

    3) The third example above begins to create a sense of anticipation. That is another excellent transitional technique.

"Let's hop in my car and go have a look at the homesites I pointed out earlier on the site plan. Remember how I was talking about trees? You can see how the trees frame the cul-de-sac. When those homes are completed that setting will be beautiful."

Notice that each of the examples above was spoken in the form of a statement, not a question. If you have enough momentum, statements can make more effective transitions. There will be times when you feel a little less confident in your customers' level of interest, so you might want to use a question instead. In this case, it still helps if you can make it an *assumptive question.*

"I'd love to take you down to see our available property if you have the time."

"You've seen the homes, but you won't really get the flavor of the community until you've seen the homesites. Would that be okay?"

Even though you are asking permission, these types of questions set up your transition more effectively than, "Would you like to go and see some properties?" If their interest has peaked in your homes, then the sites are what customers really want to see. There is no reason to feel timid about this next step. It may wind up being the most important step of the sale.

* * *

Creating Involvement At The Site

As with the initial overview and the model demonstration, creating involvement at the homesite involves the "art of selling." Walk *on* the homesite, not just *up* to it. Walking on the property is how the adventure begins. Even if you're stepping over poison ivy or between thorns, it is *land.* Walking on it is a major step toward laying claim to it. Enjoy the experience. If it is an open, bare site, that is okay. Walk across it. Stop at various points on it to talk. Use motion to help create the vision. Point to various items of significance to the buyer, even if it is only where the surrounding homes will be. Locate the home and mark the four corners. Naturally, if there is an appealing view, that is even better.

As with each phase of the selling process, preparation is of utmost importance. This step requires contact and time spent with surveyors, land planners, and your builder. Every homesite should be known to you intimately. The defects and jewels of each parcel should be etched in your mind. Features and benefits sell here as they do with product. Dreams are turned into reality on the land. This is where the romance of the sale takes place. *"Picture your home nestled in the trees with a swing on the Victorian porch and flower boxes of geraniums along the walk."* Preparation includes dressing for site-seeing. Appropriate shoes or boots for both you and your customers must be available at your center.

Show passion for the land

Allow the customer to capture the vision of the finished community. At the other end of the spectrum, talk about the history of the land. If the land was a farm, tell about the owner, or the type of farm it was. Giving the land a sense of history enriches it. There is real magic in history. Creating value and exclusivity of the land starts with the history. Add excitement by demonstrating the home's position relative to sunrise and sunset. One relatively new sales professional accompanied us to the site with compass, polaroid camera, boots, 100 foot tape, site plan and blueprints. The only thing missing was a picnic basket. What a great adventure that was. Know how each home will he sited on each lot and demonstrate diagonally to enhance space. Place stones to represent the corners of the home. Get your customers involved in discovering this beautiful piece of earth. Be sure you know where the boundaries are. Taking customers to a homesite and not knowing where the property lines are is the ultimate anticlimax. It also makes the salesperson look inept. Or, just as bad, it can appear as though the salesperson has never been to the homesite before.

If there are trees or other vegetation on the homesite, learn the types. Emphasize any little features you can. Unusual wild shrubbery, or even interesting stones can help enhance the adventure. It doesn't matter that these items will be replaced by a home. It helps to bring the land to life.

Motion and your own personal enthusiasm are more important now than ever. Walking around, pointing, gesticulating, even facial expressions are good animations to use in demonstration. You are coming down the home stretch of the selling process, and you want to be at your best. Be prepared with any *memory points* which you can relate to each particular site.

Create a sense of space, vertically, by looking up. Vertical demonstration is a powerful value "enhancer." Not every site affords a positive horizonal view. I remember that in my early days of selling, we often talked about land ownership in terms of the depth, from the mineral rights below to the air rights above. Try a little depth perception; it will open up new dimensions for you in your homesite presentation.

Down by the old oak tree

I was given a homesite demonstration recently that was memorable in terms of the emotions the salesperson stirred, and the ways in which he did it. The homesite we visited had on it several tall trees. The salesperson was always in motion, even though he maintained excellent eye contact. He walked to the four property corners, and I followed naturally. The more he moved around and I moved with him, the more of a sense of space I felt. Then he stopped at a tall tree and said, *"Isn't this old oak beautiful?"* He paused and slowly ran his eyes from the base of the tree all the way up to the very top. It was a powerful pause, and helped to convey a profound sense of the majesty of the old tree. *"It's cloudy today, but I was out here gazing up at it one day when the sky was a perfect blue — not a single cloud in sight. It was awesome!"* So was this salesperson! Then he continued. *"They're being very careful to position the home in a way that the roots won't be disturbed."*

We bought the oak tree, and yes, the home did convey.

Next he shifted his gaze toward the street. *"See over across the road? We're just starting that home. I'll be excited when those folks move in. Those are two really nice people. You said you wanted to settle by the end of the year. We don't start a home here until it's sold, and then it takes about five months. It's June now so that puts us pretty close to your time frame. This whole street will be finished about four months after that, and we'll be on to a new street. With the landscaping in front and the trees behind, it's going to be a terrific place to live. How do you like this location?"*

After just one hour with this salesperson, following him through the initial overview, two models and the homesite, we had developed a genuine sense of involvement in what we were seeing. He also kept us involved by asking questions as he led us, in order to test our level of interest.

"The privacy out back here is pretty nice, isn't it?" (Tie-down).

"You stand here where the edge of this home will be, and I'll go over and stand at the edge of the next home...Can you picture this and how it will look when it's completed?"

"Now I'm going to throw a stone as far as I can into the wooded common area behind...See where my stone landed? The next home behind you will be about forty more feet beyond that." (Memory point.) *"You don't often find that much privacy in this price range."*

Admittedly, this salesperson had an especially lovely setting for his community. But the principles he used can be applied to many types of situations in demonstrating models and homesites.

* * *

Emotional Selling

Creating customer involvement requires a certain amount of emotional selling. Start with your own enthusiasm. The examples I have been discussing appeal to the customer's emotional side, bringing the home, homesite, and community to life. Creating images as you stand on bare land, creating a vision of the finished community, and talking fondly about your other buyers are all selling techniques with emotional appeal.

However, do not rely totally on emotion for selling new homes. The role of emotional selling has sometimes been exaggerated. The rational element must be there, too. A customer can be caught up with the moment, as I was in the previous example. But as customers contemplate the seriousness of their buying decision, they must also justify the value of what they are buying. You, the salesperson, must *balance emotional selling with rational selling*. The emotions certainly trigger the decision to buy a new home, but the selling process is a rational one.

We buy with emotion, but we sell with logic. Buying is an *emotional experience.* But selling is *a logical process directed toward a specific destination.*

The best presentations we have witnessed are enthusiastic, but are well-planned and focused. They are directed, one step at a time, toward the close, reinforcing value and soliciting feedback as they progress through the plan. We have been discussing the "art of selling." It is important that we not forget the "science." The same principle applies, by the way, to "relationship selling." The relationship exists within the context of the selling process. It is the means to an end, not the end in itself. As soon as the relationship becomes more important than the sale, the process will unravel. "The customer is looking for a home, not an intimate friend." The purpose for showing homesites is to set up the close. An important step in this strategy is *getting the customer to pick out a favorite homesite.* How does the science complement the art to achieve this goal?

* * *

Choosing The Favorite Homesite

Although customers like to have a choice, too much choice can be self-defeating. Having ten homesites available, all of which fulfill your customers' needs, can diminish their sense of urgency. On the other hand, having only one available can make them feel "boxed in," especially when the customer knows that there are better homesites that will be available soon. No matter how wide a selection you are offering, if your customers have reached the point where they are ready, willing and able to buy, your goal is to compel them to choose a favorite. Once they select a favorite homesite, their level of urgency can be increased. Persuading customers to select a favorite homesite can sometimes be very easy, but there are a number of subtleties and risks that I would like to explore.

How do you convince a customer that you have one homesite better for him than all your others? Do you tell him up front? Some salespeople do. Here is an example:

"I have three homesites on which we can build the Birch home that you like. There's one in particular that I want you to see first. From what you've told me, and from the reactions I've received from other people who have seen it, homesite 36 is probably the best choice. I have to admit, I feel the same way myself. I think you'll love it. I'd love to show it to you now."

I have seen this type of approach used very effectively, although it's risky. Salespeople who use this approach often believe: "My job is to be an expert and a counselor. I'll do my best to satisfy the customers' needs. If I take a stand, it will help them to take a stand. If I act indifferent, it will be harder for me to create urgency." Spoken this way, the approach makes sense. However, let me suggest an alternative for arriving at the same destination.

"I have three homesites on which we can build the Birch home that you like. I'd be interested to know what you think. I'd like to show you all three."

In this example the salesperson did not state his own preference at first. However, he did take us first to the homesite that he thought would be our favorite. This is another issue which elicits a variety of opinions. There are salespeople who believe that if you are going to show three homesites, you should save the best for last. In general brokerage, you have "control" over the situation for an agreed-upon period of time, and this strategy can be quite effective. In new homes, however, you never know at what moment the customer's level of interest will begin to decline. Remember they drove to your site in the "getaway car." I prefer to take customers first to the homesite that I believe they will like best.

In the example of the salesperson who did not state a preference, he demonstrated the homesite enthusiastically. Based on the information we had given him, he did, in fact, take us first to the one we would have bought. When we gave positive responses, he agreed and urged us to talk more about those feelings. When he showed us the next homesite, and saw that we were not as enthusiastic, he concluded the demonstration of that homesite quickly. The same thing happened at the third site. The second and third homesites reconfirmed our enthusiasm about the first, and made us realize there truly was a difference.

After we had finished looking at all three, he said, *"You really did like the first one best, didn't you?"* When we agreed, he said, *"I just knew you would. That's why I showed it to you first. I didn't want to say anything until you'd seen all three, because I wanted to make sure it was really your choice. But now that you've made your decision, I have to tell you I feel exactly the same way."*

Reconfirming our preference with his own enthusiasm gave us a feeling of confidence about our decision. *"Just to be sure I understand, what were the things that made it your favorite?"* Make sure your customers put into their own words why they prefer a particular model or homesite. Their words strengthen their conviction. You can also refer back to their words later for purposes of creating fear of loss, closing, follow-up, or dealing with buyer's remorse.

I have shown two different approaches for leading customers toward selecting a favorite site. Both have been used effectively. The first establishes you as an expert working from a position of confidence. The second, however, allows you to react with sensitivity to your customers' choice, and then to create a sense of *synergy* with them *after* they make their selection. You become more excited as they become more excited, and soon your mutual excitement becomes a source of selling momentum.

In the first example you are persuading the customers, while in the second they are *persuading themselves.* You must, of course, be alert to their responses in order for the second strategy to succeed. In the first example you "catch fire" first and allow the sparks from your fire to ignite theirs. In the second, you create a situation in which they can spark their own fire, and then you fan the flames.

While it is important for you to display your own enthusiasm in order to arouse the customer's, be careful you don't allow "overenthusiasm" to set customers up for disappointment. This is known as *overselling.* Here is an example of enthusiasm crossing the line into overselling:

"You've just got to see Lot 40! It is the best one we have, hands down! I can't believe it's the same price as the others. If you let this one slip away you'll never find another like it!"

While this approach is designed to arouse enthusiasm and create urgency, the salesperson has raised the customer's level of expectation to the point where he will most likely be disappointed. *Disappointment is the archenemy of momentum.* You must avoid creating situations that eventually cause disappointment. As you create enthusiasm, you also need to moderate the customer's expectations so that you can meet and exceed them. That doesn't mean playing down your advantages, or watering down your own enthusiasm. It just means that you shouldn't go overboard in the other direction. Once again, the principle of *balance* comes into play.

A more cautious approach would be, *"I'm beginning to get the feeling that homesite 40 might be the homesite you like most. It's a nice piece of property, and it has a number of the features we've discussed. I'd like to get your reaction to it. I also have a couple of others for comparison, if you'd like to see them, too."*

In this example, the salesperson has still expressed enthusiasm and shown that she is trying to find the best home for the customer, but is leaving her options open. You may have exactly the type of homesite that the customer has described as what he wants, but when he sees it, he could surprise you with:

"You know, I never thought about the fact that a walkout basement requires a sloping site. I know we said we wanted trees, too, and these are beautiful, but a level yard is really our top priority." Where does that leave you? If you made it sound as though this homesite is the only decent one you have, you must now do some major back-peddling. If you said you had several good ones and then showed this one first, you have no trouble recovering by saying, *"Good, I'm glad we discovered this early. Why pay extra for trees and a walkout basement when you have to give up a more useful back yard? Remember the other two sites I mentioned? One of them is flat. It doesn't have the trees or the walkout basement, but many people prefer a more level play yard to a walkout basement, especially in single family homes. The folks in the home behind have a daughter who babysits and a son who loves to mow lawns. They're a nice family."*

The goal in showing homesites, as in demonstrating models, is for your customers to pick out a favorite. This does not mean seeing to it that they hate all of your others. You want them to buy today, so you want to create urgency. But you also need to be preparing your follow-up strategy, since their decision might require more than one visit. While you want them to select a favorite so you can move toward the close, still they want to live in your community, even if their first choice is taken by someone else.

I would like to conclude this chapter by highlighting a few additional ideas which have helped salespeople show homesites.

Expertise

Customers attach value to expertise. The same feature may be included at a number of different communities, but the salesperson who explains the item with greater impact conveys more value.

In this stage of the selling process, expertise with a site plan is one way to increase the perceived value of your homesites, as well as that of your builder. Have your manager or someone in your construction or engineering department show you:

1) How to use an engineer's ruler to measure distances.

2) How to read grading lines and points, and explain grading to customers.

3) How to explain the drainage of a site to customers.

4) How to read the variety of symbols on a site plan.

5) How to find the homesite number, street address, square footage, and basement type, if these items are shown or relevant.

6) How to identify easements.

While your explanation of these issues should not be long-winded or tedious, customers need to understand your level of expertise as well as the information itself. *People want to buy from experts.*

Homesite Sizes

Customers do not necessarily relate to square footage sizes. They need to understand how the space will work for them. Square footage can be misleading, especially where features such as slopes, odd-shaped sites, or pipestem driveways are concerned.

If you are describing a homesite with a back yard that will be 50 feet deep and 60 feet wide, you could say, *"With a yard this size you could play volleyball and still have room left over for a game of horseshoes."* Another way to explain it would be, *"Do you play golf?...Then you know what it's like to sink a 50-foot putt."*

You may also need to help the customer understand that value can mean much more than just square footage. The location, topography, view, and adjacent properties may make a smaller homesite more valuable to a buyer than a larger one. Customers need to understand how the homesite will "work" for them, not just its statistics. People don't buy facts, figures and specifications, and we should not try to sell them.

Property Premiums

Selling lot premiums requires creativity. Summarizing the premiums as you give an overview of homesites will not provide enough impact in order to convince the customer of the value of the additional cost. In slower markets customers will sometimes rebel against property premiums, or feel that they are the first targets for negotiation. Showing the homesite is the key to demonstrating the value of the premium. At the homesite you can point out the size, trees, or view which will be enjoyed by the family every day of their lives, and the value of that far exceeds the price of only "$1.00" a day for the benefit. The words and phrases used in the homesite presentation can make a profound difference in perception for your customers. Instead of referring to "homesite premiums" change your reference to "premium homesites." Homesite premiums emphasizes added cost and price increases. Premium homesites, on the other hand, suggest increased value, one of a kind, and added benefits.

Walking and Talking

As you walk to the homesites, be sure you are not talking with your head turned away from the customers. They need to see your face as you are talking, just as you need to see theirs. They also need to be able to hear you. Walking alongside them is one way to accomplish this. Another approach that we have seen is to walk just a step or so behind them. They can hear you more easily, and you can watch their body language and their reaction to what is being seen.

Be sure to divide your attention equally among all the people in the group. When salespeople focus most of their attention on one person to the exclusion of others, those others will feel ignored. You need to establish a "relationship" with everyone in the group, even non-buyers. On their trip home, the feedback of non-buyers may become a major factor in the buyer's decision. It is important that friends and family feel a sense of comfort with you as well. Always learn the name of any "non-buyer" who came along. Use his or her name in conversation. Seek his opinion. Best you hear their opinions and objections from them up front, because certainly, the customer will hear it from them later on. Beware of the "phantom buyer."

Weather

Weather should not become an obstacle unless it is extremely severe. Your primary goal is to show the homesite the best way you can, no matter what the circumstances.

Keep umbrellas handy for your customers for rain, and boots for mud. If it's hot or cold enough that you are concerned about your customers' comfort, you can ask them:

"I have a couple of homesites that I'd love for you to see. I know it's hot out but let's have a look, shall we? I'm game if you are."

While you would normally take a more assumptive approach, there may be times when you think it may be construed as insensitive for you to take them out into inclement weather without showing consideration for their well-being. Once you are outside, be sure not to belabor the issue of how insufferable the weather is. Your goal still is to make the trip as enjoyable as possible. If it is terribly hot, just say, *"As soon as we get back, I'll break out the lemonade."*

* * *

The final, and perhaps the most important topic in homesite demonstration is using this setting for your close. I am sure my passion for site-showing is coming through loud and clear. As one dynamite salesperson said, *"The best part of our job is getting close to Mother Earth. Sales aren't made in the office, they are made right out here on site. Lately, I have been demonstrating my homesites before my homes. I find that I can develop a relationship faster and it sure is a lot more fun being outside."* I will address closing on site in Chapter Eight where I deal with the entire subject of closing. In the meantime, I sense a few objections lurking around the corner. Don't you? I will move into the subject of objections so they can be resolved before the final close is attempted.

Objections

Objections are not objectionable

Great salespeople do not find objections objectionable. Objections are the lifeline to closing. The *joy* of objections is that they are often the customer's first real sign of interest. Understanding the significance of adverse opinions, in effect, customers saying to you, "I would really like to own this property except for ____," is the key to effective management of objections.

Take a mental trip with me for a moment. When one has a keen *interest* to become involved in something new, it is natural and prudent to investigate, analyze, and probe the consequences in order to determine if it is the right thing to do. My latest *interest* is snow skiing. On the other hand, there are times when we have external *curiosity* about something without any desire to become involved. My latest *curiosity* is bungee jumping. How is my behavior different in the two scenarios?

#1: *Interest in* snow skiing.

I have the desire, fear, reluctance, and motivation to want to learn more about snow skiing. I dream about gliding down the mountain, traversing like the pros, feeling the wind in my hair, being master of my skies. Talk to me about skiing, and I will tell you also about the outrageous expense, the probability of breaking an ankle, or leg or worse. However, the reason I have these fears (or objections) is that I really am interested in the possibility of snow skiing one day soon.

#2: Curiosity *about* bungee jumping.

For those of you who find bungee jumping the ultimate in feeling free, and the most wonderful experience in life, forgive me, but I have no earthly desire to "free fall" into a river. Bungee jumping does intrigue me, however. I was curious enough about this strange new phenomenon to watched Joan Lunden throw herself off a bridge in New Zealand with only a rope around her leg. I am inquiring enough about bungee jumping to visit a world famous jumping site in British Columbia, on a trip to Victoria. Do I ever plan to bungee jump? Not on your life or mine! For that reason, I have no concerns or objections or fears.

So what does snow skiing and bungee jumping have to do with objections? Objections are about involvement. To object or question anything usually indicates some degree of serious interest in becoming more involved. The difference between interest in, and curiosity about, is the difference between an A or B prospective buyer and a C prospect. It takes energy and emotion to argue, dispute, or disagree. Curiosity alone is not internalized sufficiently to produce the emotional energy necessary for debate for most folks. Giants in our business understand this. No objection means no interest: No interest means you probably don't have a prospective buyer.

Anticipate and embrace objections, don't fear them. You probably have a "live one" here. Objections signal opportunities. When salespeople fear objections, they often show it in one of four ways:

1) They ignore the objection.

This happens when a customer raises an objection, and the salesperson does not face the objection head-on. Either the salesperson moves quickly to another topic or he belittles the objection, causing the customer to feel that his concerns are not taken seriously. Failing to understand the seriousness of the concern is a major mistake because the salesperson is more focused on his own position than on the customer's needs.

A shopping couple witnessed an objection handled in a magnificent way. They were moving across town which meant a school change for their teenage daughter. Early in the initial presentation they asked about schools. The sales counselor noted this first question and concluded it was an important issue. She broke her dialogue and gave us this information. *"Tell me a little about your daughter. What are her interests?"* After learning about their daughter she continued, *"Since your daughter is a cheerleader and on the debate team I can understand her reluctance about this move and yours, too. Before we continue, let me give you the name of the chairman of the school board. We suggested to another family in your same situation that they might be able to get permission for their children to finish out the year in their current school. They were granted permission and are pleased that they could move ahead with their plans. Since Whitney is a senior, and will only have a few months until graduation, this may be an ideal solution for you."*

It is important to point out that this objection surfaced only with a simple question. The sales professional took the time to dig deep enough to find out the serious motivation behind the question, then moved to a resolution. Objections often lie beneath what is being said. One does not need to be rude or complacent to run the risk of ignoring the customer. A salesperson may only be overly focused on his presentation, and the mission to tell and not sell.

2) They agree with the objection.

The salesperson takes the customers' side in the objection because he does not want to jeopardize his relationship with them. The salesperson will sympathize with the objection without trying to resolve it. Sometimes he will even adopt this approach to the detriment of his builder. Salesmanship is about leadership. The masters that we have shopped led their interested candidates through the winding path of ownership one step at a time, careful to check along the way to see if they were still following.

A buyer was comparing new homes to previously-owned homes. The salesperson took great patience with this couple. He acknowledged that one might assume older homes have more value for the price. He did not stop there. He patiently carried the customer through a diagram of the anatomy of a house, pointing out the new and better materials and equipment in today's homes. He also graciously made the customer aware of the obsolescence of older property and the maintenance cost that continues beyond the dollars spent up front.

3) They give up too easily.

Instead of trying to help the customer overcome the objection by giving additional support and assistance, the salesperson will move to another model or homesite, or more "favorable" topic even when the first was really the best choice despite the objection. Handling objections through fear may also cause the salesperson to bury it, hoping it will go away forever.

One salesperson had a floor plan with a galley kitchen that had been very difficult to overcome. There were two other plans with large kitchens. He admitted that the temptation was to take the easy way out and work on selling the larger kitchen models and ignore the small kitchen plan. However, because he would be building ten of the "difficult" kitchen homes the problem had to be faced. The end result was a dynamic presentation illuminating the advantages of additional space in better places, such as the larger breakfast room and adjacent family room which literally increased the size of the kitchen while keeping the work station more convenient.

4) They lay stress on the objection.

As the expert, you know how wonderful your offering is. The customer does not. Sometimes there is the inclination to counter too quickly before giving convincing and persuasive information to help customers make an educated analysis of the total picture. Conflict is stressful to both parties, and builds harmful barriers to communication. The game of selling has both parties winning. One-upmanship does not make objections go away.

There are various ways in which salespeople whom we have shopped have resolved objections by:

1) Preparing for them in advance.

2) Introducing them before the customer does.

3) Dealing with the objection head-on.

4) Postponing the resolution when appropriate.

In one sense, I feel that "overcoming objections" may not be the best choice of words. Dealing with objections is not a question of winning or losing. Objections are benchmarks along the path to the close. A salesperson's approach should not be adversarial, as in a debate. Instead of "overcoming" objections, we are:

"Addressing" them;
"Neutralizing" them;
"Resolving" them; or
"Reconciling" them.

Top salespeople do not "argue" with objections. After all, customers are not necessarily motivated to argue back or defend their
position. The fact that they voiced a concern shows interest. Further conflict may be too uncomfortable for them. They are often
more likely to just "shut down" and let you have your way. However, they will not let you have any more influence over them. At
an appropriate moment, they will simply go away and not come
back.

* * *

Process To Resolve Objections

It is important for salespeople to develop a *process* for overcoming objections. An effective process not only makes objections more manageable, but it can also make you feel more confident about asking questions that bring objections out in the
open. This is important. We have seen salespeople face objections boldly, and even encourage customers to voice them early
in the relationship. We have seen others more inclined to "tip-
toe" around objections and "let sleeping dogs lie." The latter
approach can cause you to miss some of your best selling opportunities.

By bringing a customer's objections to the surface, you allow
yourself to be the one to resolve them (or at least *balance* them) .
The customer remains more focused, and you can move on with
your presentation. If you do not succeed in bringing customers'
objections to the surface, they will simply harbor them throughout
your presentation, and then bring the objections out at home when
making their buying decision. In their home environment they are
unlikely to resolve their objections in your favor. While they throw
your brochure in the trash, you are classifying them as "A"
prospects because they agreed with everything you said. Since you
dominated the interaction, they had no choice.

<u>Uncover discontent.</u>

One of the myths in our business is that everything must "stay affirmative" in order to keep the sale moving. I can remember being told that when you can see the heads moving up and down they are buying. We were taught to ask those questions which will elicit "yesses." This was supposed to produce harmony. On the contrary, forcing affirmation often creates distance, as the selling process moves farther and farther away from addressing the customer's real needs, thoughts, and feelings. Friendly customers can create distance by being friendly, just as unfriendly customers can create distance by being unfriendly. Don't assume that positive or nice answers mean you are making a sale. Honest interaction is the more direct path to the close. You need to question your customers as you go through the selling process in order to get their reactions and uncover their motivations. You don't just want "yesses." You want the truth.

* * *

Preparing Your Strategies For Objections

Once again I must emphasize the importance of preparation. When our shoppers raise objections to top salespeople, we can tell that they have already given the objection a great deal of thought. Their responses are comfortable, confident, sensitive, and deal directly with the issue.

When an objection is obvious, we often see salespeople deal with it in their "initial overview" before we have a chance to bring it up. In taking the approach that "the best defense is a good offense," these salespeople build themselves a greater position of strength, and a higher level of credibility. They also give customers the feeling that they really understand them, and are sensitive to issues which might concern them. A final benefit of addressing objections up front is that customers can now focus on your other information because they are not distracted by the objection lurking in the background.

When is the best time?

The principle of addressing objections in advance applies not only to the "initial overview," but also to later stages in the selling process. Some objections, such as backing up to a large power line, are issues which you know will be a concern for every customer. In this situation you would address it up front. While standing at the site plan and giving an overview of the community, you would say, *"The location we're selling right now backs up to a power line that sits in a large right-of-way so that there's a lot of open space."* This approach is very matter-of-fact, not defensive, but also not overselling.

As I discussed in the last chapter, you do not want to denigrate your situation, but you do want to make sure you can meet or exceed the expectations which you have created in the buyer's mind. Present the situation in as positive a way as possible without setting him up for a letdown. As I said earlier, *disappointment is the archenemy of momentum.* Creating this balance takes planning, practice, and a certain amount of trial and error.

There are other situations which create objections for some people, but not for everyone. Examples of this type of objection would be: Backing to a road or being in a flight pattern. Such objections may shrink the size of your potential market, but for some customers they will not pose a problem. Do not address these issues in advance unless you are sure that a particular customer will object to them. Instead, be very alert to the immediate reaction to the situation. If the customer's facial expression or body language causes you to sense a concern, bring the issue up right away. Tell him you observed his reaction. He will appreciate the fact that you are paying such close attention to him.

For example, suppose you are walking through a model that has a small dining room. You don't know yet whether or not your customer wants something larger, so you watch him as you walk into the room. If you believe that you see a look of concern, you can say, *"It looks as though you're placing your furniture, am I right?"* Perhaps his response will be, "Yes, I am a little worried about the size of this room."

If the dining room really is smaller than most in your price range, you could explain, *"A lot of study and thought went into our decision to make the dining room a little smaller. In this home we focused on putting the space where you use it most, which is on the first floor in the kitchen and family room. We felt that this layout would give you the best total use of square footage day in and day out. Do you plan to use your dining room very often?"* If they tell you that the dining room creates an impossible situation for them, then you can switch to another model.

Don't "tie down" objections. In other words, don't try to elicit a response by saying, "This is a small dining room, isn't it?" Make sure it's an insurmountable objection before you agree. You do want customers' opinions, however. When you don't get feedback from a customer, you could be running on a treadmill without knowing it.

If you cannot resolve the objection, you need to know how important the objection really is. Distinguishing between major and minor objections is vital, and often the best way is simply to ask. *"Is the size of the dining room so important to you that it would make it impossible for you to own this home?"*

If the answer is yes, it's okay to agree with the customer by saying, *"I understand. I appreciate any such feedback you can give me. It will help me to see if I can find something that works better for you."*

As you distinguish between major and minor objections, it is important not to get bogged-down in the "minor leagues." If you can't overcome a minor objection, just keep moving. Focus on the major ones. You do not have to overcome all objections to make a sale. You must, however, create a better *balance* of positives and negatives than anyone else. Customers will resolve their own minor objections if they like your home *as a whole.*

If you are having trouble determining whether an objection is major or minor, you can resolve your doubt with a simple, straight-forward question such as the example above with the dining room. Other similar questions we have heard include:

"In order to help me understand how important this is to you, let me ask you, is it a must?"

"How high is this on your list of priorities?"

Or the simplest and most direct of all: "How important is that to you?"

You need to get customers to state their *entire* opinions and talk the objections through. Sometimes they can rid themselves of anxiety by thinking it through out loud. If not, at least you have gained a deeper understanding of the problem, and they will appreciate your willingness to listen to their negative feelings.

When it comes to major objections, which are inevitable, it is important for your company to be realistic in its expectations. If you have one homesite with a steep grade and only a small level area, and other more attractive homesites, your company should honestly address the issue of value before placing the former site on the market. It is not fair for a company to expect a salesperson to create value that does not exist. If something is worth less, it should sell for less, unless the company is willing to carry it for awhile longer. Look for any features which may offset the objection. If there aren't any, you may want to lobby for money to create a positive feature.

Using the example above, consider landscaping the hill, or have a landscape plan drawn up to show the customer the potential for the hill, even if it will be at the customer's expense. For objections to which there are no satisfactory "answers," consider offering a real solution instead. In this case, you know that nearly everyone will raise an objection about the uphill rear yard, and you don't want to create disappointment. You would therefore explain the hill before the customer sees it, and offer the suggested landscape plan at that time. This approach creates the possibility that when the customer arrives at the site he will say, "This isn't really so bad. It will look good when it's landscaped, and I won't have to cut grass. We never use our present back yard where we live now anyway." Customers are more likely to add their own value to an item if you have not oversold it in the first place.

In preparing your strategies for resolving objections, consider that objections come from four primary motivations:

1) Price resistance,

2) Fear,

3) Lack of urgency, and

4) Lack of interest.

My bungee jumping "experience" is an example of the last motivation: lack of interest. You see this behavior in action when the customer does not like what you are selling, and has made it clear that he has no intention of ever buying it. Naturally, this motivation requires no preparation, because the objection is impossible to counter. As for the other three motivations, you should consider ways to address them in advance.

Your procedure for preparing for objections should include the following steps:

1) Determine those objections which will most frequently be raised.

2) Write them down.

3) Plan a way to respond.

4) Write or type your response.

5) Practice the response until it is automatic.

Let me break down item #3 into a little more detail. As you list the various objections which you anticipate, use the following outline to help you plan your responses:

1) Listen to the objection with empathy.

Make sure customers perceive that your goal is to make them happy, not to ignore the objection.

2) Feed the objection back in order to confirm it.

Restate the objection in a way that will help your customer to focus on the implications, and also to let him know that you intend to deal with it seriously and thoughtfully. Suppose the customer says, "This site slopes down in the back. I want a more level location. This isn't really all that usable." You could respond by saying, ***"Okay, so you are saying your top priority for a yard is that it have as much usable space as possible, and the total square footage and the view are not as important."***

3) Question it.

S: "You mentioned earlier that you liked walkout basements. Now you understand that the sloping site is needed to create a walkout basement. Level homesites usually have regular basements.

Would you like to see a level homesite with a regular basement, or is the walkout more important?"

C: "Oh, I guess I didn't realize the connection. The walkout basement is really more important."

4) Answer it.

S: "I intentionally picked the most level homesite with a walkout basement to show you first, in case that was a consideration. This one might have the best combination of walkout basement and grade, although you might prefer some of the features of other homesites. I'd be happy to show them to you if you'd like. This one is nicely situated with respect to the homes behind, and the home sits farther forward on the site in order to give you as much usable space as possible. The total situation of this homesite was very well thought-out in the planning stages. All in all, what do you think?"

C: "Well, I see what you mean. I'd probably like to see the others, if it wouldn't take too long."

5) Confirm the answer.

Make sure you really have resolved the objection in the customer's mind. If you have not, now is the time you need to know it, and you need to know if the objection is a "deal killer." This part of the interaction must be straightforward, sincere and definite. It is always important to conclude your efforts to resolve an objection by *closing the objection.*

"Okay, we can see the others now. But let me ask you this: Now that you understand why the land slopes, you're pleased with this one, is that right?"

The purpose of "confirming the answer" and "closing the objection" is to ask the question, "Do you feel okay about this?" The question can be worded in a variety of ways, as long as your intention remains clear. One salesperson was very straightforward with an uncommunicative customer by simply saying, "Okay, give me some feedback. What are you thinking?" This is really the question we want to ask at a number of different points in the sale. Why not use exactly those words?

You want to always be testing the waters as you attempt to resolve objections in order to learn whether or not you are resolving them successfully and maintaining your momentum. The balance sheet at the end of every objection is, "Do your customers like it enough to want to own it?" If the answer is yes, keep moving forward. Once the objection is resolved, however, leave it alone. There are times when salespeople cling to the objection longer than customers do. Deal with the objection as briefly as possible. Don't be long-winded unless the objection has truly demanded a lengthy explanation. When your response to an objection takes too long, it can give customers the impression that you are trying to convince yourself. Once you have dealt with it, forget it unless the customer brings it up again. This is when you let sleeping dogs lie. It is no longer an issue for your customer; don't let it be for you.

It is often appropriate to follow up an objection with a trial close such as, "Do you have any other concerns?" This is a strong question and a bold one, and can be very important in helping to set up your close. In addition to "closing the objection," the objection can sometimes be used for a trial close. This is a different strategy, and comes late in the sale after you have earned the right to close. *"Since you feel that the dining room will be okay if you place your furniture the way we discussed, and since you say you love the rest of the home, is there anything standing in the way of your moving forward with your decision today?"*

6) Move on to the next step in your presentation.

With the objection resolved satisfactorily and the resolution confirmed, you have now earned the right to continue your presentation with their approval.

* * *

Adapting To The Customer's Personality

Relating to the variety of personalities you encounter is one of the challenges of selling. It is not only important in establishing rapport, but it can also be a significant factor in resolving objections. This kind of relating does not require a profound understanding of psychology, but it does require perceptive observation. Theoretically, a robot could give an effective "presentation" from the standpoint of merely conveying information. The human element is all-important in resolving objections. Everyone, regardless of personality type, wants to feel important and appreciated. As I mentioned earlier, when we shop salespeople more than once and see them adapt their approach to the personality of each customer, we witness brilliant examples of the art of selling.

I would like to talk about four different types of customers in terms of two important questions:

1) How can we identify a personality type?

2) How can we vary our approach to overcoming objections in a way that will help us relate to customers better?

The four personality types are these:

1) The "kind" person.

These people are soft, shy, and usually friendly — perhaps too friendly. They have difficulty making decisions. It is often hard to know what they are really thinking because they don't like confrontations, and they don't want to hurt your feelings. You will need to encourage them to raise objections and to state their opinions. Initiate feedback by asking them lots of questions, and getting them to make small decisions as frequently as possible.

2) The "analytical" person.

This type needs lots of information. They are very logical and detailed, but they, like the kind person, are indecisive. They keep needing more information before they can make a decision. They will judge you on how much information you can provide. Give them the information they need in order to deal with their objections, but then, as with the kind person, you must force decisions. These people do not require as much gentleness as the kind person does, and are more likely to be candid about what they are really thinking. They are likely to raise more objections than the other three types.

3) The "antagonistic" person.

These people like confrontation. They have to get their way first; then they will cooperate. They have a higher energy level than the first two types. You will need to appeal to their egos in order to establish rapport, and make them receptive to your efforts to resolve their objections. Here are two responses we have heard from salespeople who tuned in well to this type of personality:

"I really appreciate that you're frank and open."

"I can see you're the kind of person who likes to cut to the chase. So am I. I can see we're on the same wavelength."

This type of person appreciates straightforwardness from salespeople. To this person you would say, *"I'm going to show you some homesites that back to a high wire."*

4) The "social" person.

It's pleasant to deal with these people. They have a high energy level, like the antagonists, but they are more personable. They are also decisive, but they need more help in becoming focused. You can be forthright with "socials" without worrying about hurting their feelings; they like open communication. Since they generally have a good feeling about people, they are not overly sensitive. Be very direct with them, but keep on track and help them distinguish between major objections and minor ones.

* * *

Being sensitive to your customer's personality will help you choose the most effective approach for establishing rapport and overcoming objections. This sensitivity will also help you to be able to give customers a sense of *dignity* throughout the interaction. Customers must feel a sense of dignity when they work with you — they must feel *important*. **Dignifying the customer** should always be a top priority in any sales or marketing strategy. Your product design, advertising, merchandising, selling, and customer service should all be committed to the goal of "dignifying the customer." The selling process works best when the dignity of everyone involved is protected. Salespeople should never be condescending, nor should they ever grovel. In relating to the customer's particular type of personality, it is important to deal with him "eye to eye."

It takes a lot of patience to treat a customer with dignity when he is not treating you that way, but patience is a very important selling tool. Not all customers are blessed with wonderful personalities, but they often "come around" if we have the patience. We can protect their dignity by treating them with respect, and protect our own dignity by maintaining high standards and not stooping to lower ones.

* * *

Welcome The Objection

Customers need to feel that their objection is welcomed. Make them feel glad that they expressed it. If they feel "punished" they will shut up and shut down until they can get away. Comments such as, "Thank you for mentioning that," or, "That's a good point," help keep the channels of communication open. They also give you a less adversarial environment in which to counter the objection. As I said earlier, you want all four of the personality types to feel comfortable bringing their objections out in the open where *you* can deal with them. Don't leave your customers to resolve their objections on their own.

Dave Stone, founder of The Stone Institute, teaches us to begin to address objections by "cushioning" them. You cushion an objection by giving an *introduction* to your response. Examples of a cushion are: "Let me see if I can help you with that;" "That's a good point. We could have done it that way, and we considered it, but let me tell you why we did it this way;" or, "I understand how you feel. Sitting where you are sitting at this moment, I would feel the same way."

It is important for customers to understand that you *chose* the path you did because you knew *it was the best thing to do*. At the same time, you understand and respect their position. This attitude will give you a more positive introduction to the next step, which is persuading them to accept an alternative position.

In addition to product objections, you also have to deal with their objection to moving. Change is difficult for many people. This is no time for salespeople to be shy. You need to know what *all* of the issues are — *product* issues and *emotional* issues. What are they "up to?" What motivation prompted the objection?

There could be several possibilities:

1) They could be the kind of customers who seem to have graduated from "prospect college." They know exactly what things to say to keep a salesperson at bay.

2) Perhaps they are saying, "Reassure me that I'm doing the right thing."

3) They could be "testing" — testing us, themselves, the whole situation.

4) They could really need to resolve a problem with your home before they will consider living there.

5) They may just need to talk it through out loud.

Have the courage and perseverance to follow up your customer's vague or puzzling statements with additional questions, if necessary, in order to keep your selling process moving. These questions do not have to be cleverly worded. They only have to be sincere in order for your customers to appreciate your questions and answer them honestly.

* * *

"Intimidating" Enthusiasm

I have talked previously about the dangers of "overselling." While enthusiasm is important, so is timing. If you act too enthusiastic about something that the customer has not yet seen, it can set him up for disappointment.

When resolving objections it is important to balance enthusiasm with sensitivity. One way that salespeople make customers uncom-

fortable is by being too enthusiastic. It is important to show that
you, your company, and your buyers are enthusiastic about what
you are selling. But your enthusiasm must not steamroll over the
customers' emotions. You want to know what they are feeling, and
they might not let you know if they are intimidated. Customers
actually can be intimidated by a salesperson's enthusiasm. If you
"come on too strong," customers might feel reluctant to speak their
minds because:

1) They don't think you'll hear them;

2) They don't want a confrontation; or

3) They don't want to hurt your feelings. They will keep their
   thoughts to themselves, but these thoughts will not go away.

As you listen to their reactions you need to adopt a demeanor of
objectivity so that customers will know they are being listened to.
You "dignify" your customers by honoring their opinion. You are
balancing your own enthusiasm with a sincere desire to know what
they think. Once the customer has expressed the objection, you are
then in a position to handle the concern "rationally." This is another
example of the balance between rational selling and emotional selling. You can explain how your company has already thought
through the situation, and why it chose the solution it did.

A salesperson whom we shopped justified an "undersized" fourth
bedroom in the following way:

*"We really wrestled with the design of this bedroom because, like
you, we believe kids deserve good-sized bedrooms, too. In fact,
one of our design criteria for this entire series of homes was that
any room that would be used as a bedroom must be at least
10'x10'. However, when we were deciding on the room dimensions for this home, we were thinking of families of four or less.
We realized that this would become an extra room, so we made it*

a little smaller. That way the rooms which would really be used as bedrooms could be larger, and we could still build the home for its current price. In fact, a family of your size was exactly our target family. Your kids get the two larger rooms, and this would be your extra room. What plans did you have for this room?"

The goal with this kind of explanation is to show customers that you empathized with their situation at the time you designed the home. and, even went one step farther by trying to provide them with all the functions they needed, for the best price possible without any waste.

We have seen salespeople deal with objections successfully by rephrasing them, which helps the customer rethink the objection as the salesperson addresses it. The example of the small bedroom could have begun like this:

C: "This is one of the smaller bedrooms we've seen in this price range."

S: "You're concerned about having enough space for your kids, especially as they grow, is that right?"

C: "Yes. If their bedrooms are too small now, think of what it's going to be like when they're teenagers."

You could then follow up with the explanation above by showing that they will enjoy larger bedrooms in your homes because of the way you allocated the total space. You want them to think through all the consequences of what they are requesting, and then allow their needs to evolve as they become more knowledgeable. What they need to be considering is not one room at a time, but *the best total use of space (value) for the money.* Naturally, when you use statements like this to resolve objections, you must be sure that statements which compare you to others are accurate.

Sometimes you will need to encourage customers to articulate their objections more clearly, especially objections which sound weak or illogical. One salesperson dealt with these types of objections by saying, *"Please help me to understand. What do you think would have been the better solution?"*

Remember I mentioned that timing is an important part of enthusiasm. Let your enthusiasm grow with theirs. Salespeople who use their enthusiasm to affirm a customer's decision gain more influence than those who use enthusiasm to peddle their own preferences. Once customers have made a decision, your enthusiasm for their selection serves as a "reward" that "congratulates" their decision, and helps make them more comfortable with the entire decision-making process. When a mystery shopper decided on a favorite model at one community, the salesperson gave his ego a boost by saying, "It's nice to work with someone who knows what he wants."

"Emotional selling" has more power as a reinforcement than as a persuader. Instead of trying to persuade customers, let them persuade themselves. You can still be enthusiastic about your builder, your community and your homes in general. Just don't be overly enthusiastic about the specifics until you know their preferences, or unless your own selection is very limited and you have to "go for broke."

* * *

To "Shelve" An Objection

There are times when you don't want to address an objection at the moment a customer introduces it. Three examples of such times would be:

1) When you believe that it is especially important at that moment in the sale to keep things moving.

2) When the objection takes you by surprise and you need time to think about it.

3) When you want to put your answer into the context of another piece of information that you have not yet given.

In these situations it is okay to put off your answer as long as: 1) You acknowledge the objection and tell the customer you will be addressing it later; 2) You tell why addressing it later is more appropriate; and 3) You return to the objection as promptly as possible. However, don't let customers feel that you are ignoring their objections, or that you are manipulating them or "jerking them around." If customers believe that you are giving them the runaround, they will "tune you out." Here are two effective ways of shelving objections which we have heard during shopping visits:

1) "I want to address that, and if you'll hold that thought I'll try to clarify it better in the context of our whole picture."

2) "I want to deal with that issue because I know it's important, but there are a few other things I'd like you to consider along with it. Please don't let me forget about your question if I haven't addressed it shortly."

My own personal feeling is that when a customer specifically says he wants something, you should give it to him. One example is the price list. Many excellent salespeople hold off giving the customer pricing information until they are ready. This is ideal. However, if the customer is adamant about a request and doesn't get it, a wall goes up that is very hard to tear down. The customer stays irritated and distracted throughout the presentation, and rapport-building becomes very difficult.

When everyone's dignity is protected, the customer's comfort level will rise. One mistake that weaker salespeople sometimes make is to "take the customer's side." While at first this may appear to be the diplomatic path of least resistance, the truth is that it leaves the customer with profound feelings of ambivalence. When a customer hears that we'll "go to the wall for him" against our own employer, he cannot help but doubt our integrity. Deep down, it makes him almost as uncomfortable when our dignity is jeopardized as when his is. An adversarial atmosphere still pervades, even though alliances may have shifted.

The greatest position of strength is fairness.

I know of one situation in which a customer stated a demand and then said to the salesperson, "You know that you can go to bat for us if you really want to. See what you can do and let us know." The customer was obviously trying to gain a position of strength with this tactic. The salesperson's response was perfect: *"The truth is, I'm afraid that in this case I really can't go to bat for you. I want to do the right thing for everybody, and you know I'd certainly love to sell you a home. But you have to understand that my first obligation has to be to my company. Would you really trust a salesperson who turned against his own employer just to get a commission? Would you even trust anyone in that company?"*

Taking the customer's side creates a position of weakness that never goes away. A customer who takes advantage of that situation once will take advantage of it as often as possible. It does *not* help build rapport, because it erodes credibility.

Also, be careful about "soft-peddling." This often backfires. Under-representing can be dangerous, whether in presenting information or overcoming objections. Making a problem less than it really is usually causes more problems than it solves because it also erodes credibility.

One example of under-representing is in discussing price. Give yourself a chance to exceed the customer's expectations, rather than falling short of them. If your homes start at $179,990, your position will deteriorate quickly if you say, "Our homes start in the $170,000's." One outstanding salesperson said to us, "Chances are your final price would be around $190,000, and it could be less."

* * *

A Customer's Needs Can Change

As you ask questions in your initial overview which are designed to determine your customers' needs, remember that those needs can change. In fact, they often do change. Customers become more knowledgeable and determine what they must give up in order to salvage those priorities which are most important. Many of us have experienced the situation in which a customer tells us that our home does not meet his needs, and then he buys a similar home nearby from someone else. It's not that he was lying. He simply did eventually buy the type of home that he originally wanted. He reevaluated his priorities, and those priorities changed.

The same is true with objections. Most objections are not terminal, and many are not permanent. They could simply represent what the customer is thinking at that moment. Sometimes they're just "thinking out loud," so it is important to distinguish between real objections and mere questions. Inquire directly as to the importance of the concern. Show how your homes have met the needs of other people like them, and how these people have dealt with the same concerns.

"We've had other folks raise the same objection about the size of bedroom four. But when they compared the sizes of bedrooms two and three to others in our price range, they told us they realized we had done the right thing. Their kids have more space, and the fourth bedroom is large enough for a study or guest room. Do you think that could work for you?" This final question is impor-

tant, because you need to know if your attempt to deal with their objection has been successful. If it has not, you must determine whether or not you need to deal with it further, or whether or not they like the rest of the home well enough to live with the one room they consider less than ideal.

* * *

Close The Objection, Then Close The Sale

I spoke earlier about the principle of "closing the objection." You keep your momentum alive by moving away from the objection once it is resolved, and then not coming back to it unless the customer brings it up again. You must, however, try to make a clean break from the objection, and assure that the customer is satisfied, so that the objection will not continue to lurk in the background as a distraction. Here are several ways we have heard salespeople "close objections:"

"Have I resolved this concern for you?"

"Is this okay?"

"Do you feel all right about this now?"

"Does this solve your problem?"

"Have I given you a satisfactory answer to your concern?"

"Are you still as concerned as you were?"

"Do you have any other concerns about this?"

All of these questions are straightforward and sincere. They leave the customer with the impression that the salesperson really wants to help, not simply be convincing. Not only must customers feel comfortable with your answer, and they must believe also that you feel comfortable with your own answer. Do not go back to the objection and try to justify it. We heard one salesperson say, long after an objection had been eliminated, "Although it's not quite what you wanted, it's worth it." The objection that had been put to rest was suddenly reawakened, and not by the customer.

We must realize that some objections will never be resolved. That does not mean the sale is dead. You can ask the customer if it is worthwhile to continue. In those situations where there is still hope of the sale, your goal is to minimize the negatives, accentuate the positives, and ultimately create a more favorable balance of advantages and disadvantages. After all, no one else is perfect either.

"Closing objections" is important in any phase of the sale. However, as you move closer to the end of the selling process, you can also use objections to close the sale. Once the customer has picked out a favorite model and homesite and understands the financial requirements, you are moving toward the final close. When late objections arise, *close the sale as you close the objection.* We have heard this done effectively in a variety of ways:

"Since we've resolved your concern, are we ready to move forward?"

"Do you have any other concerns?"

"Is this the only thing standing in your way?"

"While we're on it, are there any other issues you need me to address before you give your approval?"

"If there are any other issues which concern you, let's go ahead and see if we can address them now."

Writing down objections as the customer raises them can be very effective. Customers feel that their opinions are important when we put in writing what they say. This particular salesperson made a list of objections and then concluded by saying, "Is this everything?" When we said it was, he then asked, "If we can resolve these issues, is there anything else that stands in your way?"

"If we can resolve this to your satisfaction, are we ready to move forward?"

This last question brings up another issue. Do we run the risk of sounding impatient if we try to turn an objection immediately into a close? Once again, the answer to that question is, "Have you earned the right to close?" Have you given the customer the information needed in order to make a decision? Have you performed the services which you would expect someone to perform for you, before you made an investment this size? If your answer to these questions is yes, it's okay to go ahead and go for the close. There's nothing wrong with being a little impatient at the end. It's being impatient too early that causes the problem. At some point, you need to help customers to make a decision one way or another, especially if they are beginning to use insignificant objections to stall or put you on the defensive.

When you honestly believe it's time to draw the sale to a conclusion, or at least test the water, it's okay to close an objection by saying, *"If I can resolve this issue for you, are you in a position to make a decision today?"*

Dealing with objections effectively can help you move toward the close rather than away from it. We are now ready to review successful methods for completing the close.

Closing

I would like to define closing as *"a conclusion brought about by a meeting of the minds, and <u>acted upon.</u>"* With that definition in mind, I will use this chapter to explore several dimensions of closing. A close happens when a decision forces an action to move ahead. "The persuasive force" behind the action is the salesperson. I contend that closing is not only a form of negotiation, closing is negotiating. I will list a few ideas that give an overview of what my definition of closing involves.

1) Closing in the large sense is a *total process* that begins with the greeting and continues through the agreement to purchase. This closing process provides momentum throughout the sale.

2) There is also a more specific sense in which the word "closing" refers to the *final close* — a clearly defined event that occurs at a specific moment in time and draws the entire selling process to a conclusion.

3) Closing results from a *series of initiatives* by the salesperson. These initiatives include:

a) Questions during the selling process which are designed to help the salesperson understand the customer's qualifications, motivations, needs, and responses.

b) Trial closes — preliminary closing questions and statements
   which "conclude" one issue in order to move the selling
   process to the next stage. Trial closes, like the final close,
   involve a "meeting of the minds" which affirms the sale is proceeding successfully.

4) Closing involves a **series of decisions** made by the buyer, with
   the help of the salesperson. The salesperson must keep the selling process focused on assisting the customer in making one
   decision after another in order to keep the "closing process"
   moving towards the "final close." These decisions must be artic-
   ulated and agreed upon.

5) A successful close occurs when *a customer's **affirmative decision is converted into action.*** The decision alone is not enough.
   We all make decisions which are not acted upon in a timely fashion. Sometimes they are never acted upon. A decision to buy
   without action is not a sale. The acronym "AIDA" refers to the
   order in which people make buying decisions:

1. Attention,
2. Interest,
3. Decision,
4. Action.

The outstanding closer is the sales person who:

a) Enables the customer to move through a series of smaller decisions which lead ultimately to the major one.

b) Empowers the customer to convert this major decision into action.

The "action" of AIDA is where selling really comes alive, and
where closing becomes a vital skill. This is where *salespeople real-*

ly do make the difference. A certain number of sales will occur
without a close. There also are a significant number of sales that
occur because a salesperson persuaded the customer to convert his
positive responses into a decision and action to buy.

6) Effective closing demands that salespeople be willing to *climb
out of their comfort zones.*

* * *

Climbing Out Of The Comfort Zone

Closing will not always be comfortable. A certain amount of discomfort is natural for both the salesperson and the customer during
the closing process. It is so important, therefore, to establish rapport and trust throughout the selling process. If you find that closing is always comfortable, then you are probably losing sales.

It takes courage to close

Top closers have tremendous *courage.* This courage wins those
extra sales that would not have occurred without the skill and initiative of a professional salesperson. These are the sales that are lost
by average salespeople because customers are allowed to walk
away without acting on their decision. During our shopping visits
we find that top closers — the "courageous" ones — tend to speak
with more *authority* throughout the selling process. Words that
flash into my mind during these visits are strength, confidence,
fearlessness, and power. I'm not talking about "hard selling" but
rather positive persistent persuasion. I'm talking about *professionalism.*

From where does this courage come? It comes from the conviction
and confidence that you are doing the very best thing for the people

you serve. Unless a salesperson believes with his heart and soul in what he is doing, fear will stifle his courage. Fear is a debilitating animal. Some might say it is a fear of failure or a fear of rejection that keeps salespeople from closing, thus limiting their success. I believe those fears are only by-products of a less complex issue. I believe the fear of being embarrassed keeps many salespeople from reaching for their highest potential. Quite frankly, this is very sad. The fear of being humiliated — of being made to feel uncomfortably self-conscious — is a major concern for all human beings, not just salespeople. For example, the fear of public speaking tops the list of man's greatest fears — even ahead of the fear of dying.

Closing — the act of asking for an agreement — does take courage and it is not easy, certainly not for adults. Kids, now they are different. What seems like natural behavior as a child becomes very unnatural as an adult.

Our son, Kyle, is blessed with three young sons, Brandon, Travis and Tyler. They are the cutest, the brightest, the most wonderful little boys God ever put on this green earth. To truly describe them would take volumes. However, I must share with you one Brandon story. It was near dinner time and Brandon (the oldest) asked for an animal cracker. The answer was no. "Grandma Bonnie, can I just look at the pictures on the box?" Okay. "Grandma Bonnie, may I just hold some of the animals?" I guess so. "Oops, the ear fell off the bear. Can I just eat the ear? It's just a little tiny ear. Grandma Bonnie, the bear looks funny without an ear. I really think I should eat the bear, don't you?" Well, what was the harm? After all, the bear didn't even have an ear. Thinking back I realize that Brandon overcame a dozen "no's" before he finally succeeded in getting his animal cracker. I also noticed something else. He just continued asking, confident that no real harm would come regardless of the outcome. With a little luck he might even get a treat. Brandon Kyle Alfriend should be in the hall of fame for master closers. Those of you who have little ones in your life have seen how unabashedly relentless children can be when they are focused on a goal. Unfortunately, it seems at some point in life straightforward honesty and drive become stifled by shyness and fear. What will other people think? To master the art of closing we must become comfortable acting on our convictions. It also may mean bringing out the undaunted fearlessness of the child within.

"Please Grandma Bonnie, can we have some animal crackers?"

Customers expect us to close. They really do. When we ask to test drive a car, we know the salesperson is going to ask us to buy the car. In focus groups we conduct with homeowners who have recently gone through the homebuying process, we ask them to share their reflections on their buying experiences. Homeowners tell us how surprised they are when salespeople take them to the point of selecting a favorite home and homesite, then never ask them to buy it. I must admit, we see the same trend in our shopping evaluations. It appears as though some salespeople have become so concerned with "rapport building" and "relationship selling" that they are afraid if they risk closing they will destroy the relationship. Then why build the relationship in the first place? The customer knows this is the salesperson's job. They know their financial survival is tied to their ability to sell. They expect salespeople to try to close a sale. They also expect them to provide a complete presentation and a high level of service. After salespeople provide these services, and do not try to close, customers view their actions as a lack of competence and professionalism. This is one of the insights we have gained from focus groups and mystery shopping.

Are customers intimidated by closing? Sure they are. But remember, if they were *too* intimidated they wouldn't come to our sales offices in the first place. When they do come they expect to be asked to buy. It is true that nobody likes a pushy salesperson. Salespeople have to make sure they don't take that line of thinking to the point where they no longer allow themselves to take the selling process to a natural conclusion.

Asking a closing question is not a sign of disrespect. On the contrary, it proves to the customer that we value their business. Closing *can be* a sign of disrespect if we close before we have *earned the right to close*. We must put ourselves in the customer's shoes. What information would we want before we make a decision to buy? We would want to find out about the location, community, builder, homes, homesites and financing. To be closed before we are given this information is insulting. To be closed after we receive it is professional.

How much time does a customer need before trying to close him? Some people need a long time, and they really enjoy the process of shopping for a home. Most do not. The majority of people prefer to act quickly on a decision to buy once they find the home of choice, and have justified their decision. Some customers will be ready to buy on their first visit to your community, others will need multiple visits, but all must be asked. Top salespeople assume that every customer who walks in the door is planning to buy that day until the customer proves otherwise.

What about this "comfort level" issue? As salespeople your goal is to strive to help your customers feel comfortable throughout the buying process. The reason for this is when the uncomfortable moments come (and they usually will in a successful sale) they can be weathered more easily. We must find ways to make customers feel comfortable: the atmosphere of the sales office, a gentle selling demeanor, a comfortable exchange of information. We must also help them through a situation that we know will probably be uncomfortable — deciding to make a traumatic life change that will cost a lot of money in the process. You are their guide through this jungle.

When I was a child the county fair came to Danville, Virginia, every year. The fair had a haunted house. I can remember being too frightened to go through, yet I wanted to very much. It was dark inside, very scary, and, as you walked through, you would bump into all sorts of terrifying things. Talk about "climbing out of my comfort zone." I had a hard time gathering the courage to go through the haunted house. My cousin, who was older, had gone through many times by himself. He told me stories about bumping into ghosts and goblins and stumbling along trying to find his way out. After awhile he was a master at the "haunted house." He was so cool because the trip was second nature to him. Finally I got up the nerve to go through with my cousin who led me by the hand the first time. After that I was able to go alone, and then I took my little sister through. What an exciting feeling that was! My first trip was scary, but it was thrilling. I knew I would come out at the other end okay, and I was building my courage in the process. Then the feeling of leading Jane through gave me such a feeling of confidence and accomplishment!

I remembered my experiences in the haunted house many times throughout my sales career, and I still remember it in my current adventures. I remember the sense of triumph that resulted from climbing out of my comfort zone to try something which terrified me, and then to see it lead to success. Selling is a lot like that. There is trial and error and experimenting. You try out new techniques just to see what happens. Sometimes the idea fails, but you do learn from the experience. Other times you are amazed by the positive results, and it becomes a normal part of your strategy. There will be times when you feel ambivalent about the technique. "It didn't seem to work very well, but it might work better as I become more polished. I think I'll try it again with one minor change."

This is how "climbing out of the comfort zone" works in selling new homes. We should not steer ourselves away from new ideas that work just because they are uncomfortable. Nor should we stay away from techniques on the grounds that they may be uncomfortable for the customer. Change is not comfortable. The greater question to ask is, "Will it be better for the customer when the decision is made?"

You really must believe that owning your new home will improve your customer's life. Without this belief your actions and motivation are strictly self-centered and will never develop into long-term success, no matter how positive your short-term success appears. If you really believe the primary win is for your buyers and your rewards are secondary, then going through a few uncomfortable steps to arrive there will seem like the right thing to do.

You are similar to a doctor providing a remedy that may have a few uncomfortable moments in order to improve the patient's long-term state of health. The doctor would not back off from a cure because it was uncomfortable. The doctor would guide the patient through the process by keeping them focused on the ultimate benefits. This is what selling and closing are really all about

— guiding customers through the difficult parts of the buying process in order to give them a better quality of life. If this means a few moments of discomfort for them or for you, these moments are natural and are often proof that you are achieving a breakthrough.

Courage is not a natural characteristic. It is something people develop as they perform courageous acts and see positive results. In selling, "climbing out of the comfort zone" works the same way. Throughout the sale you are testing with questions and trial closes. These techniques might not be comfortable, but they are necessary for moving to the next step. The more you ask closing questions, the more courageous you will become. Courage is a part of professionalism in our business, as it is in any other business where expertise is a factor. Professionals are *straightforward.*

Let's look for a moment at the cliche, "Nobody likes a pushy salesperson." What happens if, in the process of "climbing out of your comfort zone" with techniques that are a little more aggressive, you push too hard? Will it blow the sale?

Here is a truth about selling new homes that you need to consider very carefully: *Customers will forgive you for pushing too hard as long as you are willing to back off.* They know you're a salesperson. Aggressiveness is not what customers object to. Insensitivity is what really bothers them. If you accidentally push too hard or too soon — with qualifying, trial closing or the final close — customers will find a way to let you know, and you will understand it immediately. When this happens you need to have a *pressure release mechanism.* You can show customers that you are sensitive to their comfort level by backing off. While some people accomplish this with humor, others will sincerely apologize. An apology does not have to imply shame. You can maintain your dignity with apologies like this:

"I'm sorry if I misunderstood."

"Excuse me if I came on too strong. I do that sometimes because I just love what I do."

Here is an example of the use of aggressive humor that we heard during an initial greeting used to sincerely test our buying intentions:

S: "We have some lovely homes here. I hope you brought your checkbook."

C: "Well, no, actually we didn't. We just came to look."

S: "Oh, I know. I'm just teasing you. My name is _____. It's a pleasure to meet you."

This salesperson started out aggressively and then backed off. We did not find this approach to be offensive. Your safest bet, however, is to wait to begin any closing effort until the customer has begun to give "buying signals" (I prefer to call them "attention" or "interest" signals).

The crucial point that I want to make here is that in real life it's better to push too hard than not hard enough. People will forgive you for trying too hard more easily than they will forgive you for not trying hard enough. They are especially forgiving if you back off after pushing too hard. The interesting thing about being too assertive, and then backing off, is that you don't have to back off all the way.

Some customers seem enclosed in a bubble they do not want you to puncture. I call this their "intimacy bubble." As the selling and closing process progresses, and rapport is being built, this bubble usually will shrink in size, meaning that you can move closer to the customer as they become more comfortable and begin giving those "interest signals." You should take advantage of these opportunities, pushing the bubble from time to time without puncturing it.

As you climb out of your comfort zone, you are looking for ways to help your customers climb out of theirs, so the selling process can progress from one stage to the next. This progression is called the process of closing.

* * *

Closing Is A Process

At the beginning of this chapter I said that **closing is a *total process*** directed towards a *final close* by means of a ***series of initiatives*** which lead to **a *series of decisions.***

The "final close," like the homes you sell, requires a strong foundation. The "process of closing" requires you to keep moving from one stage of the selling process to the next. You build the close in each of the three "selling arenas" — the sales office, the model homes and the homesites.

Prior to the final close you go through a number of *trial closes.* As I said earlier, a close is "a conclusion brought about by a meeting of the minds and acted upon." Every time you reach an agreement, you have executed a type of close. Each trial close leads you a little farther in your selling process.

In the sales office you "close to demonstrate the model."

In the model you "close to show your homesites."

While visiting the homesites you "close to work out the financing."

After completing the financing you "close the sale." This is the moment when you go for the final close.

While there will be times when variations will occur within your selling sequence (especially when you go back to revisit an earlier stage), you are always focused on closing for the next step in your process. This is how you keep your selling momentum going. You create a *closing rhythm* throughout the process in order to help the customer's "decision-making muscles" loosen up before you reach the final close. This is one of the purposes of "trial closes." Trial closes occur when you ask customers to affirm something you have shown or explained so you know you are able to keep moving forward.

"Are these the kinds of numbers you were hoping to hear?"

"Is this the type of community you were looking for?"

"Which home is your favorite?...What is it you like best about that plan?"

"Which homesite do you like best?...What is it that makes this one your favorite?"

"This home will be completed in about three months. Will that work for you?"

"Let's go over the customized option list and see which ones are important to you."

"With which of these financing plans do you feel most comfortable?"

These types of trial closes are each designed to accomplish the following objectives:

1) Persuade the customer to make a decision.

2) Confirm that the customer is still with you.

3) Gain feedback that can help you direct your selling efforts in an appropriate direction.

4) Make sure your presentation remains an "interaction" rather than simply a sales pitch.

Trial closes keep you on track because they open the channels of communication. They assist you in *narrowing down the customer's options* as you create urgency through *one-of-a-kind.*

Tie-downs are another type of trial close. The most trivial tie-downs will allow you to examine your customers' reactions to what they are discovering beyond simply their verbal responses to your question.

"Lazy susans are a great invention, don't you think?"

Trial closes, including tie-downs, help you to elicit "interest signals." They confirm that your customers are still responding favorably to the experience.

Dave Stone shows us how the closing process can help you lead customers safely across the "Valley of Lost Sales." He explains that salespeople use their selling skills, including rapport-building, to "build a bridge" across this valley. Each bridge is different, depending upon the needs and personality of the customer. The steps of the bridge include information, explanation of benefits, listening, reassurance, overcoming objections, and need fulfillment, to mention but a few. When the bridge is built carefully and reinforced with caring and expertise, ready, willing and able buyers are enabled to cross the "Valley of Lost Sales" to the final close. Continuing through the closing process with patience, thoroughness and attention to the customer's responses is what eventually "earns you the right" to execute the final close.

* * *

The Final Close

I stated above that "closing is a process." This process finally cul-
minates in a single moment — a moment that must not be allowed
to slip away. Trial closes are not a substitute for the final close.

The community sales representative was hired to make sales happen, sales that would not have happened without a responsible,
courageous, skilled specialist. In all communities a few buyers will
close themselves because of the simple law of supply and demand.
Those few are not sufficient numbers to keep your builder in business and you in a job. In most cases, no matter how well they are
treated, how important we make them feel or how sharp our presentation may be, most customers will never be motivated to close
themselves. They must be closed by someone else in order to put
their buying decision into action. Managing sales is not closing.
Making sales happen is closing. Ask your customers to buy and
recognize, regardless of the answer, you have opened the next critical door in the selling sequence. Your customers deserve this quality of leadership.

The final close must not be vague. It occurs at a specific moment
in time, and the customer knows at that moment that they are being
asked to buy. At that moment they *must* make — and verbalize —
their final decision whether or not they will buy your home that
day. They may say "yes" or "no," but either way you closed. By
closing, regardless of whether their response was positive or negative, you know that you maximized your opportunity for that day.
You will never have to question yourself about the customer walking away and leaving you wondering, "Is there any way they might
have bought today?" You not only will know that you have maximized the opportunity, but also you will know your next step.

How do you know the right moment to close? Often you can tell from the customers' demeanor and the presence of buying signals. You often just feel that everything is coming together and they're ready to move forward. Those are the easy ones. But what happens when there are no obvious buying signals?

Suppose you complete all the stages of the selling process up to the final close. Your customers like your community, accept your prices, understand your product, resolved their objections and qualify to purchase. They have picked out a favorite model and a favorite homesite. Everything has moved along and they have done nothing to stop the process. Yet, you have still received no buying signals. Do you close?

YES! ALWAYS!

The reason is this: just as customers are most often not motivated to close themselves, they also may not be motivated to give buying signals. Customers are not "trained" to give buying signals the same way that we are trained to look for them. They might simply be shy people, or people who are not very expressive by nature. People like that deserve to own homes, too.

Whenever a salesperson has completed all the stages leading up to the final close, he has earned the right to close, and the customer is expecting him to close, whether or not he is giving buying signals.

Timing is important in closing, but if you make a mistake it is still better to be too assertive than not assertive enough. In selling, *too much too soon is better than too little too late.* Customers will forgive salespeople for being too pushy. However, they may not forgive you twice. By backing off after moving too fast, you are showing that you are sensitive as well as diligent. If you ignore signals which indicate you are coming on too strong, it will be perceived as nothing more honorable than pure selfishness.

"Close reluctance" is a problem in new home sales. There are three primary reasons for close reluctance in salespeople:

1) They just can't gain the courage to ask closing questions.

2) They don't listen to or watch for the customer's responses and reactions to trial closes.

3) They "assume" the customer will not buy.

Each of these problems can be corrected through preparation, practice, and the courage to climb out of your comfort zone.

No matter what you have accomplished with a particular customer, be sure to draw the experience of the day to a conclusion, even if you could not lead them far enough to affirm a close.

"How do you like what you've seen today?"

"What did you like best?"

"Was there anything you didn't like?"

"Do you think you could see yourself living here someday?"

"Do you think you'll be visiting us again?"

When that moment in time comes for you to execute the final close, how do you do it? This critical stage in the selling sequence is, without dispute, the most challenging and difficult step for salespeople to master.

* * *

How To Close

In this section I will talk about "the closing moment" in general, and then give an array of effective closes *which we have actually heard on-site.* I realize that, because of some of the gimmicky closes that have been suggested in the past, there is frequent skepticism among salespeople in the "real world" as to how such techniques could possibly result in anything other than embarrassment for everyone present. For that reason I want to emphasize that *every close* that I will include in this section falls into one of three categories:

1) A salesperson used it effectively on-site during one of our shopping visits.

2) I have seen the close used effectively by a salesperson I have personally known or managed.

3) I have used the close successfully in my own selling career.

In addition to effective techniques for the precise closing moment, there are also the matters of:

1) Techniques which help you recover from a rejected close (following up the close).

2) Techniques which help create urgency.

While these two issues can sometimes relate directly to the closing moment, I will deal with them in separate sections of this chapter.

* * *

I mentioned earlier that the closing moment will not always be comfortable for everyone. If every close that you complete is comfortable, there is a good chance you could be missing some opportunities. While the close may not always be comfortable, it should always be *natural*. In other words, it must not sound "gimmicky" or contrived. Here are some characteristics of a strong close:

1) It is courteous and respectful.

A top priority of any sales and marketing effort must be to "dignify the customer." This is no less true at the closing moment.

2) It is direct.

There should be no doubt in the customer's mind that you are asking them to buy, and no way they can avoid giving you a definite answer, one way or the other. This is the only way you know if you really maximized your selling opportunity.

3) It is logical and appropriate.

You are closing because you have accumulated enough positive information to justify asking for the order. You have completed all the prior stages of the selling sequence to the best of your ability, and the customer has not stopped you. You must believe that there is some chance that they will buy your home — if not today, then someday. You are closing because:

  a) It is time to close.
  b) It makes sense to close.
  c) You have earned the right to close.

4) It is consistent with the rest of your approach.

The close should sound like "your type of close." The tone should be the same as that of the rest of your presentation, and not sound like some strange tactic you just pulled out of your sleeve.

Contrived closes that don't fit your selling style make customers feel "creepy." Your close should be appropriate for:

a) Your personality.
b) Your customer's personality.
c) The interaction that has been occurring up to that point.

To make your closing effort as smooth and natural as possible, it helps to write it down and practice it. Do this with as many different closes as you can imagine, and see which ones you think sound most natural and most effective for you.

It is equally important to be aware of how you close. Every time you attempt to close a sale, write down what you said and what you did to execute the close as soon as you have a free moment. Then write down the customer's response. Keep a running log of your closing efforts so you know the ones that are most effective. These exercises will help you to continually refine your closing techniques.

Know in advance how you will "build the close" and how you will "complete the close" in order for you to exercise your closing process with greater confidence.

* * *

Your Final Close Can Be A Statement Or A Question

Salespeople with whom I have talked express different feelings on this issue. I have witnessed both approaches used effectively.

Salespeople who prefer using "closing statements" do so because they are more decisive, more "assumptive," more confident, less risky, and less likely to stall because the customer can act without having to verbalize the commitment.

Not all salespeople are comfortable with closing statements. Some sales representatives find the statements awkward and presumptuous, and believe it is more appropriate to "*ask* for the order." They feel that closing should be a simple question that asks the customer to buy their home. They believe the question is the more direct close because it requires a definite answer. They also believe it is more respectful.

Other salespeople tell me they use both types of closes, depending upon the personality of the customer and the nature of the rapport and the flow of the presentation.

This decision is truly a judgment call. Again, the important issue is to be well prepared with the approach you prefer so when the moment comes you will feel confident to move forward.

Here are examples of each type of close. I have heard these used successfully in real-life selling situations:

The Statement Close

1) *"You've been looking for a long time and you've finally found it, so let's move forward to get this home for you today."*

2) *"I believe you feel this home has your name on it. Let's put that in writing."*

3) *"Everything looks good for you. We only have one left in the section you want. For $100 we can hold the home for two days to give you time to make the necessary selections to start your paperwork."*

4) *"You can obviously afford this. It seems to fit your needs, and it fits within your parameters. The next step is to put the paperwork together. It only requires an initial investment of $1000. That is all we really need between this point*

and the time you take ownership. I think with the situation
you are in, this is right on the number for you."

5) *"I know I've given you a lot to digest, but I hope you're not too*
confused for us to go through the paperwork now." This close
succeeded because the salesperson waited through a long silence
until the customer answered.

6) Another example of "waiting for the response" was this:
"Susan, we can take a check today for $1000 which will secure
this home for you. As you said, you really like the Haven on
the cul-de-sac."

After making the above closing statements, the salesperson
said nothing more until the customer responded. We have all
heard the following expression: "He who speaks first loses." In other words, close and "shut up." This does not mean to wait for customers to close themselves. It means *once you have made your*
closing statement, don't say anything more until the customer
responds. This is an important principle in closing, especially with
"statement closes." If you use a statement close, "don't buy your
sale back" by following up with another statement that might dilute
the first. Don't "cushion your close" and don't "justify" resolved
objections during the final close moment.

I heard one salesperson close by saying, "Let's go ahead and get
this started today." But, instead of waiting for the customer to
respond, she added, "Or, if it would be more convenient, we could
meet some evening next week when there's more time." That is an
example of "taking away your close." The cliche, "Whoever speaks
first loses," simply means that this salesperson should have made
the first statement but not the second. Be sure the customer has the
opportunity to respond. After the closing statement is made, the
person who speaks next is the one who tips his hand. This is part of
the skill of negotiating. "Know when to hold 'em, know when to
fold 'em and know when to walk away." Silence is golden in nego-

tiations. Closing is a meeting of the minds where everyone must come out a winner.

The Question Close

1) *"You've been looking for a while, and we have the home for you. Is there any reason you can't move forward to own your new home today?"*

If they say, "Not today," but indicate that buying is a possibility, it is appropriate to try for an appointment in the near future. Additionally, this saleslady questioned why another day would be better than today. She learned vital information for the next stepping stone.

2) *"You've been looking around a lot, and I can see you really like it here. Why don't we go ahead and get started making it yours?"*

3) When a salesperson wanted to get her customer back into the model to close them there, she said, *"I can see the Adams model fits your needs. Let's go back and confirm that, shall we?"*

4) *"Would you like to go ahead and write it up today so you don't lose your home?"*

5) When you want to use an objection to close the sale, or at least to close for the customer's intentions and level of seriousness: *"If we move that wall are you ready to go ahead with your decision?"*

6) Sometimes you need to help customers collect their thoughts as you go for the close. You know they want the home, but they can't seem to draw their decision together. In such a situation I heard a salesperson use a summarizing close to draw the situation to a conclusion — "a meeting of the minds:"

"You've been looking for a long time. You like what you see here. The homesite on the cul-de-sac is just what you were looking for. You love the style. The floor plan is perfect for you. You love the gourmet kitchen. Everything is right. Let's go ahead and get started moving into your new home today, shall we?" This salesperson preferred to use a "closing question." However, by leaving off the last two words she could have turned it into a "closing statement."

Closing Can Be Serious Or Humorous

Some salespeople like to use humor to close — either in their trial closes or in their final close. They find that humor improves the atmosphere and lightens the burden of the "overwhelming decision." If you use humor, just be sure you remain sensitive to the personality of the customer. Some very serious customers might find humor too frivolous for such a serious matter.

While all of the examples above were serious, here are a few humorous ones I have heard. One preliminary trial close during the greeting went like this:

C: "We're just starting to look."

S: (with a warm, pleasant smile): "Well, I'll do everything I can to make your search as short as possible."

C: "Actually, I wouldn't mind that. I've heard that searching for a new home is not exactly fun and games."

I called this a "trial close" because the salesperson used her statement to begin to determine the customer's level of motivation. His response told her he was a serious candidate, but that he was apprehensive. However, he was opening himself to the possibility of being receptive to a salesperson who could also serve as a counselor.

If, on the other hand, his response had been, "Yeah, you sales-people are all alike. You are just after one thing, your commission," she would have needed a different approach to win his credibility.

Humor can be helpful at the final close when you're not sure of your timing or of the customer's level of involvement. Sometimes you need humor to use after a favorable response, with the option to back away if the customer is not ready. Humor allows you to follow up an unfavorable attempt to close with an "I was only kidding" demeanor.

Here are a few examples of the use of humor toward the end of the selling process when the relationship or timing confirmed humor was appropriate.

"Will that be for here or to go?"

"Can I wrap it up for you?"

"Would you like a gift box?"

"Would you like me to ring it up?"

"Let met get the keys, so you can drive it home."

A common theme in all of these approaches was making light of the enormity of the decision by putting the close into the lingo of fast food or retail sales.

The Final Close Is A Simple Moment

The concept of the final close should not be over complicated. While it is the most important single moment in the selling process, it is also one of the easiest. Building the close is the hard part. Completing it is like placing a cherry on the top of a delicious chocolate sundae, or writing the period at the end of an eloquent sentence. The process is the important part, but without the closing moment the process is incomplete. The better your process, the easier your close. Completing the close may often be the simplest part of the sale, it may also be the part that requires the most courage. Preparation and practice can help that courage to grow, and reduce the fear. If they say "no" I am not going to be mortified. Learning how to follow up the close will increase your confidence in going for the moment.

* * *

Following Up The Close

Part of your confidence in closing comes from knowing what you will do if the close fails. Once again preparation is the key. Write down a selection of follow-up questions and statements that you can use in various situations when the customer says, "Not today."

This is the part of selling where I see some techniques that are "tried and true," and others that are refreshingly innovative or shockingly bold. Here are some of the ways I have heard salespeople address a variety of reasons customers use for rejecting the closing effort. While some of them will not be for you, it is worthwhile to view the panorama of options that are possible.

A) "WE WANT TO THINK IT OVER."

1) *"What exactly do you want to think about?"*

Remember when customers say "no," you need to know why, in order to have a chance to sell to them.

2) *"I understand you want more time to think about your decision. I would be interested in your thoughts about your reasons for and against buying now."*

3) *"Obviously you must have a reason for saying that. Would you mind if I ask what it is?"*

4) *"Let's think it over out loud. Sometimes two heads are better than one."*

5) *"Is it financing you're concerned about, or is it something about the location, or is it something else?"*

In certain situations the customer needs to be prompted in order to give a specific answer. Sometimes they don't know exactly what it is and you will need to throw out ideas to help them identify their reluctance. Usually it is better to sit quietly and wait for them to articulate their own reason for stalling.

6) *"Let's think about it now while it's fresh in your mind. What are some of the things you need to know more about?"*

Remember they are experiencing fear. During the final closing moment the room is filled with emotions. If you do not sense fear then you probably do not have a serious happening.

7) *"Is there anything about the home that just would not work for you?"*

This is the type of question you would ask if you were concerned about hidden objections.

Here are two closes which injected a little humor into situations when the customer had said, in effect, "We like your homes, but we have a lot on our minds right now." They may read as flippant, but in a real situation they were effective because of the nature of the rapport that had been built.

8) *"It seems life is full of decisions, both large and small. Why not save time and get this one out of your way?"*

9) *"As busy as you folks are, you probably have other things to think about that are important. Why not make the decision right now so you can free your mind to think about other things?"*

10) Another salesperson took a similar approach with a customer who said, "We like what we see, but we feel that we still need to keep looking." The salesperson's response was, *"Since you like it here, why don't we just move forward and then you won't have to keep looking."*

I want to make the point that if you have worked hard to establish rapport throughout your selling process, and proven yourself to be the expert, now is the time to take advantage of those efforts by stepping out of character with a little extra boldness, especially if assertiveness is normally difficult for you. As I said earlier, your demeanor needs to be consistent with what it has been, but you can become bolder when you have developed a relationship of trust.

This situation of seeing someone step out of character happened to my Dad and me when my Mother had emergency open-heart surgery. We had our first meeting with a doctor who showed us no bedside manner. He was matter-of-fact, even brash as he spoke. "This situation is serious and this is what I will be doing. I will be in touch with you after surgery." Afterwards he was so gentle and relaxed he didn't look or act like the same person. Even my Mother (who recovered nicely) asked him if he was the same doctor who talked with her prior to the operation. There comes a time in all professional relationships when the expert must take charge and act with boldness to accomplish that which is in the best interest of the client, patient, or customer. The specialist must get on with the business at hand. You are the expert; lead the way.

11) If you have a customer who really wants your home and is stalling for no valid reason they can explain, it sometimes is necessary to "tell it like it is:"

"Thinking it over may mean you take the chance of losing it."

This type of approach should be used sparingly, since many customers will respond, "Then I'll just take that chance."

12) Here would be the type of close you could use for the more decisive "antagonistic" or "social" personality types I described earlier:

"You impress me as a proactive decision maker. Why don't we take the bull by the horns on this one and make a decision now?"

13) *"You want to think it over. I know what you are really saying. You are saying I didn't make the benefits of owning our homes clear to you."* This is the type of statement where you then sit quietly until they respond.

14) *"Well, it may come down to the fact that you are not comfortable with what's happening right now. Let me ask you a question. When you bought your last home did you have the same feelings? I'll bet you did. So did I. Any regrets? I know within the week you will feel comfortable and proud of the decision you just made."*

15) There will be times when you are sitting in the sales office and the sale is beginning to stall. You may feel a need to move the customer into one of the other "selling arenas" to change the dynamics, rejuvenate the sale, and give you a better chance to close that day. I already discussed the example of taking the customer back into the models. Another approach would be to go back out to the homesite. One salesperson did it this way:

"While you're thinking, let's walk over to homesite 40 again and we can talk it over. Can we talk and think at the same time?" Once again, a friendly rapport had been establish so this approach was used effectively. The demeanor was casual and the customer felt relaxed. As they were walking to the site the salesperson resumed his selling effort by asking, *"Can I talk while you're thinking?"*

16) Here is another very bold approach, to be used in situations where you feel compelled to "put the customer's feet to the fire:"

"You and I have been thinking this over since the first time we met. You know that this is a terrific opportunity. You like the home. Let's go ahead now."

B) "I'M CONCERNED ABOUT THE PRICE."

When customers reject your closing efforts on the grounds of pricing concerns, you must remember that very few customers really understand pricing in new homes. General statements about value won't help your cause. Words such as "quality," "service," and "value" have been overused to the point that even uttering them risks evoking feelings of cynicism. When you use any of these three words you must be specific. You need to give a *definition* and an *example* of how your quality, service or value really is superior to that of your competition. In order to overcome the pricing concern, you must convince the customers to *rethink their approach to pricing*. The statements and questions which follow up your close must cause your customers to question their preconceptions and rethink the situation in terms of *what is really best for them*. You must help them to *enlarge their thinking*. You must also persuade them to be honest with you — and with themselves — about whether money is really the issue.

1) *"Is this really about money? If you could afford the home would you want it?"*

If their answer is yes, and they really do qualify, you could respond by saying, *"On paper you can certainly afford this home as well as most people who already live here. (Or, "Most of the people who live here cannot afford their homes as well as you can.") Are there other issues you're wrestling with?"*

2) *"If I could show you a way you could afford this home, would you want to own it?"*

3) *"It's a question of priorities. Does this home really meet your needs?"* This is another of those questions which are designed to draw out hidden objections for you to have the opportunity to address them before the customer leaves.

4) *"What you're telling me is that you really want to own it. Let's look at some ways you can."*

5) Sometimes you need to go directly to the bottom line to qualify for motivation. *"You say you can't afford it. Is that now or forever?"*

6) *"If it were less expensive, would you want it?"* Suppose their answer is yes, and they really do qualify, but simply wish the price were $5000 lower. In this situation, it may be appropriate for you to discuss the additional price in terms of its daily cost, in order to compare the expense with other expenses that are familiar to them.

Customers often don't put their homebuying dollars into the right perspective. They compare the "total" costs relating to their home with the price of groceries without factoring in the element of time. Groceries are a *daily* expense, and the cost of their home should be treated that way, too. If the difference in cost between what they are paying and what they wish they were paying breaks down to $1 a day, then that should be compared to the daily cost of a loaf of bread or bottle of milk. The method of reducing objections to a manageable level will help customers put the cost into the correct perspective. It's their *total quality of life* that's important. On the selling side, we must retain our belief that most people will buy the home they really want if you simply can help them justify the price. This can be done by pointing out how the value is greater than the price.

7) The issue may not be whether it's affordable. Sometimes it is the price of a competitor's home. If you could just bring your price down to that of the competitor, the customer would buy. Here are some of the better ways I have heard this situation addressed:

"You have to assume that every home on the market is worth what you pay for it. That's the nature of a free market economy. The question you must ask yourself is, 'Which one is best for me?' "

8) *"I have a closet full of clothes seldom worn. The price was great, but it cost me a fortune because I had to go back and buy the right thing."*

9) *"Are you saying if you can resolve the issue of price you like the home enough to own it?"*

10) *"Are you looking for the cheapest price or are you looking for the home that will cost you less? We believe the lifelong cost of our homes, which is the important thing, will be much less because of the smaller extra cost up front for better materials. Let me give you a couple of examples..."*

11) *"Price is important. But remember it's not the only thing."*

12) *"We are not the cheapest in our market, but we deliver (number) homes a year, and we wouldn't be able to do that if our customers didn't believe we were the best value."*

13) *"Why do you think they're cheaper?"* You don't want to

knock your competition, but there is nothing wrong with asking the customer to question them as carefully as they are questioning you. Naturally, if your home costs more, you need to be able to explain why in specific terms.

14) *"The sweetness of low price is quickly forgotten when you have to deal day after day with the bitterness of low quality."* Again, you would express this as a philosophical argument, not a comment on a specific competitor.

15) *"You say the price is too high. How much do you think it should cost?"* Have them articulate the specifics about their expectations. Take the spotlight off you and let them state their position in real terms. You can ask them why, and give your response to that answer in the context of their own preconceptions.

16) *"In the final analysis a home is worth what it can do for you, not what you have to pay for it."*

In following up a closing effort that has been rejected by the customer, your goal is to get them to:

1) Honestly articulate their objections.

2) Rethink their position from a different point of view.

3) Establish a way to follow up with them in the future. (We will discuss this goal later in the chapter.)

* * *

Creating Urgency

If you are fortunate enough to have any of the traditional tools for creating urgency, be sure you get the maximum benefit from them. These tools include:

Special incentives.

They could be such things as customized upgrades, grand opening and grand closing campaigns, contributions to closing costs, waived property premiums, etc. They are, of course, for a limited time only.

The right timing.

You have only a limited selection that coincides with the customer's moving timetable. This urgency tool often comes into play with inventory or completed homes.

Special financing.

Prices that will be increasing soon.

Smaller increases that occur more frequently give you more opportunities to create urgency than large increases that occur less frequently.

"This is the last of the location you prefer."

An example of this would be limited or unique property location (waterfront, golf course, trees, privacy).

When you are not fortunate enough to have any of these tools (and many communities have been forced to succeed without them), you must shift your priorities to less tangible ways of creating urgency. There are three in particular that I would like to highlight:

1) Narrowing the customer down to one homesite that they like best.

Once they decide that one is better than the rest, you can make the logical assumption that the next customer who walks in the door also will like the same one best. This situation gives you a stronger position for creating fear of loss.

2) Selling in a way for customers to get emotionally involved.

These strategies were covered in previous chapters. It is easier to create urgency when customers are emotionally involved with a particular home, and with the community as a whole.

3) Convincing customers that the sooner they buy, the sooner their lives will improve.

Help them express their restlessness with their current home so you can gain a better understanding of their motivation for seeking a new one, and then focus your selling efforts toward those motivations. Find out what they *do* like as well as what they *don't* like about their current home, and then compare your new homes with their current one as often as possible. This will be helpful as you are trying to complete your close.

* * *

The Take-Away Close

The take-away or the urgency close is the most powerful close we can use. We need to create as many opportunities as possible to bring this close into play. The reason that the take-away close is so powerful has a lot to do with human nature. If a customer decides to buy but not to act, and there are no consequences for not acting, then he feels that he has control. But once he feels he may lose what he has decided he wants, then he loses control of the selling situation. The take-away close uses *fear of loss* to convert the customer's decision into action. Naturally, if no decision has been made, the take-away close has no value.

The take-away close was self-imposed in the 80's, and fueled much of that decade's selling boom. Today it is harder. Persuading customers to make a series of decisions throughout the selling process, which leads to the selection of a single home and homesite, is now the critical strategy in setting up the take-away close.

Emotions play a large role in the take-away close. Fear of loss is one of the most anxiety-producing emotions of all. Because it is so emotional (and therefore so volatile), it is very important that we not attempt to manipulate it. Successful use of the take-away close demands a high degree of integrity. If we try to prey on this vulnerability of human emotions, we can stop a sale in seconds. The most familiar examples of using the take-away to manipulate the customer are:

1) *"These homes are selling like hotcakes. This home could be gone tomorrow."*

2) *"I've got someone else who says they want this same property. If you want it, you'd better act now."*

3) *"I can't say for sure, but there's a rumor going around our company that we're having a price increase this weekend."*

4) *"I talked to our mortgage banker and he predicts interest rates will increase by the end of the week. Act today and I will lock your rate."*

Using these tactics without basis is one of the vilest deeds in selling, and one that enrages customers the most. Any use of the take-away close must be entirely honest, and also specific, concrete and provable. The take-away close cannot be contrived.

The fear of loss must be injected into the close whenever possible because it is the strongest motivation to prompt action. I had one take-away close that I used more successfully than any other. I used it after several initial closes had not given me an affirmative answer and I wanted to make one last attempt to create urgency before the customer left. If nothing else, this would be the question my customers would be asking themselves as they went home and thought about it.

"Let me ask you one last question before you leave. In a few days, after you think it over, if you call me to say you want to go ahead with the Remington on homesite 54 and it's has been sold, how are you going to feel? Are you going to be okay with that?"

This was a question I always felt completely comfortable asking, because I was expressing an honest concern. This question was the result of observing many disappointed buyers when they did lose their favorite selection. It also had two selling benefits:

1) It was my strongest way of creating urgency without contrived coercion. I knew that it was a statement that my customers would have to consider strongly if they were close to a buying decision.

2) It always resulted in a significant answer from customers that gave me a true sense of how close they were to making a decision.

In setting up your overall strategy for creating urgency, it will help if you do not offer too much variety. It's harder to create a one-of-a-kind take-away close when you have six of a kind available. The idea that variety is the spice of life does not apply to new home sales.

Another misconception is that saying "no" to a customer makes it harder to create urgency. It depends on whether the "no" is a "sale-killer." Customers do not always have to be saying "yes" in order for the sale to keep moving, and neither do you. In fact, oddly enough, when customers always win their way, their sense of urgency declines. Telling them that you cannot customize product or negotiate price will not hurt your chances of creating urgency as long as you can justify your pricing strategy and your product decisions. Saying "no" often raises your level of professionalism in the customer's eyes, as long as you say it with sensitivity and with a sensible explanation.

* * *

Homesite Reservations
Are "lot holds" good or bad?

Anything you can do to move a sale toward the close is good. If reserving a homesite can be used to move customers closer to a buying decision, then they are serving a valid purpose. Site reservations can keep momentum alive when it might otherwise be lost. They can help move customers into a buying mode by getting them to make an initial buying decision that is less threatening than the final one.

On the other hand, reservations can hurt your selling effort if they are used improperly. You should never offer to reserve a property on the grounds that "there's nothing to lose," especially if you don't know whether they have really "bought." Lot holds can help convert a buying decision into action, or they can keep a buying decision from being made at all. Homesite reservations should be used to create urgency, not take it away.

The rule best used to determine whether or not to take a reservation should be: *Take a reservation if you know your customers really want the home, but you can't convince them to write an agreement to buy that day.* The "lot hold" is a way to back off in the latter stages of the sale in order to release the pressure *for the purpose of securing the sale in the near future.* It can keep you from pushing customers over the edge and losing them by moving too aggressively towards a written agreement before they are ready to sign. It gives customers an interim step for converting their decision into action. However, a homesite reservation should always be considered a backup plan rather than a substitute for the agreement.

As you reach the moment in time when you are ready to ask for the order, your closing priorities should be as follows, from highest to lowest:

1) Obtain a bona fide contract (agreement).

2) Obtain a written agreement with a "subject to" clause (or "kick-out" clause) when the customer is ready to sign except for one or two concerns that you feel confident can be resolved.

3) Obtain a homesite reservation.

4) If no commitment can be obtained, close for another appointment at a specific time and date.

5) If they do not commit to an appointment obtain permission to contact them again.

How long should a reservation be in effect? It must vary with the necessities of the situation, but the rule of thumb should always be as short as possible. If they seem ready to buy except for a condition that will take a week, then your decision to give the customer a full week must be a judgment call. But if an overnight reservation will work, then don't give the customer seven days to keep looking for a better situation while your home is tied up. The longer the reservation, the stronger the customer's position, and the less they will feel the urgency.

* * *

"Closing" For Follow-Up

When you reach the end of your interaction with a customer and realize that there will be no sale that day, even though the customer is clearly a prospective buyer, the last step is to "close for the follow-up." When a customer is about to leave your community for the day, your goal is not simply to conclude the interaction cordially. It is to close them to return. As discussed in Chapter Two, the incoming phone call, you are a professional running a serious business. You are entitled to set an appointment. If the customer is unwilling to set one, that is certainly his right. But it is your right to ask. The conclusion of a visit needs to be more than "It was nice meeting you. I hope to see you again."

As you are going through the selling process with the customer, you are assuming that they will buy that day until they prove to you after several closing attempts that they won't. At the same time, you are realistically aware of the probability that the customer may not buy that day, and will need to come back again in order to convert a buying decision into action. Therefore you must plan ways to set up your follow-up effort. One way to do this is to hold back some reason to contact them again. An additional piece of information or a new thought are examples of this. Hopefully the customer is interested enough that you will be able to establish a specific follow-up appointment at the end of the visit.

"I know that you don't have time to visit our homesites today, but I do have a couple of nice ones planned for the Blair model that you liked. I'd love to have a chance to show them to you. Can I set a time next weekend to meet with you again?"

When an appointment is impossible you should try to pave the way for a follow-up phone call. If you have no specific reason for the call when they leave, then simply ask them for permission to follow-up.

"I've enjoyed visiting with you today. Do you mind if I give you a call Wednesday to follow up?"

This approach is very direct and very appropriate. If they agree, which they almost always will, then your follow-up call will automatically start off more comfortably. If they don't agree, then you have at least tried. Either answer also might elicit additional feedback about their buying status.

If you have not received permission to follow up, then make sure your call is personalized and has a specific purpose. The best situation is one in which the phone call contains information that provides a pleasant surprise to the customer. Use the various stages of your selling process to begin to plan your follow-up strategy.

Suppose your customers say they are just looking and you have no strategy for your follow-up. You can use your final few minutes for several concluding questions.

"How soon do you think you'll be making a decision?"

"At what other types of homes do you think you'll be looking?"

"How about if we plan a time to talk again next weekend? We can discuss a little more about financing, customized features and some of the other specifics of what we're offering. I'd be interested in hearing about some of the other places you've seen."

"Can we set a time for you to come back with your husband (wife, fiancé, parents, children)?"

Even though the customer may not be interested in making a return appointment, they will never blame you for asking. They will appreciate your diligence and be flattered by the attention. Even when you cannot establish a specific appointment, your request will often elicit more precise feedback as to where you stand in their decision process and why.

* * *

The "Post-Sale Close"

It is very important that your level of interest in the buyers not drop off after they sign the agreement. With disillusionment and buyer's remorse being a constant threat in our profession, you must continue to sell your home to the customer during the time between signing the agreement and settlement. A thank-you note followed by periodic notes or calls providing a schedule of events and moral support will help lower your kickout rate and give you better control of your customers as settlement approaches.

Keep them apprised of any construction information important to them, even if it is bad news. The worst thing that can happen is for them to find out about a mistake, omitted option or delayed settlement date by themselves. Once this happens, you have just added an unwanted "assistant superintendent" to your staff until the day their home is completed. If there is information that is important to them, let them know what it is. If it is bad news, let them know what you will do about it, or what they will need to do. Proactive problem-solving is the best kind. It will protect your credibility better than any other strategy in an unfortunate situation. The best way to instill trust and confidence is to demonstrate through behavior that you always deliver more than your customers expect. Positive situations in life that go beyond our expectations are truly special. Protecting your credibility goes a long way toward preventing buyer's remorse. Naturally, any piece of good news is always worth a phone call.

Another way to head off buyer's remorse and reduce kickouts is to give customers a realistic perspective of what to expect as soon as they have signed their purchase agreement. This is the time they are high on their decision to improve their lives. They have done the right thing, and they have achieved the confidence that comes from completing their decision. Give them a realistic level of expectations in the following areas and remember they will need reminders along the way.

1) When they come to visit their home under construction, they could find flaws, but the flaws will be corrected. This is a natural part of the homebuilding process, and is why good supervisors "like ours" are so important.

2) There might be a few minor irritations in the ever-changing loan process, but they do not last long.

3) Periodic feelings of buyer's remorse are likely, as are feelings of momentary regret in any of life's major decisions. That is simply a part of the human decision-making process. Everyone who lives in your community today went through it during their buying adventure. Even new home salespeople experience self-doubt in the midst of so large a decision. It will pass.

4) Although other people will second-guess them, they must not allow that to cause them to second-guess themselves. People have all sorts of reasons for second-guessing the decisions of others.

In just a few months it will all be over. They will be in their new home, having moved on to their better life of the future. Be sure they understand that you are not just a hit-and-run specialist.

"If at any time between now and settlement, there's anything you need, or anything you're concerned about, or anything you want

to ask about, just call me. I don't care if it's three o'clock in the morning. I know this is a big decision, and I'm a part of it, and I want to take full responsibility for being a part of it. I know the weekends are busy, because that's when I'm working with new customers, but you are welcome to call me any time, even at home."

In addition to reassuring your customers that you are a permanent support system, you have also conveyed a subtle and well-timed message that you do not want the customer camping out in your sales office during your most valuable business hours.

Turn cancellations into opportunities

If a buyer comes into your sales center wanting to cancel the purchase agreement (or reservation) and requesting his money back, don't give up immediately. Many of these requests for cancellation can be reversed. As with other parts of the selling process, much of your success in this area will depend upon your mental preparation.

Suppose a customer calls you on the phone and says, "I'll be stopping by after work this evening. We need to talk." Suddenly a sick feeling overwhelms you, followed by seething anger that you try to suppress until you hang up the phone. Then you become dejected, and by the time the customer arrives, you already have his check sitting on the desk ready to hand to him in order to avoid prolonging a situation that is uncomfortable for everyone. Deep inside, all you want to say to him is, "Take your money and get out."

This is a natural response. I have felt like that myself. Let me suggest an alternative I found helpful. I admit it is somewhat of a mind game but it saved many of my buyers from "dying of buyers remorse."

Instead of assuming that the situation was hopeless, I began assuming that I really could save the sale. I envisioned in my mind the customer walking back out of my sales office at the end of our conversation pleased once again with his decision to buy and happy that he had come to me for counseling. Then I backed up the reel of that vision to the conversation that would cause him to feel that way. In that conversation I would remain positive and enthusiastic, assuming that his confusion was momentary. I would remind him of the day he bought, his excitement, all the wonderful things he said about the home, his confidence that day. Then I would remind him that he was that same person and that was the same home. I viewed the situation as an opportunity to sell again, only this time it was easier because I was selling to someone who bought once before. What could be easier than convincing a person to make a decision he had already made? I was not going to be argumentative, and I was going to let him speak his mind. But I would not allow him to leave until he relived the thrill and optimism of his original buying experience, and I would not allow temporary fears and second-guessing relatives derail his permanent happiness. I would remain optimistic and reassuring.

This was my new attitude. Naturally, I was not able to save them all, but with my new approach, combined with preparing customers for the realities to come in the ways that I described above, I was astounded with my ability to save sales that I thought were lost. People really were willing to change their minds again during their visit and give their great decision another chance. Many other salespeople with positive attitudes about saving sales have assured me that my experiences were not unique or lucky.

Even when the customer stays with the decision to cancel the agreement, use the opportunity to cement a relationship of understanding. By keeping the communication open you can continue to work with him for a later time and a network base for referrals. When a meeting of the minds unravels it is important for the salesperson to forgive and forget and help the buyer deal with the guilt.

Otherwise there will be no possibility of continuing any kind of relationship. These folks are valuable to you in many ways. Don't let them tuck their head and slide away.

* * *

The situation of the "post-sale close" refers to the time between the agreement and settlement, and after the buyer moves in. In fact on-site sales professionals continue to build on the relationship with buyers from the time they first meet them until the community is completely sold out and built out. Follow-up calls and visits leave customers with a good feeling that they really did the right thing after all. Buyers don't expect attention from salespeople after they settle, so when they do receive it they feel all the more grateful. This gratitude can reward you with referrals of their friends and co-workers, and also with those pleasant experiences when you walk past their homes to show homesites to new customers.

Direct closing statements and questions do not come easy nor do they come often enough. It took Brandon a long time to get his animal cracker, but persistence paid off, and it will for you if you act on the principles you have learned. I would like to challenge you to make a committment today to care enough about everyone who visits your community to ask them to live there.

Managing Follow-up

I f at first you don't succeed: Follow-up, Follow-up, Follow-up! Follow-up is a significant part of new home sales in which the salesperson can make a difference in the success or failure of a community. Follow-up continues the *series of initiatives* that keeps the selling process moving forward.

Some salespeople admit they follow up only because the boss insists on it. Others say it is their main area of procrastination. A majority of salespeople believe that follow-up is the least productive use of their time of any endeavor in the selling profession. What a shame! One of the primary initiatives to becoming a successful new home sales professional is one that many hate, others feel guilty for not doing, and the remainder do only to keep the boss off their backs. Let's face it. Most salespeople dislike the idea of follow-up. Even those committed follow-uppers confess that it is a real challenge.

These objections to follow-up are legitimate, and if you find yourself among those who think personal follow-up just doesn't work, this chapter is for you. In the "good old days," front line salespeople could keep track of their customers. The numbers were manageable. In most markets today, survival clearly depends on systematizing information. Quite frankly, and happily, the numbers are too great to manage over a long period of time. That's the good news. The not-so-good news is that the uncontrollable numbers are due, in part, to the fact that buyers are more discriminating, and less likely to act on their decisions to buy in a short period of time.

Let me clarify the term "follow-up" as it will be discussed in this chapter. I'm talking about personal after visit contacts made by salespeople. I realize that follow-up has become very high-tech in recent years, with computers spitting out form letters with instructions on when to mail generalized collateral materials to the last one thousand people who visited the community. I am not calling these efforts "follow-up." They are advertising, or direct mail. They are not follow-up in the sense that I am discussing in this chapter because they are not personal. *Follow-up must be personal to be effective.* If not it will fail. Structured programs are valuable; they can help us reach larger numbers of people more frequently. But do not substitute these programs for intimate personal follow-up. Sales follow-up is a hands-on, individualized effort by the salesperson. I might add that if an on-site salesperson does not have a computer he will have a difficult time sorting, tracking and organizing his personal follow-up. Such follow-up efforts can be handled in three ways:

1) Telephone,
2) Mail,
3) Off-site visits.

Why follow up at all? There are two key reasons to follow up with your visitors. Both are important, but it is critical to understand that they serve two entirely different functions:

1) To thank your guest for coming to see your community and homes. Everyone who visits should be sent a thank-you card, and if time permits, a thank-you call as a courtesy for being "a guest in your home." Thank-you notes and calls are professional, and they are a part of business etiquette. "Thank you's" make people feel

happy and appreciated. They do not sell homes, nor do they motivate or convince people to return for a follow-up visit.

2) To persuade customers to visit again. This part of follow-up will increase your sales opportunities. It is an effort that is directly tied to production, and needs an organized plan and strategy to be implemented effectively.

Courtesy contacts such as thank-you notes are obvious. My focus here is to help you *win more sales* by motivating your customers to return, which is a critical part of the sales sequence. In my opinion, one reason some follow-up programs are successful and others are not is that many salespeople assume the purpose of a thank you is to generate repeat visits. When they don't (and I repeat, they don't), the salesperson feels she or he has wasted valuable time. Remember the purpose of "thank you's." They are gracious gestures, but they will not motivate a person to buy your homes.

A second reason follow-up programs are ineffective is the frustration of facing the monumental task of managing customer cards with insufficient information. We see the situation of the boss dumping a pile of customer cards at the feet of the salesperson with the following ultimatum: "Here are 1000 names of prospects who have walked in your door in the past two years. It cost our company $300 to generate each one of these. I expect 10 sales from these cards." No wonder so many salespeople hate follow-up!

Your list of prospective buyers is like a garden that needs to be weeded continually. Otherwise the good plants in your garden will be covered over and choked out by the weeds. You can't afford to have valuable time taken by chasing your "C" prospects with hopeless phone calls and time-consuming letters that only serve to create a rhythm of rejection. Why program yourself for failure? It is true, "C" prospects can sometimes turn into "B's" or "A's," or they may generate a referral. They deserve some form of attention. Include them in a list for occasional mailings, if you have a staff person to commit to it, and make phone calls periodically to check for changes in status, and to ask for referrals. But let's be realistic. To be efficient and keep your sanity you will have to treat your "C's" differently from your "A's" and "B's." Searching for needles in haystacks will not motivate salespeople to follow up. Professional new home sales representatives are not telemarketers and they never will be. They are salespeople. They must see the benefits for selling opportunities in their activities.

We all need victories, even small ones. Why set ourselves up for a failure that could be crippling to our selling energy? *In follow-up we achieve a victory when we generate a commitment for a return visit.* It is important to take a more constructive approach to follow-up, in order to increase our percentage of victories.

"Thank you for calling," is not a victory. "We really like your homes," is not a victory. "We might be seeing you again," is not a victory. "If we have any questions we'll call you," is not a victory. As one salesperson told me, *"My whole purpose in follow-up calls is to motivate people to come back. When I secure a return appointment on the phone, I've hit a home run. If I'm not on the phone or in front of people, I'm out of business."* This kind of intensity and focus is evidence of a successful sales professional.

* * *

Have A Plan

The two most important ingredients of a successful follow-up strategy are:

1) Have a Plan for *you.*

2) Make it personal for *them.*

1) *Have a Plan.*

You begin planning your follow-up effort as soon as you meet a customer. You hope they will buy on their first visit, and to keep yourself focused, you even assume they will. At the same time, you are preparing yourself for the follow-up in case they don't. As you learn about their interests, priorities, and needs, you are filing information away for possible use in a personal follow-up effort.

If, during your conversation, you can develop a reason to call them back, that is ideal. Leave a question unresolved. Hold out a piece of information. Have something that you will need to check into. Your call will be easier if you can set it up by saying, "I'll call you with..."(or "when..."), and then begin your call by saying, "I promised to call you back with..."(or, "You asked me to call you back when..."). Try to make customers grateful for your call.

If you have no reason to call them by the time they leave, then, as I mentioned in the last chapter, simply ask for permission to follow up. ***"I've enjoyed spending this time with you. Would you mind if I give you a call on Friday just to follow up and see how you are progressing?"*** Customers will rarely deny this request. It is also the kind of question that provides one more opportunity for feedback before they leave.

When customers leave your office, fill out the back of your guest card as soon as possible, while the details of their visit are still fresh in your mind. Prioritize the prospective buyer based on the information you have gathered. Determine if they are NOW buyers, SOON buyers, MAYBE LATER buyers, or NEVER buyers. We see salespeople rank their customers as A buyer, B buyer, C buyer and D buyer, respectively. These categories are updated and corrected according to new information gathered. Your organization and time management skills are important here. A different plan, strategy, and time commitment should be employed based on the priority of the customer. In other words, quantify as well as qualify your prospective buyers. The information on the back of the guest card will form a customer profile and should include the following:

a) *A brief physical description of the customers.* This will help you remember them when you see them again, and it will also help you visualize them as you talk on the phone. This visualization will help you to personalize your call. Just as body language is significant in a face-to-face interaction, there is also a type of "body language" transmitted through the voice on the phone. It seems amusing to watch people gesticulate frantically as they talk on the phone, but this is actually part of their expression, and it comes across over the phone in an audible instead of visual way.

b) *Highlights of the visit.* Write down what occurred during the visit that could be significant to your rapport-building and selling effort.

c) *Personalized information.* What did you learn about them that you could refer to in a subsequent letter, phone call or return visit? This information has nothing to do with the sale, but with them as people.

d) *What would they buy and why?* These are notes you make concerning their needs, preferences, priorities and hot buttons. What did they like best, and why did they like it? Were there any unresolved objections? Try to second-guess them. What do you think they will buy if they buy? Why do you think that?

e) *A continuing record of additional contacts.* Each follow-up contact or return visit should be briefly summarized. Noting only the date of contact is not sufficient. Record new information that will be important for your action plan.

f) *Outline your action plan.* How do you plan to sell them, and what action will be your next step? Commit yourself to your follow-up action by writing it on the guest card, and write down a deadline by which your follow-up action will be completed. Transfer follow-up activities to your daily calendar.

Before you pick up the phone to make your call, you should write a brief outline of what you will say. The call should also be practiced before it is made. Plan the following items into your call:

a) What personalized information will you draw into the conversation in order to give your call a feeling of warmth?

b) What professional information will you convey that will personally benefit them?

c) How will you qualify for changes in motivation and urgency in your customer?

d) How will you attempt a close for a return visit?

2) *Make It Personal for Them.*

Personalization is the difference between a "cold call" and a "warm call." You have been establishing rapport and gathering information throughout the selling process in order to make your follow-up call *personal* and *interesting*. Like the close, follow-up calls must not sound contrived. Follow up fails when it is not personal, and it cannot be personal if you have not learned enough about the customer, or cannot remember what you have learned. If the call is just to say, "thank you," then handwritten notes may be a better medium. Even follow-up letters should be personal because they gain more attention.

For your "hot list" (A+ customers), it may be worthwhile to spend a little extra time and money on items that show your customers they are important to you as people. This would not be practical for everyone, but consider it for sales that you believe are hanging in the balance. I know salespeople who have been very successful with small gifts that provide a personal benefit to customers. For a customer with a child who plays soccer, one salesperson stopped by a bookstore and picked up a book on soccer to send with a personal note. She also sends books on gardening and other hobbies to her "hot" leads. She finds her follow-up calls are much more productive after a gift is sent. Naturally she cannot do this with all customers, but she did share that she usually sends a "special gift" once or twice a week. It's extra effort, but that's what customers appreciate from salespeople. Trying out ideas like this prove that a salesperson really can make a difference in the outcome of a sale, or an entire community.

Salespeople who are most successful at follow-up often call their customers just to talk about extraneous topics that are of interest to them. One example was a salesperson with a customer who was a golf fan. A professional golf tournament was taking place nearby, and she remembered the customer talking about being a Greg Norman fan. When the salesperson made her follow-up call she said, *"I was reading in the paper about the golf tournament, and Greg Norman's tee time is around 9:26. It made me think of you and I just thought I'd give you a call. Are you going to be able to see 'your man'?"* The customer responded favorably to the personal nature of the call. Soon the conversation wound up shifting, at the customer's initiative, to the salesperson's community. Even if the customer does not ask any buying questions, you will find opportunities to make the transition yourself.

In this example, the salesperson had been gathering information for follow-up during the customer's initial visit. Train yourself to plan your follow-up strategy during your presentation. Follow-up will fail if you do not have a reason to contact them again. The reasons for follow-up come directly from information you acquire during your time with customers. This also will help you do a better job of establishing rapport.

Interestingly, the best rapport builders also tend to be the most successful (and the most comfortable) in their follow-up efforts. As with closing, you can take a more confident approach to follow-up when you have established better rapport.

I mentioned that your closing demeanor must be consistent with the rest of your demeanor throughout the sale. The same applies with your follow-up call. If your interaction was jovial, the tone of your call should start out that way. If the interaction was serious, then start with that tone. It is okay for the tone to change during the call. But the call should begin by "picking up where you left off."

If you have any doubts about the effectiveness of your approach to your follow-up calls, ask customers to whom you have sold in the past. Have them evaluate you, and ask if they felt the call helped or hurt your chances of selling to them.

* * *

Try for the Appointment

Once again, the goal of follow-up is to convince the customer to come back. Closing for an appointment frequently becomes one of those examples of climbing out of your comfort zone. Just remember, although certain customers may not want to make a specific appointment, they won't mind that you asked. They will still appreciate the fact that you are trying to win them as a buyer. If they say "no," that is not a defeat, nor was the request a mistake. As in closing, asking for the appointment to return is what assures you that you maximized the opportunity. You can even ask them point-blank, as one salesperson did following a shopping visit, *"I'd certainly love to sell you a home here. Of course, it's my job, but also I've really enjoyed working with you. Is there any way I'll be able to encourage you back for another visit?"*

Another salesperson asked for the appointment in two questions.

S: *"Are you planning to stop back this weekend?"*

C: *"I might. I'm not sure yet."*

S: "I have my calendar open here in front of me. I have a couple of appointments in the morning, but I'll be free at three o'clock this Saturday if you are."

You could approach the appointment by testing the water first: ***"When are we going to get together again?"*** The customer's response to that question will help you decide whether to "close" for a specific appointment. Remember that customers like our directness more than we may think. An additional fringe benefit of asking for the appointment is that often it will provide an opportunity for you to gain feedback that you could not have solicited any other way.

* * *

When And Where Should You Call Them?

How soon after the visit should you make your first follow-up call? This judgment decision is based somewhat on the interaction with your customer. The best advice I can give you is to strike while the iron is hot. Follow up by phone within 48 hours, if possible. If your prospective buyers are comparing you with others, and they probably are, you want to reach them as quickly as you can to answer questions and assist wherever needed. The salesperson is, in effect, a partner with the buyer, an assistant buyer, so stay close to the scene.

Do not make the mistake of believing everything your buyers say. This does not mean that "buyers are liars," as we have heard cynics grumble. It means that when consumers are operating in an emotional state (this is where the serious ones are at the moment), even they cannot predict their own behavior. What does this have to do with follow-up? Everything! For example: If your customers tell you there is no rush in contacting them with information, don't believe them. You have given them strong reasons to buy during your presentation and demonstration. In fact, you may have set up a slam-dunk for your competition when they leave you. They may be "ripe for the picking," and not even know it themselves. Now is the time to pay close attention to your customer because they are very vulnerable.

I can remember painful lessons learned, and sales lost, because I took people at their word and allowed them to control my strategy. One, in particular, was a family of five who had plans to tour the country for six weeks in the summer. I knew they were excited about my homes. However, the parents insisted they could not make a decision until after the trip. I marked my calendar, and followed up as soon as they returned, only to hear the words that salespeople everywhere shiver to hear. *"Oh, I have been meaning to call you. We bought a home in "Green Acres" before we left. This way we can have the kids in school on time. But you were wonderful, and if I hear of anyone who is looking to move I will send them to you."* This last statement saves face for them. What they are really thinking is, "I feel sorry for you, but, too bad, you didn't do the job." I don't know about you, but I have never gotten a referral from someone who bought elsewhere. I was outsold. They knew it and I knew it. Another big "oucher." I repeat: Be careful, and don't give up your position of leadership, especially in your follow-up tactics. You know what to do; follow your logical professional instincts and act on them.

Here are some basic guidelines for when to call:

1) Be considerate. Do not call at a time that may inconvenience your customer.

2) Do not call immediately after they return home from work. People need a chance to unwind when they first arrive home.

3) Wait until after dinner if your call is in the evening. 8:30 should probably be your quitting time.

4) During the customer's visit, ask permission to follow up, and also ask, "What's the best time for me to call?"

5) Saturday morning after 10:00 is a good time to call. Some salespeople also like Friday evenings because its an upbeat time (TGIF).

6) If you are working with a couple, and one of them works at home, you can call during the day.

7) Never call customers at their office without their permission in advance.

8) Do not leave messages on answering machines unless it is a particular piece of information that you promised them immediately. In that case, leave the information to prove your diligence, and mention you'll call again.

* * *

Face-To-Face Follow-up: Off-Site

In many parts of the country salespeople will look at this last subtitle and question, "What in the world is she talking about?" In many areas off-site follow-up is unheard of. Yes, believe it or not, I'm talking about going to the customer's home. This form of follow-up is still popular with some salespeople, although it is not as widespread as it used to be. Twenty years ago I did it all the time — with excellent results, I might add. Even if this idea is foreign to you, my plea here is, Why not try it once or twice just to see what you think? I'm betting you'll be pleasantly surprised with the reception, and the results.

Yes, we make house calls.

My suggestion to you for off-site visits is not to call ahead for an appointment. Just drop by. It is important to have a reason for dropping by. Your reason could be an answer that you promised them, and you decided to deliver it in person. It could be information or collateral material that you decided to drop off. Or it could be a small gift: flower bulbs, potpourri, a promotional key chain with your company's logo or community name. Remember the salesman in the garden center? He drove by my house to see how my flowers were growing. What a powerful statement of care and concern.

Stop by on your way to work or on your way home, depending upon the hour. As with the phone call, you don't want your visit to be disruptive. Saturday mornings are a good time. Certainly, this is something to consider with a special candidate who lives close by. Time may not allow you to travel too far out of your way, and don't take time away from other selling activities that you deem more urgent. If the customer isn't home leave a note with your business card. One salesperson I know likes to write a note on the back of his card that reads, "Sorry I missed you, give me a call, and I will bring *it* out, or you may stop by the sales office to pick *it* up," without telling them what *it* is. Curiosity will cause most people to call or stop by. The *it* should be something of importance to them. It could be a new design that you think they will like, news that a new phase just opened, school information, or any number of reasons to stay in touch. Prospective buyers will appreciate the gesture, and for sure they will be surprised. You can say, "I'm like the old fashioned doctors. I love to make house calls." One of your greatest benefits in visiting them at home is for you to see your greatest competition — their home.

During my own experiences with off-site follow-up I found people very receptive to these visits, and they often turned into some of my most pleasant selling experiences. I found prospective buyers more open and personable during these visits than they were on the phone or in my sales office. They were more honest, and gave more

meaningful feedback. They were on their home turf, so they felt
more comfortable. I found the experience enjoyable and invigorating. It was a great way to start off the weekend on Saturday morning. These visits are not meant to continue the selling process but
rather to continue the relationship and bonding sequence. If you
plan to visit during the evening, then it is best to call in advance.

The greatest show on earth

One of the most creative and successful off-site follow-up programs I have seen is the following: A young salesperson, the father
of two small children, rented a theater on a Saturday morning for a
private showing of the Walt Disney movie, *The Littlest Mermaid.*
The buyer profile in his new home community was young families
with small children. He invited his entire customer base plus his
homeowners to the matinee. Unlimited popcorn and soda was on
the "house." The only stipulation was kids must bring mom or dad.
Of the 275 families invited, 300 parents and children attended and
filled the theater. Before the movie he introduced himself, his wife
and children, then relaxed and enjoyed a fun time with some very
nice folks. This superstar reported that he has made great friends
from this event, he has sold three homes that were a direct result of
this activity, and received numerous leads and referrals. For those
of you who are wondering, the cost was under $500.00. And who
said follow-up couldn't be fun?

As with other parts of selling, customers appreciate initiative and
diligence. It allows you to do a better job of "differential selling"
against their current home. You will be able to compare your benefits with specific elements of their home that you have personally
seen. If you can't stop in, drive by, if you are near. Check out their
neighborhood and create ways to help them "leave one neighborhood" and move into another. If you have buyers with purchase
agreements subject to the sale of their home, it is a good business
practice to check out their home and determine the marketability.

Increase Your Sales

By gathering information, organizing your systems, developing a plan, and creating a personalized approach, you will be able to develop one more "initiative" beyond the final close. Sound follow-up practices will generate more return visits, give you greater confidence in your total selling ability, and increase your selling opportunities 100%. Guaranteed! Be sure to keep your plan simple, fun and manageable.

Increasing Your Customer Base

"Get out of your mental rut, think new thoughts, acquire new visions, discover new ambitions." — Dale Carnegie

"It's the middle of the month. Do you know where your next buyers are?"

Developing a continuous customer base is another in the *series of initiatives* that fuel the momentum of the selling process. Networking for referrals is initiative in its highest form. Yes, I am speaking here of *generating your own customers over and above that which is generated by your company's marketing effort.*

The quantum leap into "superstardom" is taken by those salespeople who are not content to place their future in the hands of others. They are not satisfied allowing the amount of success they will enjoy to be directed exclusively by the marketplace or the marketing department.

One superstar shared with me his attitude of *"if it is to be, it is up to me"* said it this way. ***"I am a family man with obligations and*** *commitments. I love selling new homes, but I cannot exist in a world of feast or famine. I will not put my family's existence in the hands of chance. What I have discovered is that the real joy of this business is the security of knowing that I can attract buyers regardless of any outside influence. In fact, the only limitations are those I place on myself. I am grateful to be with a company that can add to my self-prospecting efforts, but I consider those sales a bonus. Being a prospector is not work, it is just a matter of telling everyone I meet who I am and what I do."*

"It's just a matter of who I am."

For many salespeople, self-prospecting offers a whole new world of opportunities in selling. It is my desire to make the world of networking for customers easy for you. Do not turn away from this chapter, even if your community is providing you with great numbers of qualified customers *today*. Your good fortune may be short-lived. Great prospectors tend to be people who truly enjoy their careers, and I know that you are one of those. Salespeople who don't enjoy selling new residential homes rarely succeed at networking and rarely make a commitment to it. They also rarely survive long in this business, after the "cherry picking" is over. Generating a customer base is a very natural activity. It grows out of an enthusiasm for what you do, and the *habits* you form based on that enthusiasm. It is social and enjoyable. In fact it is the most fun of any activity a salesperson does outside of direct selling. If you are not enjoying prospecting, you are doing it wrong!

Remember the 1000 customer cards thrown at the feet of the salesperson? If you approach your networking efforts in the same way, you will set yourself up for failure. By now you are aware that I am not a proponent of "cold calling" unless, of course, you are comfortable calling complete strangers or you live in a world isolated from any other humans. Chances are pretty good that neither one of these is true. My philosophy has always been that it is a much smarter strategy to do those things that are fun and enjoyable, than to set up barriers that will make life more difficult, and limit success. We have seen too many salespeople fail at the goal of "cold calling" or "knocking on cold doors." Generally, they are successful with only one thing, adding additional stress to their lives—guilt!

"Hey Boss, can I switch to phone solicitation next month?"

"Reach out and tell someone"

The movers and shakers in our business demonstrate their belief in home ownership to everyone they meet. This is not a matter of having to think about business all the time. They *are* the business. Salespeople who have the most success at prospecting are the ones who not only *love* their business, they *live* their business. Being a new home salesperson is part of who they are. They don't divide their identities into the different hours of a day. They can be a parent, a daughter or son, a sibling, a friend, a little league coach, a club member, a book reader, an exerciser and so on. And they embody this total identity 24 hours a day. In addition, they are also a new home salesperson 24 hours a day. At the grocery store, the golf course, the poker game, the hair salon, the cocktail party, the PTA meeting and the gas station, they are still a new home salesperson. This does not mean their whole life is one perpetual sales pitch. It simply means that everyone they meet learns quickly where they work and what they do. This is why from time to time some salespeople wear their business name tags outside the office. They realize an important principle of life, and of business: *If people know you and like you, they'll help you succeed.* Let's look at how the most successful prospectors find buyers right under their noses.

* * *

You Can't Expect Me To Sell, I Have No Traffic!

"Who, me, prospect? It's not my job."

One of the major changes to occur in markets which prospered during the boom of 80's was a "division of labor" between sales and marketing. The job of marketing was to generate traffic, and to create an environment to appeal to that traffic once it arrived at the community. The salesperson's job was to sell. In fact, the battle was continuous between those in charge of advertising and those charged with closing sales. "Your ads are not working." "If you would just advertise more, I would sell more." "How can you expect me to reach this quota when you won't spend any money?" "The problem is nobody knows we are here, do something." "Of course the competition is outselling us, look at *their* ads." Sound familiar? I remember wars like this myself. What a waste of time and energy!

Self-prospecting is necessary in good times, and in challenging times. The first step — like it or not — is to realize that prospecting is essential to continued success and longevity in this business. From grand opening to grand closing your neighborhood is constantly going through shifts and changes brought about by the marketplace. Employment, the economy, the political climate and changing consumer trends and attitudes can shift suddenly in any community. The marketing effort, though much appreciated, will not be able to react to every situation in a timely fashion. Frequently the quality of traffic is not the caliber you need, and, when it is, the numbers are not great enough for you to accomplish your goals and reap the rewards you so richly deserve.

In times gone by

The idea of salespeople establishing a base of working referrals is certainly not a new concept. In fact, prior to the accelerated interest in home ownership created by the "boomers," it was an established practice to hold salespeople responsible for generating up to one-third of their own sales through self-prospecting methods. New home sales, like general brokerage, was a networking business. New home salespeople were recruited, in part, because of the people they knew. Many sales were the result of who the sales representative knew in the community, and those people telling their friends. This chain reaction I call *"pyramid networking"* is phenomenal, and has continued to be an integral part of the salesperson's selling success.

Another secret to excellence: Salespeople, who consistently work to increase their customer base through self-prospecting and networking, are not plagued with frustration from the peaks and valleys of the market. They are in total control of their destiny at all times. What a great way to limit stress! Their personal goals are met each month regardless of the time of year, interest rates, economic impact or consumer trends.

First, let's look at three aspects of prospecting that concern salespeople:

1) There is no immediate gratification from networking efforts.

Forming good prospecting habits will pay off for you tenfold, but it does require patience. *The purpose of prospecting is not to generate sales. It is to build a network.* The network generates leads and the leads generate sales. Don't wait until you are hurting, and in need of new customers to start looking for referrals. To be most effective you must plant seeds daily, and fertilize them often. The principle behind prospecting is not that you will sell a home to the person you are speaking with although occasionally you will, but that you and your company will become a familiar and positive influence with as many of these people as possible. I told you about David, who sold me my car. The car with "my name written on it." He and his wife are enjoying a lovely new home they bought from me.

The principle is that "people tell people." Don't frustrate yourself with short-term *sales quotas* for your prospecting program. That is not the immediate goal of cultivating a client base. Fruits of your labor six months ago are ready for picking today. Rather than becoming frustrated by the lack of immediate results, try to monitor your progress by tracking the source of your inquiries. This may not be easy, but probe a little deeper to find out how your visitors found the trail to your door. The sign outside is not the only source of business, it's just the last thing they see before coming in.

2) Leaving the comfort of the sales office is frightening.

When developing a customer base, your initial contact with prospects should be made in person, if possible. Follow-up with these initial contacts should be done in writing and by phone in addition to face-to-face encounters. Off-site prospecting can be a very uncomfortable situation for many salespeople. The oft-held belief that salespeople are the most bold, aggressive and adventurous risk takers in society is a myth of stereotyping. In fact, personality studies have shown that salespeople as a group are not very different from other groups in our society in terms of their forcefulness, fearlessness, and dominance. The fact that many salespeople have low prospecting activity is because they are, quite frankly, scared to death. The fear is real for them, and fear is the number one deterrent to motivation and action. The concern about appearing too pushy, overbearing, or self-serving not only limits networking but also closing efforts. Although courage is an important characteristic of successful salespeople, the key to overcoming the fear of prospecting is to recognize that *people really do respect initiative.* Poor prospecting habits are usually the result of poor goal setting. Establish goals that you intend to keep and keep them simple. An insatiable desire to accomplish realistic goals will reduce the fear of prospecting.

Remember, no matter how knowledgeable, talented or skilled you are, it is the extra push that makes you a superstar. Your desire to achieve your goals must be intense enough to "trip the fear switch." The fear of prospecting can strike anyone at any time; even veterans are not immune. In fact, they may even be more susceptible. While some salespeople start out with fear and must overcome this fear with willpower, the fear quickly vanishes as soon as the rewarding experiences begin.

3) It takes a time commitment.

Networking does require planning and organization. The good news is that networking is actually not as time-consuming as one might think. Most activities serve dual purposes, and are activities you are already doing, but not gaining the ultimate benefits. Networking also trains you to manage your time, and accomplish more than one result at a time.

Developing the plan is the easy part. Implementing the prospecting plan takes a *consistent* commitment. You need to plan a certain period of time *every day* to commit to some form of prospecting, and you must stick to that daily objective. As soon as prospecting becomes a "leftover" activity to be pursued in your spare time, your program will fail. Caution yourself; don't get caught up talking to people about things that don't make money.

The networking suggestions in this chapter will create warm, comfortable contacts for you. Your most difficult challenge may be how to cut the conversation short, and stay on with your plan. Learning about other people, and sharing with them what you do is very enjoyable. Just be careful with your time management.

Have you ever wondered why your high volume months are usually followed by a low volume month? The reason is quite simple. You probably stopped your prospecting and follow-up activities during that busy time. For high production months, continue to network by using creative, less personally involved methods such as notes, newsletters and other mailings. The best time to be most productive in your networking plan is right after a sale, when your self-esteem is at its peak and your fear is nonexistent.

* * *

Benefits Of Networking

When you consider the benefits of networking you will put away yours fears and concerns.

1) It helps make your "down time" more productive. As busy as salespeople are, there really is some quiet time. In some cases it may even be worthwhile to bring in an assistant on days you are normally scheduled to be at the sales office so you can devote the day to prospecting outside of the office. It is important to have your

builder or manager's support and encouragement.

2) It allows you to target your market. You can go after a specific market more effectively *in person* than through media or direct mail. Bringing a portion of this market to your sales office gives you that special satisfaction which elevates your performance. These are your "special customers."

3) It increases your selling opportunities. The more qualified candidates you can see, the better your chances of finding a buyer.

4) It helps you to begin establishing rapport with customers *before* they walk in your door. Just as the initial phone call from the customer requesting information or directions gives you a head start on building a relationship, the same principle applies here. Customer leads which you have generated are more relaxed and comfortable by the time they meet you.

5) It gives you identifiable victories of your own. Here is another opportunity for a personal win. The most satisfying victories of all are the ones we achieve without help from anyone else.

6) Prospecting makes salespeople feel good about themselves. If this sounds a little far-fetched, think of the last self-generated sale you made. There really is a unique sense of accomplishment in self-generated leads that does not exist in your other sales. It builds confidence. It energizes you. It gives you a feeling of having done something entrepreneurial as well as productive. It's *EMPOWERMENT!*

7) Working with the customers you have generated can be especially enjoyable. Not all customers are fun to work with. Networking presents opportunities for you to select some of the people you want to work with.

8) Prospecting is great for "slump" recovery. When you are in a slump, take baby steps to bring yourself out. It's much safer to make five calls to your referral network than to say, "I'll make a sale tomorrow." Congratulate yourself when the task is done.

* * *

Realtor Referrals

Proof is in the pudding

The greatest opportunity ever to sweep new home marketing and networking efforts is the relationship built with Realtors over the last decade. Who would have imagined this incredible success story in such a short time? *That's networking!* Many salespeople boast that 50% of their business is the result of Realtor referrals. Yet there was a time, not too long ago, when new home salespeople would not have considered networking the Realtor community for leads. Today, salespeople not only invite Realtors to their neighborhoods, but also make presentations in the Realtor's office. How sad, for all those years, that 50% of our business was right around the corner, and we did not see it. You can use the same dynamics you use in prospecting Realtor referrals to expand your horizons into other arenas. The opportunities are limitless.

Turn over every rock

Terry and I were touring Colorado several years ago. We took a ride on The Silverton steam train (the ole 473) amidst cinders & smoke through the San Juan Mountains from Durango to Silverton, to get a taste of history in the little mining towns. This was the same route the silver traveled from the mines back to the city. We also learned a rather sad story about the little town now known as Silverton, Colorado. Prior to the silver rush it was populated by prospectors looking for gold. Families rushed to this little town in hopes of finding their fortune that was not to be. In fact, the condition of the people was so bleak and the poverty was so great that many died from exposure and malnutrition. A stranger to the area stubbed his toe on a "rock" that attracted his attention. He had not seen anything like this before. The mining office examined the rock and thought it might be silver. The man approached the property owners to join him in search for this possible treasure. All refused to stay and sold out for a pittance. From 1852 to the decline of mining over $300 million dollars in silver ore was shipped out of Silverton on the little steam engine number 473. These people were living in poverty and sickness on top of the greatest riches imaginable, and all they had to do was to look at things a little differently. What a shame! Prospecting for customers is like that. Our best opportunities are often where we least expect them, such as with our Realtor friends.

* * *

How To Succeed At Networking

There are as many opportunities for prospecting as there are stars in the sky. I have listed below some of the most frequently used ones in new home sales across the United States. My hope is that these will inspire other great ideas in you.

1) *Realtors.*

I could devote an entire chapter to the activities possible to gain Realtor referrals, but since that is not the purpose of this book I will simply include a few ideas. Realtors are, in effect, your customers. Treat them as such. Get to know them, and help them get to know you. Just like our customers, the more Realtors know you, like you and trust you, the more likely they are to bring their customers and clients to you.

Of all the elements of Realtor prospecting, the most effective activity is considered to be the visit to the Realtor's office, especially if you can get a few minutes for a brief presentation during their sales meeting. The highlights of this presentation should include:

a) Demonstrating the primary benefits of your community, builder and homes.
b) Explaining factors that can help make the sale relatively easy for Realtors.
c) Providing assurances to the Realtors that their customers will be pleased with a purchase at your community.
d) Guaranteeing protection of their customer and their commission when they bring someone out.
e) Fielding questions and answers about how you both can work together for more sales.
f) Recognizing Realtors who have visited you or brought you buyers with a token of your appreciation.

Recognition, appreciation and, of course, the opportunity to gain more sales is what will endear Realtors to you. Above all, however, you must create a sense of trust and integrity in their minds.

Create a top ten hit list of your most promising Realtors. Invite your hit list out for a "meet the builder day." Treat them to a demonstration of your community and a special lunch or brunch.

2) Homeowners.

Keep in touch with your homeowners. Visit them after they move in as part of the periodic service you provide to your buyers. Ask if they know anyone among their circle of friends who may be looking for a new home. Ask them to keep you in mind, and to spread the word. Let them know about specific homes you have available. Again, people respond to requests for help. In fact, they respond to these requests just as much as they respond to incentive programs such as referral fees and gifts. They sometimes feel more honored by personal requests than by corporate promotions. These visits also make it easier for you to call them in the future if you have a sudden special request for help. Seek out your community "bird dog;" every neighborhood has at least one. These are people who are knowledgeable about everything that goes on in the neighborhood, and they will keep you in the loop.

3) Past Sales.

Look for patterns in your past sales, and use these patterns as the basis for your prospecting. There are specific market segments for every community. People tend to run in packs. It is not unusual, for example, to have a number of people from the same company move to the same community, especially if they are transferees. Also keep your eyes open for people coming from the same community or apartment complex. If you find such patterns, then consider personal visits, phone calls, and mailings to these sources. Take a look at your life, and find an opportunity to be where they are.

This kind of prospecting is an example of how to bring "niche marketing" into the prospecting arena. Once you know your market profile, target that market in both your advertising and prospecting efforts. Several years ago we were marketing a small community of 28 homes. Our first sale was to a family moving in from another state with a corporate move. Eventually nine homes out of the 28 were sold to employees from the same company.

4) Visitors to your community. Ask everyone who walks in your door for a referral, whether they buy from you or not.

I know of a small company where every on-site interaction, every phone call, and every letter to visitors concludes with this request: **"If you know of anyone else who might be interested in our homes, we'd appreciate it if you would tell them about us."** They offer no rewards; they simply ask. The #1 source of sales at this community is referrals from people *who have not bought homes from them.* Their #2 source is from people *who have bought homes at the community.* Think about that for a moment. That is an awesome statistic, and testifies convincingly to the power of asking for referrals from customers who have been treated well, even if they do not make the decision to buy.

5) *Circle of Influence. Make a complete list of your own personal "centers of influence."*

Write down the names of all the people whose lives you touch in a significant way: relatives, friends, co-workers, people in your church, people you exercise with, etc. Consider ways in which your circle of influence can help you gain more customers and sell more homes. I have read that every person touches approximately 200 other people in a significant way. Check out these numbers. If you have your 200 "significant others" spreading the word to their 200 "significant others" you have made 40,000 contacts while staying within the safety and security of people you know and like. I realize that it's not quite that simple, but the power in numbers is mind-boggling, and you don't have to go far from "home" to find them. At the very least, be sure your influence circle knows what you do, and knows that you would appreciate all the help you can get. We assume that everyone in our sphere of influence would automatically think of us when opportunities arise, but they don't, especially if they're not in a sales or service business themselves. Your responsibility is to continue to nurture these folks along. "Out of sight, out of mind." As a salesperson I trained my family to keep their "radar" out for leads, and they did, most of the time. Even so, I remember many dinner conversations that would reveal opportunities my family was not aware of. And rightfully so; it's not their business. *You* must keep *your* antennas up at all times.

Terry: "We just hired a new engineer for my division. Boy, am I in need of help right now with all the research facing me. I talked to him today, and with luck I can have him on board by next month."

Bonnie: "Honey, that's great. Does he have a family? Where do they live? Will they be looking to buy a home?"

Terry: "Oh, I didn't even think of that. We were so busy going over details of his position. I'll ask him the next time we talk."

An important and wonderful aspect of networking your circle of influence is the opportunity to know more about your friends, and to discover ways you can help them. A friend of mine is a high school teacher. During one of our "networking chats" she asked if I would speak to her class about a career in new home sales. I was able to send some of my buyers to another friend, who is an interior designer. She, in turn, gave a class for my new owners, to help them with ideas for their homes. Exchanges like these are the ultimate benefits in networking.

6) Chamber of Commerce.

The Chamber of Commerce offers wonderful opportunities for salespeople. Visit them periodically, tell them what you are selling, and ask if there are ways they can help you promote your business. It is important for you to be known in your community. Public speaking is not for everyone, but offer to give a brief overview of the market and housing trends at Chamber events and trade association meetings. The homebuilding industry is of interest to everyone. This will give you a chance to network as well as share your expertise with community leaders.

7) Personnel directors of major companies.

Make sure all personnel administrators in your area know about your community and you. Supply them with brochures to hand out or mail out to incoming transferees. This prospecting source you should meet personally, and follow up periodically. There is a great deal of difference between them knowing you personally, and simply being aware of your community. Personal contact is at the heart of successful networking.

8) Retail businesses in your area.

Stop by and introduce yourself to the employees, particularly with any new stores that open. One of my salespeople used this dialogue: *"I am the sales counselor at Timber Wood Forest. I talk about your store as part of my sales presentation, and I just wanted to meet you personally. I'll try to send you as many people as I can. If you meet anyone who might be looking for a home, it would be great if you'd remember me."*

9) Mutually beneficial service businesses.

Accountants, lenders, financial planners and attorneys are examples of this type of prospecting source. Make contact with them, offer to help them and ask them to help you. There also may be opportunities for you to use "partnering" on activities and promotion. We have conducted "How To Buy" seminars with speakers from this source.

10) Schools in your area.

This is an area where networking is coupled with an activity you already do. As you learn about the schools serving your community, meet with the principal, and ask for his or her sales presentation on the school so you can inform your customers of the benefits. School administrators appreciate this kind of effort to help them with their own PR. At the same time, you can ask the principal and faculty to send you people moving into the area and looking for a home. Ask if they would like brochures to keep on hand. Parents will often contact schools prior to looking for a home when contemplating a move.

11) Newspaper stories.

The more you keep yourself abreast of what is going on in your area as it relates to people, the more sources of contacts you will gather. Subscribe to all local papers, and pay particular attention to human interest stories and pictures. When positive stories about people in your area are featured, cut out the articles and take them to the people. Introduce yourself and congratulate them. If this is too cumbersome, you could mail the article to them with a personal note. One salesperson I know laminates the articles (or pictures) and mails or delivers them in that form. It's a special touch. Sending pictures of young people in the news to their parents is well received. Your note might read, "I thought you might want one more copy for Grandma."

One superstar sends copies of awards and recognition about local Realtors featured in the paper to the Realtor. She shared with me that this has won her great friends in the real estate world. In fact, her hit list includes the Realtors she has met with this activity. "They are my most loyal Realtors."

Are you trying to sell a home to that person? No. You are **widening your circle of influence.** They will be surprised by the gesture, and they will appreciate your efforts. If they meet someone who is looking for a home, they will remember you. This more time-consuming intense prospecting should be limited to areas you have identified as a specific target market.

12) The Criss-Cross Directory.

Many areas have a criss-cross directory. In addition to listing names as a phone book would, it also lists names, addresses and phone numbers *by street and telephone number.* If you decide to experiment with cold calls in a particular area, the criss-cross directory is your tool. Your call could be patterned along these lines:

"Hello, my name is Bonnie Alfriend. I am the sales representative for Timber Wood Forest. We've sold several homes to people in your area, so I was calling folks nearby just to let them know

we're here, and to invite you out to see us. Is there any chance you'll be looking for a new home in the future?"

As you conclude this conversation, remember to say, "If you know anybody else who might be interested..."

Always follow up your calls with a note thanking them for their time. You also might send some additional information and materials to whet their appetite. This strategy is used frequently for calling rental communities.

13) *Everyone you do business with.*

This one is great fun. This is a business-to-business contact, and you are appreciated as a customer or client before the networking starts. One salesperson told me that her networking activities were full just spending time with everyone from her dry cleaners to the owners of the restaurants she frequents. I know you can gather another list of a hundred or more names here. After you make your list and check it twice, you will find out who is a willing networker and who is not. Don't worry about those who do not respond; there are more people than you could possibly ever need. Work with the few who are most productive for you.

14) *Organize or join a networking circle.*

The idea behind a networking circle is quite basic. You join together with a group of people from all walks of life who have a common interest. It could be gardening, jogging, foreign language, single parents, golf, bridge or any other activity shared by the members. Your time together is twofold. You expand your mutual interest, and develop relationships that will enrich each of you in both your personal and professional life. A secondary mission of the circle is always to do business or refer business to a member of the circle.

Keep networking manageable, realistic and achievable. As with follow-up, keep your prospecting program manageable. Many salespeople like to keep a special focus on their top ten prospective buyers. In the same way you can keep closer tabs on your top ten Realtors and top ten "bird dogs." I was in an office recently and noticed a sticker on the salesperson's phone which read, "Have you called a Realtor today?"

Keep your goals realistic. Don't overwhelm yourself with the "numbers game" in prospecting. The most important part of your goal-setting, in the early stages, should be your *commitment of time,* and what you plan to achieve in terms of *contacts* (not sales) during that time. Many salespeople believe that at least half of their time should be spent prospecting and presenting (including on-site sales presentations). The other half to be spent in preparation for selling, in handling the details involved in managing a new home community, and getting your sales to settlement.

Make sure that your goals are achievable, and that your strategy is one that is *fun* and *natural* for *you.* Sure, there's reluctance at first, but your fear must be put aside if you are to achieve ongoing success. Remember, your most important function is the time spent face to face with a prospective purchaser presenting your community, whether on-site or off.

The ideas above are intended to help you create your own networking program. Don't try to accomplish them all, unless you have the energy of ten people and an 80-hour day. Pick a few that look the most comfortable and most promising for you. Better still, create a strategy of your own. Experiment with different programs, one or two at a time, until you find those that will yield the best results. If you're looking for more sales, there really is a way. Your buyers are out there just waiting for you to find them. I hope you stub your toe on a few. Increasing your customer base will make the difference between an average year and a great year.

Selling Without Models

Is it for everyone?

C an all salespeople sell without models, or is this a special gift
of a chosen few? I have heard this question debated by
builders and managers alike. In reality, all new home salespeople sell without models. That is, unless they have an identical example of every home offered. When salespeople
understand this fact they increase their confidence and belief that
they can and, in fact, do sell without models. No one would argue
with the tremendous benefit of model homes, and the importance of
them in given markets based on the expectations of the buyers and
the custom in the area. It goes without saying, if builders could present the public with a model of every floor plan, the consumer
would have an easier time with the selection process. That is Fanta-
sy Island. In today's financial climate many builders feel fortunate
to have one or two representative models, and those may only come
after several agreements have been finalized. Even large merchant
builders are being forced to trim back.

Having stressed the importance of model demonstration in Chapter Five, I now find myself writing a chapter in which I say that
models are not necessary in order to sell. Which chapter is telling

the truth? They both are, because both situations are a reality in new home sales. Models provide a valuable selling tool. They help the salesperson bring his presentation to life, and make his message tangible. Model demonstration gives you the opportunity to engage all of the customer's senses, and it gives you an additional selling arena in which to learn your customer's needs and responses. Does this mean that selling without models is a handicap? No, it is not. Believe it or not, many salespeople actually *prefer* to sell without models.

An award-winning superstar told me that she was concerned about next year. When I asked her why, she said that her builder would have a model for her to demonstrate. *"I fear that I will let my model take the place of the selling skills which have brought me the success I now enjoy."* Another salesperson shared with me her concern that she was being transferred to a community without a model and her fear of selling without a model. After talking with each of them I began to realize the anxiety that salespeople have relative to model homes. Surprisingly the attitudes do differ about the benefits of a model in the minds of salespeople. Selling, in the true sense of the word, is the process of bringing goods to the market, and taking them back out again. Selling new homes carries an added dimension because product is purchased "sight unseen." Whether you demonstrate with a merchandized model or use floor plans and blueprints, new homes are bought without the owner physically seeing the actual finished product. There are two distinct and different circumstances which may cause you to sell without having a model home.

1) Communities that will never have models. You will sell from an on-site trailer or an off-site office. The only homes you can show are those under construction.

2) Communities that begin without models in what our industry jargon calls a "presale" situation. Perhaps a more correct term would be "pre-model sales" or "pre-grand-opening sales." In

these circumstances, prior to model completion, you have displays, brochures, blueprints, site plans, raw land and perhaps a few product samples.

* * *

Customers Can Buy Without Models

Contrary to what we might think, not all buyers need to see a model in order to make a buying decision. There are certainly some who do, and we need to retain those names for a later time when we have a model or homes under construction. But many customers are willing to buy from floor plans and they rather enjoy it. For example, look at the luxury home market. There is a misconception that for more expensive homes a model is essential. On the contrary, for the most expensive homes of all — top of the line custom homes — there is almost never a model. The home is purchased through "vision" rather than through "sight," and built uniquely for the owner. If a million-dollar custom home can be sold without a model, anything can.

The customers do need to *see* what they are buying, but they may not need to see it in the form of a model home. They also need to *understand* what they are buying. In communities without models we witness some of the most sublime brilliance in all of new home sales — getting customers to understand what they cannot physically see. How can we make this miracle happen? I like to call it *subliminal seduction.* Bringing visions and dreams to life is what selling new homes is about. The mind is extraordinary. For instance, it is much faster than the speed of light; it can go to Mars and back in a split second. Plugging into your customers' minds and "seducing them" into taking this wonderful trip with you is more powerful than any model could ever be. As with each skill in new home sales, ***success begins with preparation.*** You must know your message, and you must know how you will orchestrate it. In selling without models, the script is not only important but it is different. Dramatize to help them fantasize, as the saying goes. You are creating seductive visions, therefore, hand motions, facial expressions and voice modulations will help you convey the enthusiasm necessary to stimulate emotion as you paint your verbal pictures. Preparation also includes knowledge. An understanding of construction details, architectural drawings and engineering plans is critical to conveying correct information and establishing credibility.

* * *

Salespeople Can Sell Without Models

The more comfortable *you* are without models, the more comfortable the customer will be. If you are conveying your information and benefits with ease and confidence, you will help the customer realize they do not have to rely on the theory that "seeing is believing." The most realistic and effective presentations without product are those where the sales professional actually "walks" the customer through the home room by room. They use their fingers to slowly lead the customer through the home, working from a floor plan, pointing out the features and advantages. It is not as important to be polished as it is to be positive and glowing. In fact, if your presentation is too "slick" it can appear to be a "sales pitch" that is disagreeable to most buyers. The words you use are important.

"Come with me while I take you through the Jefferson colonial to see if the spaces are what you and your family had in mind."

"Notice here we feature dentil molding and wainscoting in the dining room."

"The family room features a vaulted ceiling with a drop ceiling fan. How does this size and layout meet your needs?"

"I would like to start outside and bring you in through the foyer. How familiar are you with Hometown Builders? The owners are (name owners) and they are both on the board of directors of the Brick Institute. We are famous for our total brick homes."

"The distance of your back yard will be the same as from here to that tree."

"The size of your bedroom is the length of this room you're standing in plus two and a half feet."

"Let's pause and take a look at the many cabinets we offer in this kitchen."

"What size is your master bedroom now? This one is 3 feet longer and 2 feet wider. You mentioned that you would like a larger master; is this what you had in mind?"

As you explain the features by painting "verbal pictures," you need to know for certain that the customer understands what you are saying. The best way to be sure is simply to ask them as you go. The most effective salespeople we see during shopping visits are those who pace their conversation carefully. You are persuading the mind and it is better to "overdramatize" and "undertalk." Absorption of conversation happens rather quickly. If they are on information overload or confused they will shut down. Pace your talking, and ask questions to confirm that they are still following you.

As part of your presentation, be sure you convey advantages of buying without models. These advantages become their incentive for buying at your community under your current conditions. Here are several possibilities:

1) Financial advantages.

   a) If you are in a pre-opening situation, you could be offering incentives to early buyers to help establish credibility and gain selling momentum. One serious mistake we see builders make is starting prices too high without allowing for a phasing in of price increases.

b) If you are selling an entire neighborhood without models, then you are saving the customer that portion of the total expense for models that would have been prorated to each home.

2) Selection advantages.

a) Pre-opening offers a larger selection of choice homesites than you will have later.

b) Models would not adequately convey your variety of homes. Perhaps the reason you do not build models is because you offer a wide range of customizing possibilities.

3) Representation advantages.

a) You feel you can represent your complete line better by selling on the level playing field of blueprints than if you modeled only one. How many times have you seen the model home become the most favorite floor plan and the easiest model to sell? The model has an advantage over the others, doesn't it?

b) You feel you can convey your homes more accurately by showing the actual homes in the field than by using merchandised models.

Whatever your rationale, be sure that your customers believe there is a benefit to them by buying without merchandised models. Do not let them believe they are simply having to settle for second best at your community by buying from plans, while your competitors show models.

* * *

Different Strokes For Different Folks

A critical step in home ownership for your customers is to help them recognize and evaluate their motivation to buy. A clear perception of the advantages of why they should buy now will help them to move on to what to buy. In pre-model sales this becomes a major issue. Without anything to see, the customer must be led to discover things which they never before realized. The way you position and dramatize your presentation will depend on the information you receive from them. People are not robots; they need individual attention. In addition to the four types of personalities I discussed in Chapter Seven, I would also like to discuss several types of situations that you may frequently encounter. It is important to know how to communicate effectively to these groups as well.

1) The Rich and Famous.

Despite a trend to downsize and watch those dollars, sales of large and elegant homes are rarely affected by housing slumps. The wealthy will continue to buy comfort and extravagance, and in every community there are buyers who fall into this category. They are the folks that have a bit more than your average buyer. I use "rich and famous" here in relative terms. These folks will be more motivated by the ambiance and flair of your home than by practical issues.

2) The American Family.

Husband, wife, a couple of kids and at least one pet still make up the largest number of home buyers. They are interested in community, schools, and activities that will bond a growing family together as well as convenience to shopping and services. Highlight family gathering rooms such as eating areas, family rooms, kitchens and recreational rooms in your verbal demonstration.

3) The Struggling Modest.

These are the folks who believe in the importance of home ownership but are forced to buy less than their dreams. Wrap your home in a pretty package for them and help them see the gold in their castle.

4) The Young and the Restless.

They are moving fast — starting out with a small place and changing as often as they move up the corporate work ladder. Recreation, amenities and, of course, the investment aspect of your community are high on their list. Thirty-year mortgages are impossible to comprehend. Point out convenience in the home and areas for a den, study or library.

5) The Retiring Society.

America's maturing population are buying everything from condominiums to large single-family homes, and everything in between. Security and convenience is very important to them. Macro community facilities such as hospitals, doctors and other services should be pointed out. They also like to know that their lifestyle will be as worry-free as possible. Quality of construction will impress them, as well as step-saving conveniences in the home.

6) Single-minded Professionals.

Their motivations run the gambit, but certainly they are interested in other single folks with like interests to theirs. Find out what they love to do when they are away from work, and fill those dreams, such as golf courses, jogging trails, painting classes, horseback riding, theater, etc.

Some Salespeople Prefer to Sell Without Models.

I have met a number of salespeople, like the young national award winner I mentioned at the beginning of this chapter, who say they actually prefer to sell without a model. Here are the three reasons they give:

1) There is more *selling control* in an alternative on-site environment such as a sales trailer.

Salespeople have contact with the customer at every moment. They can carry on an uninterrupted interaction where the customer *needs* them in order to understand what is being conveyed. Customers "see" the homes and community through the message of the salesperson without interference from outside influences, while the salesperson is able to get a more thorough understanding of the customers' responses every step of the way. An example of an outside influence would be distracting decorating that is not of the customer's taste.

Salespeople also like the fact that they are able to persuade the customers to sit down more quickly in a trailer than in a sales office which is located in a model home. After all, there is nowhere to go. Remember, having the customer seated early in the interaction will help you to establish a more productive "business rapport." I have had a number of salespeople tell me that the selling atmosphere is comfortable when they are "walking and talking" or "sitting and talking," but that "standing and talking" is more awkward.

2) The trailer environment gives them a better opportunity to *demonstrate their expertise.*

Expertise is a more important part of the selling strategy when you are in a trailer. When you can show a higher level of expertise than your competition you actually gain a more significant selling advantage than you would gain in a furnished model. By showing your proficiency with architectural drawings and engineering plans, you can show customers that you, and your company, really understand the craft of building a better value and offering a better total quality of life.

3) Better quality of traffic.

When a prospective buyer visits a sales environment without a merchandized model you can rule out several possibilities. The curious looker probably will not bother, and the folks looking for decorating tips have no reason to stop by. A real safe bet is that your traffic is seriously interested in your location and what you have to offer. The benefits are great if you position yourself correctly. The beginning of a community takes planning and strategy which cannot be taken lightly.

* * *

Bringing Your Product To Market

For several months I passed a sign every day which read, "Coming soon, The Estates of Burke Lake." Since this property was near my home I was more than curious; I had a personal interest in what was going on. I made a call and was asked if I had received any information. I had not. I was told that the initial invitations were sent to potential customers who had shown an interest in previous homes by the builder and a list of people who fit the buyer profile. Could this be true? A limited V.I.P. list which excluded the general public? In fact, that is exactly what was occurring. If I wanted additional information I could contact a sales representative in another community, which I did. She told me that they were considering candidates for the new community, and if I had an interest she would be happy to schedule an appointment. I did not opt to do so. Last week I noticed the ground clearing and the beginning of construction on an entry feature. This week another sign went up. "On-site sales office coming soon, over 50% sold prior to grand opening." You talk about creating urgency. I was impressed and so was the rest of my neighborhood. The impact this neighborhood had in the market was phenomenal. The builder is a friend of mine, and she shared with me her philosophy. "We believe that the key to opening any community is to build momentum that begins with a little mystique. There is nothing more powerful than knowing that others have gone before you. Our first candidates were invited to join us with the added benefit of preconstruction prices. Once they were on board the rest was easy. The mistake that many builders make is hitting the market before they are ready with a plan and strategy of how to introduce the new community."

* * *

Selling Homes Under Construction

You should demonstrate homes under construction the same way you demonstrate a model. If the home is far from completion, don't feel inadequate about it. The customer realizes that seeing a home under construction is a different experience. If you do not have models, your goal is to convince customers that seeing a home under construction is a *better* experience. They are seeing "the real thing." Don't be reluctant to explain technical items to customers who may not appreciate them. Sometimes you must teach customers how to appreciate quality, but once you have, you have created a selling advantage for yourself. Your goal is to sell them on your expertise as well as your product. They will perceive value in both.

Even if the home is just a shell, you can convey "living" benefits as well as construction benefits. You can still convey room sizes in meaningful ways, and you can still create verbal feelings for the home as you are walking through. Many people employ emotional selling more effectively in a bare shell than they do in a furnished model because the former offers an unlimited range of possibilities, while the latter is often limited by what the customer actually sees. I have seen salespeople draw chalk lines on the subfloor of homes under construction in order to show furniture placement and to demonstrate the true size of the rooms. As with selling from blueprints, it is important to convey that you are completely comfortable with the idea of selling from homes under construction, and that there are real benefits for the buyer in purchasing under those conditions.

* * *

Presales

In the present economic environment preselling is not only practiced by many companies, it also is often a condition of bank financing. Companies who have a pre-model selling phase find that there are four benefits to "pre-selling" which outweigh the potential loss in presale prices on the first few homes:

1) It gives them a chance to *test the market* and make any revisions in product, price or strategy before the models are completed.

2) It enables them to *generate initial cash flow* more quickly by having the first settlements occur closer to the completion of the models.

3) It helps them to *create sales momentum* by showing that a number of homes have already been sold prior to the model opening. This momentum helps to establish the credibility of the community more quickly, boosting consumer confidence and possibly allowing for higher sale prices once the models are completed.

4) It gives them an opportunity to *perfect their selling approach* so it is smooth, powerful and flawless by the time the community officially "opens" with the completion of the model.

To help maximize the selling opportunities of the presale situation, consider the following ideas as you organize your sales strategy:

1) Be able to promise an investment advantage to presale buyers.

Be willing to accept a lower profit margin on your first offering so you can assure pre-sale buyers that there will be a price increase when the models are completed. The investment advantage is one of the primary incentives for buying at a presale stage. This incentive must be protected, and even guaranteed whenever possible.

2) Place extra emphasis on selling the builder.

Selling the credibility and prior successes of your builder may be even more important during the presale campaign than later on, because the builder's reputation can be a primary key to overcoming the customer's fear of the unknown.

3) Keep track of presale traffic so you can contact them again at the grand opening.

There is certainly a portion of the market that is incapable of buying a home without seeing a model. They are even willing to pay more to see what they are buying. Keep records on all your visitors, and call them when your models are completed, even if your prices have increased. The combination of your sales success and the increased value of your homes might create the urgency needed for them to come back, and act quickly.

4) Go through the same selling process in a presale situation that you would pursue with a completed model facility.

Throughout this book I have discussed ways that top salespeople have used their skills and their brilliance to make sales. The basic principles of successful new home selling are the same whether you are in a model, a trailer or an off-site office. Specific techniques will change, as will logistics. But the process of selling a new home is always *a series of initiatives on the part of the salesperson that result in a series of decisions on the part of the customer.*

Make the most of the incoming phone call by *beginning the selling relationship,* and then *asking for an appointment.* When customers walk in your door, *get to know them.* In addition to qualifying them, learn about their personalities and their needs, and then tailor your presentation accordingly. *Establish rapport* as you *present an initial overview* on who you are and what you have to offer including important information on your *builder, location and community.*

Whether or not you have a model, the *product demonstration* is a critical part of the selling process. While touring homes under construction or looking at blueprints, you must *bring the product to life* as you *convey its value.* Customers will relate value in the *benefits of the homes,* and in the *expertise of the salesperson.* Sometimes you will have to "show your homesites" without having access to the site. A knowledge of engineering plans can help you to help them *decide on their favorite homesite.*

Above all, when you reach the closing moment and have earned the right to close, take that one final, all-important initiative: close for the sale, whether you feel certain that the customer will buy that day or not. If they do not buy, continue to maximize the opportunities that exist in follow-up.

Some people find selling without models intimidating, but there is no reason why it should be. Think of it as the same process you follow with models with the added opportunity to control the selling environment and convey your message the way you want it to be conveyed. Remember, when you don't have models, the customer needs you more than ever.

Reflections On New Home Salespeople

"There is nothing more difficult to take in hand, more perilous to conduct, or more uncertain in its success than to take the lead in the introduction of a new order of things."

Niccolo Machiavelli, *The Prince*

The days of simply putting in your hours and collecting a pay check are over. A new age is upon us and many sales professionals are meeting the challenge. I am exhilarated by those who are riding the wave, and saddened by those being left behind. What can you do to make sure you are not left behind? The first thing is to pay close attention to what is happening, and try not to dismiss or excuse it as just another trend that will pass. Accept the fact that you cannot continue to do business as before. If this sounds negative it isn't meant to. I believe that true optimism is the ability to read the signals, accept the truth, and seize the opportunities that are brought about by change. Let's take a look at these changing times.

The dream of home ownership is alive and energized. This dream, which was brought to life in the 1920's, was challenged in the early 1990's, and is once again reviewed as a new century nears. Baby boomers are moving up, perhaps for the last time, and the baby busters are moving in behind them. There is a shift, however, in the rules and regulations that dictate behavior, and set boundaries. *Home* has taken on a fresh new meaning for families. At the same time, we are facing the challenge of dealing with an educated consumer who is more discerning, has higher expectations, and has a powerful influence on the market. These changing attitudes are creating great opportunities for salespeople who are eager to meet the demands of the latest movement and understand the paradigms in the market. Success for the future means being able to sense the big changes in the wind — and to stir up a few for yourself.

Being good is not good enough

The most intense competition for salespeople may not be the builder down the street, or the buyer's present home or even resale homes. Most likely, the greatest competition is the growing trend of professionals seeking opportunities in new home sales. New home salespeople are among the highest paid professionals in any sales field. The competition is fierce. There are a growing number of dynamite salespeople around the country. You heard from many in this book. There are also a large number of qualified people wanting to move into new home sales. The rising rate of unemployment has sent many great achievers into the entrepreneurial world of selling.

Recently, I was assisting a developer in selecting and recruiting a salesperson for his community. We placed a simple ad in the newspaper for three days. There were over 200 applicants, from several states, who sent resumes, and requested an interview. The story doesn't stop there. On paper, all were brilliantly qualified, currently employed in outstanding jobs, and 90% had a degree in either marketing, sales, public relations or business management. It was difficult to narrow the list to 50 candidates and then to 10 interviews. I was amazed. It seems the word is out. New home sales is the place to be. Gone forever are the days when folks can just "fall into the business because of a southern accent." There is no longer room for those who will not change the way they are doing business because, "it was good enough then, and it should be good enough now." My friends, good enough will not cut it today. *Good enough* will not guarantee success, or survival, in the world of selling new homes. Look over your shoulder; the movers and shakers are behind you and they are gaining ground because they are willing to do whatever is necessary to be the best. They want your job.

The superstars I have encountered are not holding back. They are not content with mediocrity in themselves. The great ones are relentless about their search for excellence. As I watch winners win, I see a distinct difference in their behavior. They not only establish strong goals, and realistically evaluate their strengths and weaknesses, but also they take active steps to reach for new benchmarks. For many years I honestly believed that success begot success. I don't hold to that generality any longer. In fact, often success and achievement breed complacency, which turns to apathy unless it is followed by a commitment to seek new targets and a focus on a plan for achieving them.

The real joy in life is the *journey* of moving toward the finish line. I was told this by a good friend as I was preparing to run a marathon, a bit late in life to be doing such a thing. It was this same friend (a reformed couch potato) who convinced me that running would not only change my life, but also would keep me living more abundantly for many years. Up to this point I considered exercise against my upbringing. Actually running was my rebellion against Jane Fonda and her discovery that women over 40 should sweat to live longer. I must share with you a revelation, which prior to this time was unknown to me. When the race was over I was, at that moment consumed with the greatest feeling of power, and self-worth you can ever imagine — the essence of human achievement. Yet, when the focus on my efforts ended, and the dust settled, I reverted back to my old behavior. The trophy stood alone collecting dust. Success, in and of itself, does not sustain us for any length of time. I had to find new races to run in order to keep the momentum alive, and so do you.

"Mom! You did it! And guess what . . . there's another one next weekend!

* * *

Standards For Excellence

Selling is as competitive as any athletic event. For every customer who buys a home, there is one salesperson who is a winner.
A salesperson's goal is to win on as many of the real *opportunities*
as she or he is able. This means developing a competitive edge in
as many areas as possible. Let's review.

*   Have great impact on customers who call your community.

* Make an unforgettable first impression.

* Deliver a memorable selling message and deliver it with impact.

* Make a convincing argument for why your homes are the best alternative.

* Establish rapport, and develop a strong bond with every customer.

* Strive to identify and fulfill needs.

* Help people dream dreams and paint pictures of a better life.

* Conduct a demonstration that creates involvement, and conveys superior value.

* Help people feel like they belong in your community.

* Help people feel comfortable making decisions that lead toward a purchase.

* Initiate the closing event as often as possible.

* Develop and implement an effective follow-through program.

* Generate a strong customer base through self-prospecting.

In each of these situations your goal is to *win the sale* by being better than anyone else. It is easy to come in first when you are the only entry. The playing field, in the game of selling, is filled with those who take their responsibility seriously, and are racing for first place. For those who do not, there are folks in the wings waiting to take their place.

* * *

Words Of Wisdom From Superstars

I asked several salespeople to share with us their personal secret to success, and this is what they had to say.

Integrity: "Above all else salespeople must have a strong sense of right and wrong. I adhere to moral principles and practices at all cost. There is no sale worth jeopardizing my moral character. When I go home at night I rest well knowing that I have maintained the very essence of who I am — a trustworthy and honest person."

Responsibility: "The game of life and work is not about crediting success to ourselves, and failures to fate. I take responsibility for it all — the good and the bad. I enjoy the accomplishments, and grow from the mistakes, but they are all mine. Don't ever let anyone take either from you because it is the total that makes you whole."

Accountability: "This may be an old-fashioned word but I like it. Everything we do affects other people. Our business is complex. I must be answerable for what I do and say. I have an obligation to those I serve because they have placed their trust in me. I believe in a strong work ethic and I demonstrate that ethic to my builder and my customers. That is the basis for my success. There are times when I could easily pass the blame to someone else, but doing that would only make me a lesser person."

Commitment to Grow: "This is a challenge I must admit, especially when you are looked upon by your peers as someone who has arrived. Though it is not always easy, I know that if I stand still I will lose my place. I have been in this business for ten years, yet I work hard to find better ways to enhance my performance. You might say I believe you never reach your peak performance."

Self-Management: "If you can't manage yourself you will never succeed at managing a community. The great thing about this business is that we do not have the boss breathing down our neck. It can also be a pitfall if you are not organized, time-managed and self-motivated. It is much easier to be told what to do than to create your own work agenda. I am tougher on myself than any manager would ever be."

Knowledge: "Knowledge is our most important tool. We are dealing with the single largest investment made by people. You must understand clearly every aspect of your community, your sites and the homes. The comprehension of product, people and systems is enormous. I will never stop learning, and I help myself daily by listening to tapes, attending workshops or reading. I always learn something useful even when I have heard it before. Knowledge comes from the anticipation that what you are hearing will have a positive impact on what you do. Some veterans do not believe they can learn anything new. I would say to them that they have lost their way, and will be out of the business soon."

Balanced Life: "I chose selling because it offered me an opportunity to learn more about people in general, and myself in particular, and how to live an abundant and joyful life. My world outside of new home sales is very important to me. This is a career that offers me the opportunity to co-mingle many aspects of the business with my personal life. My wife, children and friends are an integral part of my success and work. We share much more together than if I were in another field. Yet there is a part of my personal life that is held separate and apart from my selling. I believe that we must balance a well-rounded life to enjoy the fruits of our labor. I am learning to play the piano, a dream I have had since I was a child."

Select your Mentors: "The frustrations and stress of any career can be overwhelming. Selling is no different. I really hate to elaborate on this but it is true. We live in a negative world, inhabited by some

very negative people. Many of them live and work around me. I
would never be able to block out this influence if it were not for my
mentors. They are trusted professionals, chosen by me, whom I can
go to when the going gets tough. They not only extend a hand to
help me up, but they will not allow me to wallow in self-pity. They
are tough, compassionate, and fair. They are my oasis."

   In addition, I would like to add one final note on my observation
of the wonderful superstars I have met. They all seem so happy. I
really mean it. They are a fun group of people who work hard and
play hard. They live life to its fullest and enjoy ever minute of it.
As Mom would say, "They don't let any grass grow under their
feet." What pleases me most is that professional new home salespeople are finally *beginning to gain some, the status and recognition they deserve.*

Appendix: Recommended Resources

A Passion For Excellence. Thomas J. Peters and Nancy Austin. Warner Books, New York, NY.

Action Selling. Jim Mills. National Association of Home Builders, Washington, DC (1978).

Aggressive Selling In A Defensive Market (Video). Thomas Richey/NAHB/1984.

Anatomy of a Successful Salesman. Arthur Mortell.

Art of Negotiation (The). Gerald L. Nierenburg.

Body Language. Julius Fast.

Building For The Market. John A. Hébert and William R. Smolkin. NAHB. 1985.

Building Sales Through People Motivation (Booklet). Thomas Richey. NAHB. 1980.

Bulls, Owls, Lambs & Tigers (Video). Charles J. Clarke III.

Championship Selling. Grant G. Gaid.

Closers, The. Pichins. William & Steven Co.

Complete Book of Closing Sales. Sal T. Massimino.

Comprehensive Guide To Real Estate Finance. Jeff Elias.

Construction Marketing and Strategic Planning. Warren Friedman. McGraw-Hill, Inc. (1984).

Creative Real Estate Financing (audio tapes). David Stone, Los Gatos, CA.

Dress For Success. John T. Malloy.

Essential Dictionary of Real Estate Terminology. Hemphill & Hemphill Prentice-Hall Inc.

Establishing A Builder/Relator Cooperative Program (video). Thomas Richey. NAHB. Washington, DC. (1986)

Fair Housing Compliance Manual. National Council of the Multifamily Housing Industry NAHB. (1990).

Fundamentals of Selling. Richard D. Irwin, Inc. Homewood, IL. (1988).

Get Ready To Manage (video). Dave Stone & Tom Richey. NAHB, Washington, DC. (1986).

Getting To Yes. Roger Fisher & William Ury. Houghton Mifflin Co.

How To Become A Successful New Home Sales Manager (manual & tape series). Dave Stone & Tom Richey. Los Gatos, CA.

How To Get More Business By Telephone. Schwartz. The Business Bourse. New York, NY.

How To Master The Art Of Selling. Tom Hophins. Scottsdale, AZ., Warner Books. (1982).

How To Organize Your Work and Your Life. Robert Moskowitz. Doubleday and Co. Inc. (1981).

How To Sell New Homes & Condominiums. David Stone. McGraw Hill, Inc. New York, NY.

How I Raised Myself From Failure To Success In Selling. Frank Bittger. Simon & Schuster

If It Ain't Broke, Break It. Robert J. Kreigel.

In Search of Excellence. Thomas J. Peters and Robert H. Waterman, Jr. Warner Books, New York, NY. (1982).

Integrity Selling. Ron Willingham. Doubleday Publishers. 1987.

Marketing New Homes. Charles R. Clark and David F. Parker. NAHB. Washington, DC. (1989).

Megatrends. John Maisbitt. Warner Books New York, NY (1978).

New Home Sales. David Stone. Longman Publishing Group. Chicago, IL. (1982).

New Home Sales (video). David Stone. Lumbleau Stone Productions, Burbank, CA (1983).

New Home Sales Insights (newsletter). Richard Tiller. Tiller Marketing Services, P.O. Box 531. Herndon, VA 22070. (1993).

New Home Sales Training: A Complete Program. Richard Tiller (1992).

No Bull Sales Management. Trishler. Business & Finance Publications. New York, NY (1985).

Organized Executive (The). Stephanie Winston W.W. Norton & Company. New York, NY (1983).

Sales Closing Power. Edwards. National Tall Tree Marketing. Washington, DC (1983).

Sales Closing Techniques. Dane. Parker Publishing Co. West Nyach, NY (1982).

Secrets of Closing Sales. Charles B. Roth and Roy Alexander Prentice-Hall, Inc.

See You At The Top. Zig Ziglar.

Selling In The 90's . . . The Official Handbook For New Home Salespeople. Bob Schultz Boca Raton, FL.

Selling Personality: Persuasion Strategy. Walter Gorman. Random House.

Selling New Homes. Charles R. Clark and David F. Parker. NAHB, Washington, DC. (1989).

Shut Up and Sell. Don Sheehan. Amacom New York, NY.

Success In New Home Sales. Richard Tiller. Tiller Marketing Service, Herndon, VA. (1991).

Super Natural Selling For Everyday People. Danielle Kennedy.

Swim With The Sharks Without Being Eaten Alive. Harvey MacKay. William Marrow and Company.

Telephone Techniques That Sell. Charles Bury. Warner Books, Inc. New York, NY (1980).

The 5 Minute Professional (audio cassette tapes). Bob Schultz.

The Official New Home Sales Development System (video). Bob Schultz.

The Seven Habits of Highly Effective People. Stephen R. Covey. Fireside. (1989).

The Power Of Positive Thinking. Norman V. Peale.

The Secrets of Power Negotiating. Roger Dawson. Nightingale-Conant Corp.

The Winning Edge. Dr. Dennis Waitley.

The Official Guide To Success. Tom Hopkins.

Think And Grow Rich. Napolean Hill.

Training Sales People and Prospecting (video). Dave Stone & Thomas Richey. NAHB, Washington, DC (1986).

Unlimited Power. Anthony Robbins. Ballantine Books, New York. (1986).

Using a Host/Hostess In The Sales Office (video). Nicki Joy. National Association of Home Builders, Washington, DC (1983).

Your Blueprint For Selling Success (audio tape series). Thomas Riley. Richey Resources. (1986).

Zig Ziglar's Secrets of Closing Sales. Zig Ziglar. Risell Publications Dallas, TX. (1979).

About The Author

Bonnie Alfriend brings to us an exciting and unique glimpse into the world of successful high achievers in New Home Sales. There has never been a residential sales book like this one—a precise, comprehensive and richly detailed sharing of actual situations and dialogue that you, the reader, can use to gain a greater advantage and win more sales.

The author knows first hand the challenges that face on-site sales professionals, having spent many years as a successful top producing sales representative. Her career as a sales manager won her much acclaim with her hands-on approach to management and coaching techniques, that generated over one billion dollars in total sales.

Bonnie is president of Alfriend and Associates, a company specializing in sales and marketing evaluations, and skill development for sales professionals. She holds the CRB and MIRM designations, is a licensed real estate broker, as well as a nationally approved IRM and CSP instructor, and is currently serving on the IRM board of trustees for the National Association of Home Builders. She is co-editor of New Home Sales Insights and a columnist for the New Homes Register. She is a well-known seminar speaker, writer and educator.

Bonnie and her husband, Terry, divide their time between Fairfax Station, Virginia and Monterey, California where she continues to pursue her passion of working with salespeople and sales managers.